The Instinctiv

CW01497201

Sam North

The Instinctive Screenplay

Watching and Writing Screen Drama

© Sam North 2017

All rights reserved. No reproduction, copy or transmission of this publication may be made without written permission.

No portion of this publication may be reproduced, copied or transmitted save with written permission or in accordance with the provisions of the Copyright, Designs and Patents Act 1988, or under the terms of any licence permitting limited copying issued by the Copyright Licensing Agency, Saffron House, 6–10 Kirby Street, London EC1N 8TS.

Any person who does any unauthorized act in relation to this publication may be liable to criminal prosecution and civil claims for damages.

The author has asserted his right to be identified as the author of this work in accordance with the Copyright, Designs and Patents Act 1988.

First published 2017 by
Palgrave

Palgrave in the UK is an imprint of Macmillan Publishers Limited, registered in England, company number 785998, of 4 Crinan Street, London N1 9XW.

Palgrave® and Macmillan® are registered trademarks in the United States, the United Kingdom, Europe and other countries.

ISBN 978–1–137–60750–8 hardback
ISBN 978–1–137–60749–2 paperback

A catalogue record for this book is available from the British Library.

A catalog record for this book is available from the Library of Congress.

Contents

Introduction

The genesis of storytelling is found in gossip, as will be explored in Chapter 3, but the roots of dramatic *performance* are in primitive rituals, dances and games that mimic the hunt for food (seal, kangaroo), or the battle with predators, or flight from predators, or they simulate the sexual act. 'The Water dwellers of Tierra del Fuego, for example, have their canoe play, the Bambuti pygmies have their jungle-hunting game, the Tasmanians a seal game, and the Kemirai of New South Wales a kangaroo game.' (Weimann 1967/1978, 2) In rituals, dances and games the audience and the performers are the same; the spectators take part. For this reason music and dance are important ingredients in the performance: they act like drugs, and are sometimes accompanied by drugs, to reduce people's inhibitions.

> At this level of culture *mimesis* arises out of a community in which there is little division of labour; the 'spectators' take part in the game or join in the acting. The unity of player and audience is complete when each participant shares in the indivisible process of primitive living. (2)

Catapulted into a hypnotic, enchanted state, when participants indulge in ritual or carnival they both perform and observe the performance at the same time. They create metaphor, practise instruction, reveal meaning, all of this by virtue of their taking part in the mimesis for a short, intense period within the inescapable, long-term performances of their own lives.

Two thousand five hundred years ago ritual evolved into theatre, which created a new way of delivering these acts of mimesis – it separated the participants. One group (the audience) merely watched while another (skilled actors) interpreted and performed. Both groups were in the same space, both were engaged in consuming the drama, but the audience adopted a passive role. It might seem unfair that they were the ones who were asked to pay.

The cultivation of dramatic technique lies in this dichotomy: the audience wants to feel as involved as if the mimesis were in fact their own lives and they are *in* the drama, whereupon they will enter the enchanted space of the story, all the while remaining seated in the dark, hiding behind their inhibitions. They want to take part in the drama, but at the same time remain safely hidden.[1]

Technology added another mode of delivering performances: in 1896 the Lumière brothers shot a moving picture sequence from the back of a train. In 1899 Eastman, Goodman and Carbutt managed to paint light-sensitive emulsion onto celluloid. It was a technical and an economic transformation: no longer were actors required to interpret and develop the text each night. The interpretation was created in one unique version. The dramatic performance could be captured and, more significantly, copied and distributed. Projectors carried the drama onto cinema screens. The actors and the audience were no longer in the same room or even the same country. They were separated by perhaps thousands of miles and by as much as a hundred and twenty years in time.

Within a few decades the medium of film became, by far, the most popular form of drama enjoyed by the human animal.

Delivery mechanisms proliferated. The television signal evolved during the 1920s; by the 1990s drama could be encoded in binary. The enchanted space of the auditorium has to compete for an audience who might choose to remain in their own homes; and a member of that audience might even be alone, watching the performance as the kettle rises to the boil on one side, while on the other hand a fingertip swipes past

---

[1]At the time of writing people in different parts of the world are being arrested for various reasons while playing *Pokemon Go*; the new storytelling world of interactive game narratives and immersive theatre is demanding once again that the audience take part in the drama.

a recipe. The screenwriter must work even harder to gain and hold the attention of the audience.

> Our minds can only focus on a few things at once. To hold an audience, in a world of competing demands on attention, an author needs to be an inventive intuitive psychologist. Yet criticism has tended to underplay the 'mere' ability to arouse and hold attention. (Boyd 2010, 232)

With all its competing distractions the home audience demands from fictional dramas even greater concentrations of dramatic technique that insist the audience is involved.

It is increasingly likely that the home audience has paid little or no money to watch the performance; none the less they want to walk through the screen and take part. They want, at the same time, both to be in the story and in the audience. In 'Dramaturgy of the Spectator' Marco de Marinis warns us, ' ... there clearly exists a dramaturgy of the director and a dramaturgy of the performer. However surprisingly it may seem at first, we also can and should speak – not just metaphorically – of a dramaturgy of the spectator', and he advises –

> The partial or relative autonomy of each of the different dramaturgies (the director's, the writer's, the performer's, the spectator's) all work together in the composition of the performance and must be seen as mutually setting and occasionally adjusting each other's boundaries. (2003, 220)

It makes for an increased demand on the dramatist's magical abilities, especially considering to what extent, over the last decade, the audience's expertise in 'reading' drama has accelerated due to the enormously increased number of hours we practise watching it. Therefore dramatic techniques lose their transparency; the writer's hand can be seen even before the mouse clicks on Final Draft; and under such conditions it is easy for the writer-as-puppeteer to lose his or her black cloak of invisibility.

With exhilarating speed dramatists have learned to write more powerfully, subtly and over a greater number of hours. Philip Parker, in *The Art and Science of Screenwriting*, describes the amount of work being done – 'Screenwriting is the most industrialised form of dramatic writing we have yet invented' (2006, 3).

'Industrialised' is right – the American artist J.F. Weir, in works such as *Forging The Shaft* (1874–1877), captured the force of human work and industry during the Industrial Revolution, while on the other side of the Atlantic the British artist William Turner was compelled to do the same in works such as *Rain, Steam, and Speed – The Great Western Railway* (1844). Their vision of industry offered a torrent of light and smoke and action and, above all, images of human ingenuity; likewise currently we are building great factories of story, of screen performances. We are in an artistic foment of screenwriting. There is so much of it, it is so powerfully insistent and so widely consumed, that it divides people just as did the Industrial Revolution. Some would say it is progress and the mark of humanity's excellence; others would claim that so much television and film, so much *story*, impoverishes and enslaves a human spirit that has become addicted to its consumption to the exclusion of real life, real events. And yet the following pages will describe how 'story' is, and has always been, of central importance to our real lives, and real events.

Dramatic techniques, when put together, constitute the writing of plot. If there is a spectrum of writing, just as there is a spectrum of light from white at one end through the yellows and greens to the higher frequencies of red and eventually to black, then such a writing spectrum might suggest that poetry occupies one end, where plot is of little concern (except in narrative poetry), and image, language and the logic of the poetic machine are the required frequencies. The reading vibrations, if you will, at this poetic end of the spectrum attract those who will develop an elite sensibility specifically for this purpose, and they are fewer in number. The spectrum will then move through the middle ground of prose fiction, where some novels tend towards the poetic – wherein language, image and observation take pride of place – and those in which plot begins to vibrate more powerfully, and the readership becomes crowded.

Plot is difficult to do well, and here, in the middle of the spectrum, among prose fiction writers, some are for it and some against. The word is often expressed in a derogatory tone. In his Editor's Preface to *The Essential James Joyce*, the scholar Harry Levin defined plot as 'the unscrupulous manipulation of surprises and coincidences' (Joyce 1948, 21), but plot is the *scrupulous* manipulation, not only of surprises and coincidences, but of desire, logic, morality and emotion (Chapters 1–4 herein); it is the scrupulous manipulation of events.

E.M. Forster wished that plot were not important, and made his famous distinction, in his 1927 collection of essays *Aspects of the Novel*, between story and plot.[2] 'The king died and then the queen died'[3] is, Forster claims, a story, whereas 'The king died and then the queen died of grief' (Forster 1962, 93) is a plot. It is an enigmatic conundrum; the difference between the former sentence and the latter are those few words, 'died of grief', which add cause-and-effect, and moreover create an opportunity for inference (she loved him), which together make up a display of logic (the subject of Chapter 2); and those few words also add love, an emotion (Chapter 4). The emotion, as all emotions do, carries an action-tendency, a desire (Chapter 1). Thus Forster goes three-quarters of the way to describing 'plot'. However, most people would conflate the two terms and say that story *is* plot. McKee's famous analysis of plot is called *Story* (1999).

Further along the spectrum prose fiction gives way to drama, and plot vibrates more strongly. Included here are novels that are essentially written in the dramatic form, with plot as their central concern, as well as stage plays and radio plays. At this end of the spectrum it is not the poetry of language that most concerns the writer, nor the accuracy or facility of the observation (although these are important qualities); it is the plot.

The very furthest end of the spectrum is occupied by screenwriting and plot becomes the essential skill. Because of the financial risks associated with its production, a TV or cinema film simply must win the attention of every man, woman and child, of any class, whatever sensibility, against all the competing distractions, in a dramatic performance that is utterly involving.

To think about either end of the light spectrum and the special, colourless qualities of black and white, in terms of this analogy the 'white' of

---

[2]See page 61 of Bordwell and Thompson's *Film Art – An Introduction* (2001) for their description of the difference between plot and story.

[3]For an insight into what a logician will do with Forster's concept, see Apostolos Doxiadis's 'A Streetcar Named (Among Other Things) Proof' (Doxiadis and Mazur 2012, 288–331).

poetry is vocabulary, language, whereas the 'black' of plot is events, what happens. Plot is the poetry of events.

Plot is a workmanlike term for something that is intensely difficult to write, and furthermore plot is, like poetry, 'a machine for remembering itself' (Paterson 2000, 286). It is happenstance arranged with such dexterity and understanding, and with such a graceful application of inventive forms of logic, that it transforms our own experience of life. A large audience gathers at this dramatic end of the writing spectrum, made up of all types of sensibilities, elite and otherwise, low brow and high.

Tiffany Stern, a historian of early modern theatre, makes the argument that plays were patched together out of a number of different documents, often scrappy and utilitarian in nature. She unearthed three types of manuscript in archives of theatre history that can, for the dramatist and screenwriter, illuminate what is plot.

Stern first draws attention to what is termed a 'back-stage plot' (2009, 3), which –

> hung in the tiring house detailing entrances and 'personals' (the properties that actors were to take onstage with them). They were written to govern onstage performance from backstage, and were some of the theatre's most important manuscripts: they alone of all play fragments were mounted on special boards and penned with several quills for clarity and beauty. (7)

The 'backstage-plot' described the movements of an actor, holding onto whichever properties were necessary, while he was on the stage – the character must first go there, do this, and speak such-and-such a line, and then perform that event – and so on, always with the necessary props to hand.

Such a definition of the word 'plot' reinforces a decision the screenwriter must inevitably make – to write with the actor in mind, especially the lead actor(s). In addition, it reminds us of the importance of objects (properties) in the construction of plots, the reasons for which will become clear later.

The second document that Stern offers as a 'plot' was found on the other side of the 'fourth wall'; it was given out to the audience, front-of-house. She describes it thus –

> an abstract of a play's story, a passage that would never be spoken on stage, might be an important performance document though not part of the

performed play. Known as an Argument, it was written to be handed to the audience – something akin to a primitive theatre programme – and would 'interpret' the play while it was being enacted. (2)

It was a resume of the story such as might be found in an English programme for an opera sung in Italian or German. The significant phrase for screenwriters is 'known as an Argument' – because a plot, if it can be described as the journey of a lead actor through a set of events, will have its antithesis: the forces at work (however gentle or vigorous) that might obstruct, complicate, delay, argue with or prevent that journey.

Most significantly, the word argument implies what will always be found in the fabric of a plot: the interplay of right and wrong (described in Chapter 3).

Thirdly, Stern discovered many plots that could be 'judged, sold, stolen, and waved in front of a company as promise of a play to come' (5). They were ideas for stories, a precis of what happens, and there was a fierce trade in them. Often they were rewritten by other writers. Stern finds that a Latin university manuscript play, *Senilis Amor*, was given a new ending by a different writer – 'Titubis and Collosus having cheated the woman of her henns, make a feast and sing Io Bacche Venus: & Catt: are sett in the stocks being drunke' (21).

As Stern describes, there were writers who wrote only plot ideas, and sold them as such – undeveloped. Once purchased, a plot might then travel through a number of writers' hands. Shakespeare wrote very little that was original in the way of plot *ideas*. Most were borrowed, or lifted from history. Only two, *The Tempest* (1610) and *Love's Labour's Lost* (1598), were his own.

It is the same today – a film, most especially among the dramatic forms of texts, is created using a patchwork of different documents, using a variety of people's input. Sometimes the most important contribution is the editor's. There is still a lively trade in plot ideas (pitches or treatments). And the distinction holds good between people who are good at plot ideas, and those who are good at writing them into screenplays. Steven Price, in his *A History of the Screenplay* (2013), advises that to write screenplays is to work in a crowded, collaborative space, not in the solitary garret occupied by the novelist. He quotes Claudia Sternberg's description of the screenplay as 'literature in flux', where screenwriters jostle for position among many others, including actors, directors and editors, with the scripting 'as a continuous, unpredictable, series of stages in the production process' (Price, 235).

Plot is a mimesis, an imitation of life, but engineered for effect, and under conditions that are inevitably complicated given the industrial process. It is this engineering, this manipulation, that is difficult to perform, and it is then again difficult to make such manipulation appear invisible, and steer it through the controlled chaos of production. A plot will lead the audience to where they urgently want to go, however placid the rhythm of the drama, but none the less it is a place that will be surprising. It will do this with subtlety – invisibly, inaudibly, and with good grace.

There are hundreds of books about screenwriting, about plots and plotting. Ian W. Macdonald, in his *Screenwriting Poetics and the Screen Idea* (2013), conducts an audit of screenwriting books from industry gurus such as Joseph Campbell, Christopher Vogler, Syd Field, Linda Seger, John Truby and Robert McKee, as well as from famous practitioners such as William Goldman. Macdonald concludes that – 'there is no analysis in these sources of why audience and readers might respond emotionally; only that they must' (53).

This book answers that question 'why' – and therefore it can be regarded, in part, as a 'how to' manual.

However, the following chapters won't concern themselves with the screenplay as a document, nor with the three-act or five-act structure, or with the way a 'there-and-return' narrative hinges on its mid-point, or with the single, multi or plural protagonist, or the single linear narrative or the multi-stranded narrative. Successful analyses have been written on these subjects; it is often a matter of common sense, as one might sensibly divide a meal into three courses.

In order to write the poetry of events, it is the human hunger for story, and the food itself, that must be the screenwriter's first concern – she or he must reach the human animal in his cave and understand why we are 'The Storytelling Animal' (Gottschall 2013) and how that has led to the evolution of dramatic techniques.

Everything we need to know about dramatic writing is inside our primitive selves and contained within our instinctive experience. To take from Boyd's 'evolutionary perspective on storytelling' (254), we should comprehend exactly *how* our instincts control, inevitably, our attention, how our judgements work, how we meet drama, and how drama meets us and others around us; and once we can feel, in our bones, how and why our human instincts are brought into play in a narrative, then we can use these insights to create potent arrangements of events, as they pertain to character, in the writing of screenplays.

1

The Map of Desire

In *Joanna Lumley Meets Will.i.am* (Sibley 2014) the actress Joanna Lumley escorted Will.i.am, co-founder of super-group The Black-Eyed Peas, around his home territory in south Los Angeles. She witnessed his good works: he had started a company that developed fabric out of recycled plastic bottles; funded educational initiatives for underprivileged youths; designed a building devoted to the art of music.

Will.i.am appeared to be a man at peace, content, and, for someone who exhibited such drive, such purpose, and who offered so many different accomplishments, he was relaxed in his demeanour.

Towards the end of the programme Lumley asked him what single quality was it, did he think, that was responsible for his success? He replied, 'Will.' Joanna Lumley was initially confused, but then he added, 'Will I am. Will.' Joanna Lumley understood – and the logic behind the chopping of his name, William, into three different sections, Will.i.am, became clear. The single quality responsible for his success was willpower.

Schopenhauer went further and claimed that willpower is everything. At the outset of the first volume of *The World as Will and Representation* (1818/2010) he promises to explore, 'a truth that must be very serious and alarming, if not terrifying to anyone, a truth that can and must be maintained … namely this: "The world is my will"' (24).

Willpower derives its energy from the survival instinct. The European eel *will* swim three hundred miles to the Sargasso Sea in order to breed. The Arctic tern, every year, *will* migrate from one pole to the other in order to maintain its pattern of survival. Schopenhauer noticed this conscious-less power of will in animals –

> the larva of the stag beetle chews a hole into the wood where its metamorphosis will take place, and the hole is twice as big if it is going to be male than if it is going to be female, in order to accommodate the horns it has no idea it will acquire. The will is clearly at work in this kind of animal behaviour. (139)

The human animal, also, must survive, and beyond that, thrive. Willpower is the muscle that works this instinct. It drives our lives with more or less vigour as is the case. Screenwriters can build willpower into the shape of the drama, lift it across from real life and use its energy to drive a narrative.

A more romantic word for willpower is desire; it carries all the emotion and longing attached to the human heart. Desire is the engine of our lives and it will therefore be the engine of our narratives, and the desires that most directly, without complication, tap into our survival instinct are the strongest. In a developed, sophisticated world such desires might be dressed up. The instinct to mate, to breed, might transform itself (in a species that can take survival for granted) into love. The desire to eat and to gain shelter in a society that is organised and successful transforms itself into the urge to thrive, or make money.

What we want, desire, creates our forward momentum, our personal survival and our thriving; furthermore it creates our expansion as a race and as a species.

It offers the same quality to a story: forward momentum. Agents, producers and script editors call it 'traction'. It is a good word: the tyres grip; the story moves. The sensation given to an audience by the desire principle, when it is artfully constructed in a story, is sometimes described as 'pulling you through' or 'like being carried along'. And we expect to be carried along when we engage with a dramatic narrative.[1]

---

[1] For the difference between 'want' and 'need', see page 45.

For any screenplay that aims to harness this force of nature it is as well to do so quickly, deftly, and with increasing intensity, in a manner that allows its most virtuous force, taking into account the style and content of the writing.

Much has been written on the subject already. McKee's words almost have a warning tone, 'A protagonist is a wilful character' (137), and he goes on to explain, 'The energy of a character's desire forms the critical element of design known as the *spine* of the story.' (194) Kenneth Thorpe Rowe, the MIT lecturer who taught both McKee and the playwright Arthur Miller, in his work *Write That Play* (1939) defines it as 'attack' (54) and goes on to advise, 'the character must exercise his will' (54). John Yorke, in *Into The Woods* (2013), is unequivocal: 'Almost all successful plays, films and novels are about primal human desires' (10); furthermore he finds in the work of the acting coach, Stanislavski, 'that characters are motivated by desire' (9). Exponents of the neo-Aristotelian monomyth, such as Campbell and Vogler, would describe desire as the quest. In *The Art of Dramatic Writing* (1942/2004) Egri names his Chapter 5 'Strength of Will in a Character' (1942/2004, 80). Bordwell and Thompson emphasise the importance of 'Goal orientation' (2011, 114). Boyd, examining the dramatic power of Homer's *Odyssey*, is emphatic – 'An understanding of others in terms of desires and intentions has been a major force, perhaps *the* major force, in evolving intelligence in all social species. Without it stories would be impossible and the *Odyssey* incomprehensible.' (257) Truby advises, 'Once a character has a desire, the story "walks" on two "legs": acting and learning.' (2008, 2) In looking at the architecture of desire in prose fiction, Rene Girard points out, 'Desire ... can always be portrayed by a simple straight line which joins subject and object.' (1961/1976, 2)

I hope to contribute to the subject in two ways: by concentrating on the matter of recruitment to the desire; and by looking at three different shapes or varieties of the desire principle found in drama.

Firstly – recruitment. If a protagonist's desire is the engine of a narrative, then of greater importance than the desire itself is the pattern of recruitment (and/or non-recruitment) to that desire – whether it's the recruitment or involvement of the audience (essential) or the recruitment of the surrounding characters (who might be either allies, opponents, or disinterested).

It is only a first step, therefore, for a writer to shoulder the responsibility for inventing a character's desire, understanding its quality, its psychological shape, and how it maps onto other characters.

This second, additional requirement is more important: to engineer the audience's involvement, interest, in the desire. This is not to say an audience must necessarily share the desire or approve of it, but their recruitment is essential.

Their taking part.

To *increase* the audience's involvement is a third requirement, if only because without such an increase their involvement will lessen.

It is not as simple as it looks to write into a script the events that secure an audience's *increasing* involvement in a character's desire. It might appear to be enough to summon a character, imperiously attach a desire to him or her, and thereby put in place the engine of the narrative. But – we are no longer in that primitive ritual when we are both the audience and the performer, when our circumstances are the same, and we want the same thing, when we are the writers of the drama and its actors and its audience, all at once.

Moreover we arrive at the drama with our own desires, and our desires are the engines of our own private narratives. We observe this other character, in this other space, with this desire attached to him or her by the writer, and the writer's initiative (we probably don't even know her or his name) exists on the other side of the membrane that divides us, in real life, with our real involvement, from them: mere characters in the world of fiction. Why should we care?

Also, even as an audience takes their seats they exert a moral sensibility that filters their involvement in any narrative enterprise.

The following examples[2] will show how other screenwriters have succeeded in recruiting an audience and then intensifying their

---

[2]The examples of films that I've used in this book are from different countries and eras; they are chosen because they demonstrate well the principles under review and they are also distinguished by their effect being felt on repeated viewings. In this sense I will spend significant time in 'Telling the Pictures' (Delaney 1993/2001). In order to access this effect on the page in as direct a way as possible I have omitted the scholarship available on some of the titles.

involvement in the desire of a character; furthermore the examples offer three different models or varieties of the desire principle at work. These models can be distinguished one from another by asking three questions.

1 Is the desire habitual, or singular?

A singular desire emerges when circumstances gather around a protagonist in such a way as to sponsor in him or her a unique objective, a desire that can be answered in one way or another: granted or denied. And such a desire also has a singular starting point. Yorke finds that A.W. Schlegel, in 1808, describes these starting points as 'first determinations' (14), and McKee will later categorise them famously as the 'Inciting Incident' (181).

On the other hand, a habitual desire is constant whether or not it is answered, and, just as there is no end to it, there is no unique starting point either. A protagonist will have this kind of habitual desire every day; he or she cannot imagine not having it. The desire to eat, to make money, to improve at basketball, to maintain the happiness and well-being of a family; such desires, if a protagonist has them, can be expressed in the habitual mode – merely built into daily life. There will be no particular end point when this desire can be said to be fulfilled, because any satisfaction is no sooner granted before the desire re-asserts itself. The habitual desire is therefore extraordinarily stable. It has a natural credibility, because it has a history within that character. It is often more low key, but exerts a constant pull – rather like gravity itself. It is this relentless quality that gives it its power.

Either way, we can use a habitual or a singular desire to be the engine of a narrative.

The qualities of both types of desire can be observed in a film that has two protagonists, two desires, one of which is singular and the other habitual: the Coen brothers' thriller, *Fargo* (1996).

A singular desire in *Fargo*

Circumstances gather around Jerry Lundegaard (William H. Macy) in such a way that he conceives a singular desire: to arrange for his own wife to be kidnapped and therefore earn a share in the ransom that will be paid by his wealthy father-in-law.

The desire has been put in train before the film begins; the engine is already turning and the audience is invited to latch onto it immediately. A mere two minutes are allowed for us to settle in our seats and feel how chronically cold is the winter in Brainerd, Massachusetts, how it grips the slow-moving motor car and the second motor car, the tan Oldsmobile Ciera, that is towed behind it, before the driver of that car, Jerry Lundegaard, walks into a small town bar and searches among the pool players and barflies for the two men he's come here to meet. His hat is ridiculous, and so is his scarf. His gait is tentative and his expression is woebegone. His gaze settles on the two least salubrious men in the bar who appear to have been waiting for too long: one of them has his head tipped back, asleep. The other looks cheesed off.

Jerry approaches and introduces himself. There is a scuffed-up bit of dialogue; and out of this deliberately confused back-and-forth up pops Jerry's singular desire. He doesn't say it out loud, although his every agitated movement betrays his anxiety about it. Instead it is a confused Carl Showalter (Steve Buscemi), showing his snaggled teeth, who declares it for him, in a tone of disbelief, 'Let me get this straight, you want to kidnap your own wife?'

This is Jerry's singular desire,[3] and it becomes the spine of the drama. The traction is already pulling, the wheels turning, and every scene on Jerry's side of the narrative serves to pour fuel into this engine. The kidnap happens quickly; the remainder of the film concerns itself with Jerry's

---

[3]Jerry's singular desire – to kidnap his wife and thereby earn a share of the ransom that will be paid to the kidnappers – is, in fact, rooted in his habitual desire to make money by any means possible, because the writers have given him a long history of other get-rich-quick schemes. The narrative therefore benefits from the excitement and immediacy of the singular desire while at the same time it is rooted in the stability, and credibility, of a habitual desire.

attempts to get his hands on the ransom. The film ends a few minutes after his singular desire is finally and catastrophically denied to him: he doesn't even possess the shirt on his back when, groaning with pain, he is pinned down by police officers in a motel bedroom.

Jerry's singular desire is used by the writers as an organising principle. It gives them a beginning to this particular strand of story (a beginning that isn't shown and takes place before the timescale covered by the film) and also prescribes its end: Jerry face down on that motel bed.

The remaining, more difficult task is to arrange events and circumstances in such a way that they contribute, increasingly, to the intensity of the audience's involvement in Jerry's desire. Because it is true to say that most of *Fargo's* audience, with a disturbing gaiety of spirit, almost in disbelief at such goings-on, step through the screen and take part. So – why is the audience glued to Jerry Lundegaard and his deplorable ambition?

It helps that a quality of distinctive humour is shot through the character of Jerry, and his story, that makes the narrative beguiling. Fargo is not a comedy (it announces on the cover of the DVD that it is a thriller) but it sharpens every moment on an angle of humour that somehow manages not to puncture the excitement. It is a difficult balancing act to develop and maintain this tone.

A second reason for the audience's involvement is the way in which the moral compass is set, and how the writers steer the audience's reaction by way of this moral compass.

On the whole, any audience will be against the idea of anyone kidnapping his own wife, or anyone else's, for whatever reason. They would think it morally wrong. However, the writers perform various pieces of work to swing the needle from 'wrong' towards 'right' and thereby obscure the audience's overall, theoretical position, and recruit them instead to the individual circumstances that make this case different. In the middle of this film, especially given the humour, an audience might almost go so far as to admit that they applaud the kidnap of Jerry's wife, and wish Jerry success in getting his hands on the ransom.

Most significant among the devices that achieve this effect is the writers' placing of Jerry's character alongside the characters of Carl Showalter and his sidekick, Gaear Grimsrud (Peter Stormare). In comparison Jerry comes off as a paragon of virtue. Jerry insists from the outset of the kidnap plan that no one should be hurt, and therefore Showalter and Grimsrud's increasing violence shows up Jerry's character, to the audience's relief, as more definitively incapable of violence.

The writers also place Jerry next to the character of Wade Gustafson (Harve Presnell), Jerry's ungenerous, opinionated, wealthy father-in-law, who is pompous and cruel in his superiority and who ostracises Jerry – behaviour that is selfish, that of an archetypal bully. Next to Wade's wealth and calculating confidence Jerry's money troubles and his loser's demeanour – the hat, the woebegone expression, the history of his failure written in the lines of his face – cast him as an underdog and therefore demanding of our moral support.

It is an example of an anachronism that is always present in the workings of narrative: in real life our moral position can be locked in position by our upbringing, by the stories we've been told, by our experience or by a belief system that we ascribe to; and generally speaking it will hold firm for an extended period of time unless it undergoes some kind of revolutionary change. In our engagement with a fictional story, however, because it isn't real life and because we are inclined to enjoy a story if we can, we give to the writers the licence to lift up our entire moral compass and move it into a separate moral universe, one that in real life we would refuse to inhabit. However, within this new moral universe that we've agreed for the time being to adopt we search for what McKee calls (his italics) the '*Centre of Good*' (347). We don't mind if that centre is miles away from where our own centre is located in real life. In the play-world of narrative it is refreshing for us to share (safely, and not for real) the moral universe of petty crooks and murderers. But within this new world that we happen to find ourselves in, we search for the least worst character – and we find Jerry Lundegaard.

The Coen brothers created the nastiness of Showalter and Grimsrud, and of Wade, so that when Jerry Lundegaard is placed alongside them we compare what's on offer and choose to side with him.

Part of our agreement in moving to a separate moral universe is that in return we demand the writers look after our moral sense. Moreover we know – our narrative experience tells us – that we are being deliberately manipulated in this way, but unlike on other such occasions when we might sense the writer's hand and react adversely, under these circumstances we applaud the writers for their humanity in understanding the way we work, and in so effectively handling us.[4]

The Coen brothers engineer additional refinements to our moral position with regard to Jerry Lundegaard. Jerry does *try* to be good: when it later appears, for a while, that he's going to get the money from another source (a land deal for a parking lot), he attempts to call off the kidnap. Furthermore, he's not that good at being bad – the hopeless, cack-handed way in which he attempts his various frauds earns our sympathy because of their comic failings. Moreover Jerry's wife, the victim of the kidnap, has an unfortunate voice and a crass manner, and when the kidnappers appear at her patio doors she is chewing gum and watching daytime television; therefore we might think she deserves to have her world shaken up.

Likewise our disapproval of Jerry's mean-spirited father-in-law means the latter should be the victim of Jerry's scam; Wade deserves to have some of his money taken off him.

Within the context of a bullying, cheating, thieving, selfish world Jerry exhibits the least amount of skill and so we rush to support him.

Meanwhile Showalter and Grimsrud become steadily more violent. They perform the kidnap and promptly shoot a state trooper, and then two innocent passers-by, before hiding out in the cabin by the lake. It is so cold that the breath puffs from their mouths as they wait for the money to be organised.[5] The final image of the mortal, cold cruelty of

---

[4]Perhaps the highest form of satisfaction that comes from watching drama is obtained by our being able to admire the writer, the actor or the composer; we take pride that we are, together with them, members of the human race. It's a celebration of what a beautiful thing can be achieved in art. In the National Theatre's stage adaptation of Michael Morpurgo's 1982 novel *War Horse*, for example, the audience's emotional reaction was generated as much by intense admiration for the large-scale puppetry as by the story itself. Without the puppetry, Spielberg's 2011 film failed to arouse this more exceptional degree of satisfaction. It pertains to the idea of 'elevation' as a feeling, described in Chapter 4.

[5]The production could have used a studio set and kept the actors comfortably warm and saved some of the budget, but they wanted that cold to be visible, hence the real puffs of breath. Money pays for warmth, and without money there is only cold, in a Brainerd winter. It's an important element in the way in which the desires of the film's characters tap into our collective instinct to survive.

Showalter and Grimsrud is Showalter's foot sticking out of the top of the chipping machine, as Grimsrud shreds his partner and blasts the bloody remains against the frozen white snow.

Their increasing selfishness has cast Jerry almost in the role of a hero, albeit a foolish one, as he both tries to stop the kidnappers and earn money out of the situation at the same time.

These writerly decisions create our empathy: we allow Jerry his kidnap attempt and furthermore become more intensely involved in it. Our desire is not aligned with his, we don't approve of it and we know it is the wrong way for him to go about things, but we intensely desire to see its outcome, finding pleasure in the irony that the one thing that Jerry wants, that he is chasing after, he should, if he has any sense, stop and let go.

It can be judged how important to the story is this irony, and this delicate positioning of the moral landscape, with reference to the character and the events and the lines drawn between them, if we imagine it with the polarity reversed: if the two kidnappers had been the woebegone amateurs and Jerry had been the murderous one, we would quickly have refused to take part in the story, unless the author had centred our recruitment on the woebegone amateurs.

It speaks for the writers' skill in *Fargo* that the script doesn't relax having secured our involvement in Jerry's singular desire. Instead it intensifies our involvement – and it does so simply but with great effect. We learned in the opening scene that the ransom demand will be for eighty thousand dollars, to be shared equally between the kidnappers and Jerry himself. Around halfway through the film, Jerry meets his father-in-law, Wade, in a roadside cafe in order to discuss handing over the money to the kidnappers. 'No police,' confirms Jerry, 'they were very strict about that.' A further condition laid down by the kidnappers, of course, is that it should be Jerry alone who hands over the million dollars.

With a lurch, our commitment to Jerry's desire intensifies. Jerry, and, by proxy, we, the audience, will receive not forty thousand but nine hundred and sixty thousand dollars. Jerry has lied to the kidnappers about the extent of his father-in-law's wealth and will cream off the majority of the ransom. The kidnappers will receive what amounts to a tip – less than five per cent. Given that Jerry is the (anti) hero, the audience experience that 'lean forward' moment as their involvement increases.

It is exactly *how* the map of desire is drawn – with what skill – that ensures our increasing involvement in Jerry's singular desire. The writers, director and the actors perform with ironic good humour and psychological insight; the film carries us faster and deeper.

A habitual desire in *Fargo*

Opposite Jerry Lundegaard, the other protagonist in *Fargo* is Marge Gunderson (Frances McDormand), the police officer. She has a singular desire as well: to investigate this murderous chain of events and catch the perpetrators. In this respect the 'inciting incident', or the 'first determination' that disturbs the equilibrium of her life is a phone call that wakes her in the early hours and tells her of the murders. The ending of her singular desire comes with her wounding Grimsrud and incarcerating him in the back of her police car. Marge's singular desire operates as the most obvious part of the opposition to Jerry's singular desire.

However, what is remarkable about *Fargo* is how the writers have demoted Marge's singular desire; they have made it of secondary importance. Instead they have promoted a different, habitual desire: for Marge (along with her husband) to sustain, keep warm, and nourish a newly emerging family. The reward that the writers seek in dramatising this habitual desire is the emotional charge carried by the ending of the film.

The audience doesn't encounter Marge until they are thirty minutes into the story. In a darkened room, they first of all see a painting of a mallard duck, and then a pile of books, and a marriage bed that contains a peacefully sleeping couple. The man's arm is thrown around the woman, and the audience knows from its own experience the comfort of such human warmth. Marge and her husband, Norm (the name so close to the word 'normal'), are spooning.

The phone rings and her hand reaches out to answer. The audience can work out just from her side of the conversation that she's listening to a report of the murders of the highway patrol officer and two passers-by.

Brainerd is a small town and we expect some register of alarm on her part; we expect her to mention these cataclysmic events to her husband when she puts down the phone and he awakes. But there is not a word of it. She must climb out of bed and deal with the situation, but the dramatic space is occupied by the warmth of the marriage bed, the warmth in her tone of voice, and his voice, especially, as he repeats his offer to his wife to 'fix you some eggs'. During the gaps in the dialogue we are waiting to hear her account of the telephone call and of the three murders. Instead, three times, one for each murder, we hear Norm's determination to feed his wife. 'I'll fix you some eggs.'

When she rises from the bed, the audience notices her heavy pregnancy.

The writers deliberately make remarkable what Marge *doesn't* say – that a triple murder has been discovered and needs solving. It wrong-foots the audience's expectations, but that's not the writers' motivation for the not-writing of this dialogue. They want to establish Marge's habitual desire: to keep warm and safe (in this cold world) both herself and her husband, and their unborn baby.

An audience might expect Marge to move fast, with urgency, but instead she takes the time to sit down to a very early breakfast. She doesn't finish the plateful that her husband has put in front of her, but with the ironic humour that's never far away in this film, he'll finish it for her. She leaves the house to climb into the prowler, while the camera lingers and watches Norm eat.

In one sense we are impatient for the film to accelerate: three people are lying dead in the snow. On the other hand, this (unrealistic) sequence starts to grow in the audience its love for Marge and Norm and, wordlessly, the story recruits the audience to her habitual desire.

As a final grace note to this scene, Marge reappears. She opens the front door and says, 'Prowler needs a jump.' The same human warmth that saw Norm rise and cook eggs for his pregnant wife also sees him helping to start the frozen police car.

When Marge attends the crime scene, her first concern is a cup of coffee. Fur hat close around her ears, warm gloves pulled on, steaming coffee in hand, she walks down to the car that rests on its roof in the field. She leans down to peer inside. She takes a step back, doubles over and says, 'Think I'm going to barf.' An audience will presume she is sickened at the sight of the dead body inside the car, but, as before, the writers correct the direction of our thinking, and point us towards Marge's habitual desire. It is morning sickness. She is looking after her pregnancy. After a moment she recovers.

It takes a mighty hauling on the wheel, but throughout the film the writers steer the audience towards Marge's habitual desire, the one that must occupy the dramatic space if they are to achieve the ending they want, with its charge of emotion. Therefore the police investigation and the pursuit of the murderers, which is her responsibility, her routine job, a singular desire that forms part of the map of desire for this film, is underplayed in order to favour the habitual one.

The audience's involvement in Marge's habitual desire is first of all secured, but then it is intensified by virtue of the characters with whom the writers have surrounded her – characters chosen with the same care as those who surround Jerry.

One character in particular is positioned next to Marge solely in order to intensify the audience's involvement in Marge's habitual desire, and this character is written by the Coen brothers in a subtle and remarkable way.

Once again Marge is woken in the middle of the night and reluctantly answers the phone. This time, it is someone from years ago, from her schooldays, Mike Yanagita (Steve Park). He saw Marge on the television and is calling for no reason, just to catch up. She does remember him. And she agrees perhaps they could meet, given she has to go to Minneapolis anyway.

The encounter between Marge and Mike Yanagita is one of the longest scenes in the film and at first glance has nothing to do with the story. It might be thought extraneous. On movie websites like www.stackexchange.com a host of opinions are offered as to the narrative function of this scene. Most commentators judge that the scene is there in order to prompt Marge not to trust people, and therefore lead her to interrogate Jerry Lundegaard again about the stolen car (StackExchange n.d.).

The scene is of a more fundamental importance: it intensifies the audience's involvement, their taking part, in Marge's habitual desire.

Mike Yanagita has chosen a better than average restaurant ('It is a Radisson, so it is pretty good'). When Marge arrives, he smiles broadly and rises to greet her. 'Marge? Jeez … ' He embraces her, and his eyes roll in a kind of delirium. He squeezes too hard, and finds it difficult to let go. She has to prise him away – 'Easy, there,' she says. He notices her pregnancy and exclaims, 'That's great.' He sits opposite her. 'Sooohh … Chief Gunderson, then!' He is anxious for the conversation to go well.

They are all smiles.

He asks about her life, and is quick to admire her job, and the fact that she is married and about to have a baby; he congratulates her. She's done so well.

'What about you, Mike? You married? You got kids?'

He replies that he *was* married – but suddenly he leaves his side of the table and slides next to Marge, and puts his arm around her – 'D'you mind if I sit over here?' he asks before adding, 'I was married to Linda Cooksey.'

Marge interrupts and sends him back to his side of the table, 'No, why don't you go over there, I'd prefer that.'

Hurriedly he obeys, and is profuse with his apologies.

Marge is quick to be generous, to allow him to escape with his dignity, 'Oh, no, just so I can see you, so I don't have to turn my neck.'

He moves the conversation back to where they were before. 'I was married to Linda Cooksey – you remember Linda?'

'I think I remember Linda … ' Then Marge's eyes widen. 'Oh yeah!'

It is clear that Mike was married to the school beauty. And he works for IBM – 'It sounds like you're doing really super,' says Marge.

The expression on Mike's face drops. Sadness overcomes him. He reveals that Linda, his wife, died of leukaemia; and there were no children. 'She passed away. It was, ah … tough … it was long … She fought real hard, Marge. What can you say.' Tears blink from his eyes. 'I'm so lonely.' He openly cries in front of Marge. It is awful; and we look back over the story and we realise – that's why he called Marge so late at night; it is why he put his arm around her so clumsily.

The events translate into emotion: we feel our own loneliness in Mike Yanagita's. Such loneliness that surrounds him might be our fate, and it would be Marge's, too, without her marriage. Her habitual desire to maintain the warmth and security of her about-to-be-family is not only something that we admire and approve of, it has intensified to being absolutely necessary, the root of any happiness for us or for Marge, because without it we turn into Mike Yanagita. Thus our commitment to her desire intensifies by virtue of a character whom the writers have placed alongside her.

Far from being an extraneous scene, it is one of the most important, and it carries the film's meaning.[6]

The audience's involvement is increased further, because it is not the last that's heard of Mike Yanagita. Thirteen minutes of screen time later, Marge packs her belongings in an overnight bag and at the same time talks on the phone about him to an old friend. The friend tells her, 'No! No, they never married ... '

The information drops on us with extraordinary poignancy. Mike Yanagita was never married. He made it all up. There was no wife, no cancer, no bereavement.

Previously we felt sorry for him, but that sorrow is now replaced by a sense of dread at just *how* cold is the state of loneliness inhabited by Mike Yanagita. We latch onto Marge's habitual desire with renewed commitment, for her sake and for our own.

In *Fargo* the Coen brothers place a habitual desire opposite a singular one, and they recruit the audience's involvement in both, and they intensify that involvement over the length of the film.

The habitual desire wins over the singular one. The ransom money is buried beneath a cold, snow-covered roadside; no one will find it. Jerry ends up wearing only his underpants, pinned down by law officers on that motel bed, his face stuffed into a pillow, groaning. As for Marge, the closing scene of the film demonstrates her victory. It is a small domestic episode that exercises her habitual desire. In these closing minutes it delivers the emotional value of the drama.

Marge joins Norm in the warmth of the marriage bed. It might be thought that the dramatic events of the day (her discovering the deaths of Jerry's wife and Showalter, and her shooting and taking into custody of Grimsrud) might get a mention, but, as in Marge's first scene, the murders are not given screen time. Instead, Norm says, 'They announced it.'

'They announced it?'

'Yeah.'

'So?'

---

[6] See page 29 for how this technique is also applied in *The Shawshank Redemption*.

'Three-cent stamp.'

'Your mallard?'

A slight expression of pride crosses Norm's expression. 'Yeah.'

Marge congratulates Norm on winning a competition that will see his illustration of a mallard duck (the first object we saw in their house) appear on a three-cent stamp. 'That's terrific.'

'It is just a three-cent.'

She says with more certainty, 'It is terrific.'

'Hogman's blue-winged teal got the twenty-nine-cent.' Norm is mildly piqued that his picture wasn't chosen for the larger denomination. 'People don't much use the three-cent.'

Just as Norm cooked breakfast for Marge in the middle of the night, now it is Marge's turn to support her husband. 'Oh for Pete's sake, of course they do. Whenever they raise the postage people need the little stamps.'

Given prominence over murder and greed are the qualities of humility and humanity (and art) – qualities that are expressed by this tiniest of items, a stamp of the lowest possible value, that people will rarely have cause to use. At the opposite end of the scale from Jerry's one million dollars, the three-cent stamp brings to Norm and Marge everything (nearly) they could wish for. Norm's benign grumble that he didn't get the twenty-nine-cent stamp is the final humorous and ironic grace note, and the audience embraces the meaning that the narrative has so generously and emphatically reinforced in us.

2   Is the desire vigorous or placid?

On an Ordnance Survey map the closeness of the contour lines denotes the steepness of the land.

One might also understand a desire as being more or less steep, accelerating us either quickly, or, in a gentler landscape, more placidly. A vigorous desire agitates the surface of events, whereas a placid one has less kinetic energy, which doesn't mean it lacks depth or power.

Either a vigorous or a placid desire will serve equally well for the purposes of narrative traction. (In *Fargo*, the placid, habitual desire of Marge is a more powerful force than Jerry's singular, vigorous one.)

It might seem logical to think the singular desire is likely to be vigorous, and the habitual one will surely be more placid, but it is not always the case. In *There Will Be Blood* (2007), directed and with a screenplay by Paul Thomas Anderson from the novel by Upton Sinclair, the protagonist, Daniel Plainview, is driven by a vigorous but habitual desire to make money.

It will be tempting for a screenwriter to seek out the strongest, most vigorous desire because she or he wants to inject the greatest possible energy into the script and thus be certain to carry the audience along; however it is a mistake to search for a vigorous desire when the placid one will deliver a more credible reality and a stronger emotion.

Placid desire in *Wings of Desire*

In *Wings of Desire* (1987), written by Wim Wenders and Peter Handke, silent angels wearing dark overcoats look down on the inhabitants of Berlin, and can hear the thoughts of those people to whom they come close enough. The angels can't be seen except by children; their role is merely to watch over the population, to witness human experience.

A woman takes a break from decorating her apartment; a teenager wonders at there being nothing good on TV; a man visits the apartment of his dead mother; a youth considers the lover who does not love him while, in the next room, his father despairs of the son's choice in music.

The angels can't interfere. They are observers, merely – and have been for countless years.

They can be anywhere they please, and so it is inevitable that they occupy odd places from which to carry out their observations. Two of the angels, Cassiel (Otto Sander) and Damiel (Bruno Ganz), dressed in their uniform of dark overcoats and scarves, have chosen for their meeting place a brand new convertible car, still in the showroom. Occupying the front seats they compare notes on the day's events, as well as events that happened on the same day long ago; and through the showroom's large plate glass window they can see, walking along outside, mortals who must deal with life itself, human feelings, human failings, humans who have their very own portion of time allotted to them.

It is as if the human race is on display, and much admired by Damiel. He admits to his companion –

> sometimes I am fed up with my spiritual existence, of forever hovering above. I'd like to feel a weight in me, to end the infinity, and tie me to the earth. I'd like, at each step, each gust of wind, to be able to say now, now and now. No longer: 'Forever' and 'for eternity.'

Damiel describes, in a lengthy monologue, his singular, placid desire: to enter into the flow of time as it is experienced by humankind, to be mortal and to shoulder the suffering of mortals, because without suffering, pleasure isn't possible; together they constitute human feeling, human life. Damiel wants to become human. The poetic expression of his desire in this scene is a remarkable, long monologue that uses mostly concrete nouns to anchor itself in the reality of being human, rather than in the abstract idea of 'life'. It uses the conventional power of imagist poetry, which in effect is a verbal expression of one of the two modes of film writing, action, to create in our mind's eye a montage of ordinary events that together make up a concrete description of real life as it happens. Damiel wants to 'feed the cat like Philip Marlowe, to have a fever, blackened fingers from the newspaper, to be excited not only by the mind, but by a meal. By the line of a neck, an ear'. When he allows himself the luxury of including the abstract in his account of his desire, he still attaches it to a concrete image – he wants, 'To lie. Through one's teeth.'

It is a singular, placid desire.

In *Fargo* we snatch a momentary glimpse of Jerry's singular, vigorous desire as it is trawled past our noses by a different character, and we have to work to understand it; and moreover the writers have to do some heavy lifting in order to recruit us to its movement. In *Wings of Desire* Damiel himself expresses his desire at length in a monologue that invites us to take pleasure in the description; and our recruitment to the desire is easy and immediate. We are human beings, and the poetic celebration of the sensual, commonplace pleasures afforded to us, along with the suffering that comes as an inevitable accompaniment to the experience of life, strikes us the more deeply because of the length and intensity given to its expression. It is a useful example of a monologue performing essential work in a drama. It is also an example of telling, not showing, which allows us to throw out the conventional dictate ('show don't tell') that is so misused in the discipline of creative writing.

The intensity of Damiel's singular desire can't be doubted after his speech, yet it is still a placid desire rather than a vigorous one. It doesn't disturb the surface of the action, unlike the vigorous desire of Jerry in *Fargo*. After such uncountable numbers of years at their task (before human life was evident), nothing is vigorous for the angels; all their actions have become smoothed down, and appear with the same placid, deadpan surface. Yet, as in the case of a deep pool situated between more turbulent stretches of a river, the placid nature of the surface is evidence of its depth, of the sheer weight of desire that has gathered in this enormous reservoir over time.

In the way of singular linear narratives this desire now becomes the spine on which are hung the actions of the film. Yet the actions are as minimal as they can possibly be: the angels can only observe, passively. They play no active role. One of the reasons for such a long and poetic description of Damiel's desire is that no actions are available to him (within the rules of the world of the film) to demonstrate the desire-in-action. His longing to be human is dramatised only by the expression on his face as he observes human beings and overhears their thoughts. The most he can do is put his hand on a person's shoulder, to give them a slight shift, in their thinking, towards the positive.

The desire is also remarkable because there isn't any opposition arranged against it, to speak of. Commonly, conflict is assumed to be necessary both to create the drama (the greater the opposition to the desire, the more conflict, and thus the more powerfully dramatic it is) and create the extent, the length, of the film. Without wishing to underestimate the importance of conflict, or opposition to the desire, I agree with David Terruso (2007) when he applauds his tutor, the writer Justin Cronin, and says –

> The conventional wisdom about how to keep a screenplay moving along is to cram it full of conflict. Conflict, conflict, conflict. Conflict in every scene. Well, not only is this nearly impossible, it is also misleading.

> What keeps a screenplay moving along is not conflict, but tension. Conflict is two forces in opposition ... Tension is simply this: The question of what happens next.

The writers of *Wings of Desire*, Wim Wenders and Peter Handke, chose not to use conflict as a means of exploring and intensifying Damiel's desire. There is no internal conflict, even, within Damiel, which would have been easy for the writers to have invented: his choice could have been dramatised as a difficult one to make, between a painless, eternal existence and a painful, yet also pleasurable, short one. But the writers do not put him in a state of internal conflict. He merely wishes to be human. And certainly there is no external conflict: the other angels make no objection, and the rules of the story don't provide any obstacle for Damiel to overcome in order to achieve his desire. These would have been the more conventional methods for a writer to use in order to explore and intensify Damiel's desire, and create the film's extent. Wenders and Handke eschew this method but concentrate none the less on the primary task faced by the dramatist: to express the desire, explore its argument, air its psychology, and, most importantly, intensify our involvement in it, and thereby deliver its meaning.

In *Wings of Desire* our involvement in Damiel's desire is intensified with the use of the characters who are put alongside him, in this case primarily the trapeze artist, Marion (Solveig Dommartin). If Damiel is an angel who complains that any role he might currently play in people's lives can only ever be a pretence, Marion is a human who complains that she must pretend to fly like an angel. When she comes down from the trapeze she describes her wings as 'chicken feathers' and, we are told, 'these wings bother her'.

Damiel watches Marion carefully as she folds herself into different shapes on the trapeze, and watches equally carefully as she waits, alone, in her caravan. But it is beyond any possibility for him to fall in love with her or demonstrate any emotion. He is interested in her just as in anyone else. But we, the audience, see the possibility of a love affair because she is someone who feels strongly the absence of love. In her caravan, while she alters position from sitting to lying down on her bed and then to sitting again, Damiel overhears her thinking, 'That's what makes me clumsy.

The absence of desire.' And then she adds, as if talking to him directly, 'Desire to love.' In this sense they are the same; they don't have in their lives that 'longing, longing … ' that they both identify as being the true value of life, akin to hope. We recognise the philosophical truth of this even as we are within the middle of a fictional construct that uses desire as its engine. The intensity with which we are involved in Damiel's intention doubles, now, because we understand that the fate of two people, both of whom we admire, depends on the outcome of Damiel's singular, placid desire to become human, which in itself is to suffer from and to enjoy desire.

Instead of being argued with the use of conflict, the desire is expressed – and delayed – by way of philosophy and metaphor. The circus, of which Marion is a member, is losing money and has to close early; its time is cut short. The news throws Marion into uncertainty: she will probably have to become a waitress again. The circus acts as a metaphor for life and its cruelties, its hardships, as well as its music and celebration and excitement (and art). The character of the storyteller, Homer (played by Curt Bois, the actor who also played the pickpocket in *Casablanca*), in his search through the library's archives, allows the story to collapse time and bring together the past history of Berlin and the present day. Homer turns the pages of a book of photographs in the library and sees rows of dead children; meanwhile the angel, Cassiel, hears his thoughts, 'What is wrong with peace that its inspiration doesn't endure, and that its story is hardly told?' Later, as Homer bumps along the graffiti-covered boundary of the Berlin Wall, he thinks, 'I cannot find the Potsdamer Platz.' The bringing together of images from the past and the present collapses time and explores its nature. And it is time – his own, singular experience of, and involvement in, time – that is Damiel's desire. Marion says, 'Time will heal everything. But what if time was the illness?' Time is also collapsed by the use of a film-within-a-film: a film set is visited both by Cassiel and Damiel. The production is a comically ridiculous story set in Nazi Germany and therefore the images seen and remembered by Homer are echoed in this film's costumes and fight sequences. By collapsing time, and by offering a rich, dense pattern of moments in many people's ordinary lives, the film explores the philosophical nature of Damiel's desire to live, to occupy his own time, for good and ill.

The desire is intensified by this philosophical discussion: we can see that, despite the drawbacks, our lives (our time), as human beings, are so much more desirable than the eternal, pain-free, uninvolved witnessing of the angels, and therefore our approval of Damiel's desire is increased at the same time as we feel the wonder of our own lives, a wonder that we wish to share with Damiel.

Our involvement in Damiel's desire is also intensified by the use of the character of Peter Falk (playing himself), who was once, we come to learn, an angel like Damiel, and years ago made the same transition that Damiel wishes now to make. Leaning an elbow against a trailer selling coffee and snacks, Falk is one of us, a mortal, but his previous history as an angel means he can sense Damiel's presence. Falk talks into thin air in order to celebrate with Damiel the simple pleasures that will become available to him: rubbing his hands together to warm them; drinking a cup of coffee and smoking a cigarette at the same time.

By virtue of this imaginative and philosophical exploration of Damiel's desire, the film delivers what the screenwriter and Russian formalist Viktor Shklovsky described in *Theory of Prose* (1925/1993) as the purpose of all fiction, all art: to refresh our practised view of life, make it strange, and thus allow us to achieve once again the sense of incalculable wonder at our surroundings that was given to us when we were first born. (2–13)

Damiel's desire has been philosophically explored in such a way that our involvement has been distilled to a more intense state. It's been done mostly with the use of two characters positioned alongside Damiel: Peter Falk, who has already trodden the same path and proven the worth of his change from angel to human, and Marion, who unknowingly waits for him and is the concrete expression of what many of us will claim to be life's greatest pleasure: sexual love.

Without opposition, merely by desiring enough to do so, Damiel crosses over from eternity to take up ownership of his very own portion of time's flow. His singular, placid desire is answered. The filmed image changes from the binary of black-and-white to the multiple vibrations of colour, and immediately, in a comically heavy-handed metaphor, a suit of armour lands on Damiel's head and injures him: red blood flows from a real wound. He will need the metaphorical suit of armour to protect him from life's blows.

At an hour and a half's extent, the film could end here with the achievement of Damiel's desire, but we have become invested in the concrete expression of that abstract desire – which is to meet, and love, Marion. This logical extension to Damiel's desire takes us onwards for a further thirty minutes.

The first of those minutes is taken up with Damiel finding his way to the pleasures that were first signalled by Peter Falk; he leans against the same coffee stand, rubs his hands in the same way, drinks that same black coffee. He buys some horribly colourful clothes to replace the dull angel's uniform of overcoat and scarf (although Peter Falk has kept to the angel's uniform). But when Damiel visits the site where the circus once stood, it has gone. There is only a circle of sawdust left behind. For the first time Damiel feels pain and disappointment.

A curious child asks him, 'Are you sick?'

He replies, 'Yes.'

'What's the matter?'

'A need.'

Fate leads him to go to the same music venue at which he saw Marion previously, where she is dancing to a performance given by the singer Nick Cave. Damiel sits quietly at the near-empty bar, adjacent to the room where the music is playing. As if a magnet draws her away from the music, Marion moves to that same bar where Damiel waits. They were always going to meet and the film is quick to bring them together. She sits on a stool next to him; and slowly, with a sense of portent, he takes off his hat. Without a word he lifts his glass of wine with both hands and offers it to her, as if it is a libation. 'At last it is becoming serious,' she says. 'We incarnate something.' He leans close to her; and she speaks as if they've been together for a long time. 'There is no greater story than ours, that of man and woman. It will be a story of giants.' She stares directly into the camera, into our eyes, 'I am ready,' she says. 'Now it is your turn. You hold the game in your hand. Now or never.' Thus she invites us, the audience, to work on our own story, our own time.

Damiel's last words, spoken at the same time as he writes them down, are, 'I know now, what no angel knows.' It gives us, the human race, the audience, a sense of privilege, of riches.

The expression of Damiel's desire occupies every moment of the story, even in its perambulations around the people of Berlin; in this case the drama is effected without conflict but nonetheless the desire is expressed, it is argued philosophically and, most importantly, our involvement in the desire is intensified even as we arrive at a more complete understanding. The desire's placid quality, its depth, is its strength.

3   Is the desire hidden, or evident?

In *Fargo* and in *Wings of Desire* the characters' desires are in plain sight. In both films, the actions and the words of the characters express and prosecute their desires. The writers choose to make the desires evident both to the audience and to the characters themselves.

In writer-director Frank Darabont's *The Shawshank Redemption* (1994) and in Mike Leigh's *Secrets and Lies* (1996) the protagonists' desires are, in different ways, hidden.

In *Shawshank*, the desire is hidden from us (for the first two-thirds of the film) but not from the character; in *Secrets and Lies* the opposite is true: the desire is repressed, hidden from the character herself (for the first half of the film) as well as from other characters, but not from us. It is written as the character's *unconscious* desire.

In the preceding pages it has become evident that morality, right and wrong (the subject of Chapter 3), contributes heavily to a writer's successful drawing of a map of desire; and in this following section it will likewise become evident that the notion of logic, the subject of Chapter 2, also makes an indispensable contribution to the narrative power of the hidden desire, whether conscious or unconscious.

Hidden desire in *The Shawshank Redemption*

The Shawshank Redemption, adapted by Frank Darabont from the book by Stephen King, starts by planting the idea that Andy Dufresne (Tim Robbins) might or might not be guilty of the murder of his wife and her golf-pro lover.

It is the final moment in Andy's trial for murder and the judge describes him as 'an icy and remorseless man' and orders him 'to serve two life sentences back to back, one for each of your victims.'

The desire for justice is set in train – especially in us, the audience. The writing, and the performance of Andy, steers the audience towards making the opposite judgement from the court's: Andy might well be innocent. There is reasonable doubt. And if Andy shouldn't have been convicted, the audience has a tentative desire that he shouldn't, perhaps, be in jail.

But the audience are expert at narrative: they understand that they've been coached into the position of thinking Andy might, or might not, be guilty. They are ready to hear the truth, either way. They trust the story will tell them, for certain, before it ends.

Andy arrives at Shawshank prison along with a bus-full of new convicts. Everyone in Shawshank claims they are innocent, and yet there persists, gently, in the audience, a desire that Andy, in particular, shouldn't be in here. From the outset the writers are working on the audience's recruitment to the central desire of the protagonist, while at the same time hiding that same desire, preventing the audience from seeing it, in the character of Andy Dufresne.

Prisoners gather to watch the new intake arrive. A group of them bets smokes on who 'will be the first to go'. Ellis Boyd 'Red' Redding (Morgan Freeman) bets on 'That tall drink of water with a silver spoon up his ass' – Andy Dufresne. The audience don't know yet what it is they are betting on, but soon find out. That evening, after lights-out, the inmates begin to call out to the newcomers, warning them of the dangers of male rape visited on them by the prison's so called 'sisters'. Their bet was on who among the new intake will be the first to break down and beg to be let out. In particular the energetic Heywood (William Sadler) is determined to win the bet and, in a cooing voice, he plants horrible images in the mind of his neighbour, the 'chubby fat-ass' that he's chosen as the likely candidate. Red's bet was placed on Andy as the first who will crack due to the latter's class and race. Instead, it is Heywood's 'tub of lard' who breaks down and blubs, 'I don't belong here! I want to go home!' His sobs echo through the cells in Shawshank, and his words resonate with the audience's emerging desire that Andy should escape from this prison if he can.

Heywood is gleeful, 'And it is fat-ass, by a nose!' He's won the bet and tomorrow he will smoke.

The night's business is done, and Heywood warns his man to shut up. The lights are switched on; the wardens are here. The blubbing continues; the man is too far gone. He can't heed the warnings of the guards and continues his own desperate pleading to be let out. His claims that he shouldn't be in here, as well as his noisy sobbing, puts into sharp relief Andy Dufresne's silence, his lack of an expression of this desire. But the begging and pleading words enter the minds of the audience and stick to Andy Dufresne because of his *refusal* to say them.

Prison officers are gathered around, chief among them Captain Byron Hadley (Clancy Brown). They haul out the 'chubby fat-ass,' and Hadley beats him to death.

With this example of murderous, sadistic cruelty, the audience's desire on Andy's behalf grows – he, and everyone else, must be got out of there. The audience's moral sense is invoked. Andy's crime of passion (if indeed he did commit it) looks innocent next to the brutality of Hadley and his guards. And yet there is still no desire evident in Andy himself. His expression is deadpan. He doesn't talk to anyone.

A first hint of the desire already held by the audience on Andy's behalf – that he should escape – becomes briefly evident in Andy himself twenty-four minutes into the film, only for it to be immediately hidden again.

Andy sidles up to Red in the prison yard and says, 'I understand you're a man who knows how to get things.'

'I'm known to locate certain things, from time to time,' answers Red.

'I wonder if you might get me a rock hammer.'

Our ears prick up: perhaps Andy will now express this desire that we wish for him, and this desire will then carry the film along in the manner of a traditional single linear narrative.

'What?' asks Red.

'A rock hammer,' repeats Andy.

Any idea we might have of Andy using the rock hammer as a weapon, or as a tool for digging his way out, is, the next moment, covered over, obscured. The rock hammer is 'six or seven inches long' – ridiculously small. Andy then reveals his reason for wanting it. He sinks to his haunches and fingers the dirt of the prison yard. He picks out fragments of rock and names them, one after another. 'Quartz. Some mica. Shale. Limestone.'

'So?'

'So I'm a rock-hound. At least I was in my old life. And I'd like to be one again, on a limited basis.'

The list of proper names of the rock samples confirms the audience's belief: it is a hobby. The authority, as usual, is delivered by the detail.

Red tries to pull the audience back to what they initially thought. 'Then I'd guess you'd want to escape? Tunnel under the wall, maybe?'

Andy gives a short sound that might have been a laugh.

'Have I missed something here? What's so funny?'

'You'll understand when you see the rock hammer.'

He doesn't want to escape, at all. Instead, over the following years, he will use the tiny rock hammer to carve, beautifully, a chess set – piece by piece. It is arduous, painstaking work and uses up vast stretches of time. Evidently his desire is not to escape but instead stoically to bear the punishment of being in jail.

Meanwhile, writer-director Frank Darabont realises that he's composing a story that features a main character without any apparent desire, which risks leaving him with a story that lacks traction. He therefore composes events that will evoke the desire in the audience – these events will secure and intensify the audience's recruitment to this desire that Andy should escape. The irony is that its very absence in Andy invigorates its growth in the audience. They already think that maybe Andy shouldn't be in Shawshank, by rights, but now the writer will move the audience from just concern – Andy shouldn't be in there – to a passionate belief: Andy must escape.

The writer achieves this by orchestrating three particular sequences.

The first of these is the unwelcome attention of Bogs Diamond (Mark Rolston) and the 'sisters' or 'bull queers'. Bogs and his 'sisters' are inhuman sadists.

Andy is at work in the prison laundry when he's sent back to the store room. Bogs follows him in – it is a trap. Another sister appears. Andy grabs a handful of soap powder from a drum. A third sister comes from behind him and grabs his arms. Andy fights back and manages to plant an elbow in Bogs's face. He struggles and kicks until they get him on the ground and lay into him, kicking and stamping. The injuries he has inflicted on them mean that his punishment will be worse. The camera's eye tactfully withdraws so the audience can only imagine the subsequent rape.

The sense of injustice is further invigorated with each of the sisters' subsequent attacks, and, given the continual bravery of his fighting back, the audience wishes with *increasing* fervour for Andy's escape from Shawshank.

The second sequence of events that intensifies the audience's desire for Andy to escape is orchestrated around the idea of the prison library.

For over forty years the character of Brooks (James Whitmore) has pushed his trolley up and down the gantries, poking the same tattered volumes through the cell bars to those few prisoners who want to read them. But now, after a lifetime in prison, Brooks has been granted parole.

He stands at the gates of Shawshank, an old man, with his small case, and wearing a civvy suit. He steps over the threshold, and he's out. It is strange to follow a minor character, and leave the enclosed world of the story – the jail.

He has been found a room in a halfway house in a nondescript town, but he has trouble even crossing the road. 'Dear fellas,' he writes to his friends in Shawshank. 'I can't believe how fast things move on the outside. I saw an automobile once when I was a kid, but now they're everywhere. The world went and got itself in a big damn hurry.'

They've given him a job packing grocery bags at the local Foodway store. 'It is hard work,' he writes, 'and I try to keep up, but my hands hurt most of the time.'

A querulous housewife points a finger at Brooks and complains, 'Make sure your man double bags. Last time he didn't double bag, and the bottom near came out.' In front of her, the manager ticks off Brooks, 'Make sure you double bag, like the lady says, understand?'

Brooks is humiliated; and he's lonely outside his native habitat of Shawshank. He has no friends; he doesn't fit in. Shawshank took his life already. He has become institutionalised and cannot thrive in the outside world.

We understand that even after he is let out, he cannot escape.

'I have trouble sleeping at night,' he writes. 'I have bad dreams, like I'm falling. I wake up scared. Sometimes it takes me a while to remember where I am.' And then he muses, 'Maybe I should get me a gun and rob

The Foodway, so they'd send me home.' That word 'home' is heartbreaking: Shawshank, a hellish place, is Brooks's home. He adds, 'I could shoot the manager, while I was at it, sort of like a bonus.'

He dresses smartly in a suit and tie and writes to his friends, 'I don't like it here. I'm tired of being afraid all the time. So I've decided not to stay.' He unfolds a clasp knife and steps onto the chair, and from the chair he steps onto the little square table. Using the knife he carves something into the plaster above the roof beam. After this small act of defiance, he folds the knife shut. On the table his polished shoes move up on tiptoe, although the audience can't see what he's doing.

The shoes settle into a comfortable stance. There is a short pause.

The polished shoes then dance sideways, once, to tilt the table, and on the return journey the table slips sideways and falls from under him. The shoes are left hanging.

Carved into the plaster are the words, 'Brooks was here.'

Meanwhile, in Shawshank, the audience can see that Andy has stepped into Brooks's shoes. Andy is the new librarian, and moreover he is a better librarian. Every day for many years he has written a letter to the prison authorities always to make the same request: for more books, for music, maybe, and for writing equipment. After nearly twenty years the prison authorities' irritation with these letters reaches a conclusion: to shut him up, they give him what he wants.

Boxes of books, records and study materials arrive. Andy now magnifies the good work of the library. It turns, in effect, into a school for prisoners.

Andy, put alongside Brooks, and heading down the same path, is set to become Brooks – except the library is so much bigger. Andy is a better version of Brooks, is headed down the same road, towards the same fate, but more so. He is becoming institutionalised. No escape will be possible.

With an intense sensation of sympathy and dread the audience wishes so *hard* for Andy's *escape*.

It's worth pausing to notice how this sequence from *Shawshank* that features Brooks's release is remarkable in its similarities to the sequence in *Fargo* featuring Mike Yanagita.

In the Coen brothers' *Fargo*, the writers foreground a minor character and deliver an apparent digression that is, in fact, a central plank in the story's design, and they do it for the same reason as Darabont: to place two characters alongside each other (in *Fargo*, Marge and Mike Yanagita; in *Shawshank*, Andy and Brooks) in order to increase in the audience, to an enormous extent, their involvement in the desire that operates as the story's engine and provides the traction that will more powerfully carry them along.

It would be satisfying to hear that the Coen brothers observed the technique at work in *Shawshank* and borrowed it for use in *Fargo*.

There is a third sequence in *The Shawshank Redemption* that helps to intensify the audience's desire for Andy to escape: it starts with the arrival of a new inmate, Tommy Williams (Gil Bellows).

Tommy is a cocky Italian youth with a rebellious spirit and history of aggrieved violence.

Within the context of the library Andy is now running an education programme, and he takes Tommy under his wing, to get him through his exams and maybe set him on the right road. Andy is working hard for someone else to escape the system, even as he himself is becoming more entrenched in that system (so much so that he's even working for the governor of Shawshank, running the governor's corrupt system of bribes and pay-offs). It is a determined effort that Andy makes on Tommy's behalf: he doesn't want this young man (who's only on a two-year sentence for breaking and entering) to offend again.

But the writer's purpose, as far as Tommy is concerned, is to drop into the story a crucial piece of information that will intensify the audience's desire for Andy's escape from Shawshank.

Tommy sits facing backwards on a chair, and tells the story to a small number of prisoners, including Andy Dufresne. The film admits the audience to Tommy's memory, and they watch as Tommy's cellmate, from years ago, in some other prison, makes a confession. 'I got me this job one time,' says the cellmate, called Elmo. 'Bussin' tables at a country club. So I could case these big rich pricks that come in. So I pick out this guy. Go in one night. And do his place. He wakes up. Gives me shit. So I killed him.'

This part seems to amuse Elmo – it was fun to kill someone.

'Him and his tasty bitch he was with,' he goes on, with a horrible, mirthful giggle. 'That's the best part. She's fuckin' this prick, see, this golf pro. But she's married to some other guy. Some hot shot banker ... and he's the one they pinned it on!'

Andy didn't shoot his wife and her lover; the audience knows it now, for certain. Andy has been in prison since 1947, nineteen years, for a crime he didn't commit.

This information has been held back until now in order to use its power most effectively to *increase*, more strongly than before, the audience's desire for Andy to be released. And here is the chance that might allow *the audience's* singular, vigorous desire, a desire that has never been demonstrated in the character himself, to be granted.

Andy goes immediately to Warden Samuel Norton (Bob Gunton)'s office and tells him the news. Norton's face is impassive. The irony hits home: the work that Andy Dufresne has done to help Norton in his illegal sequestering of funds now means that Norton cannot afford ever to allow Andy to leave Shawshank. Instead of instigating an appeal against Andy's life sentence, Norton throws Andy into solitary confinement for a month.

The audience feels despair. Continually their desire is thwarted, or 'Denied,' as Red's parole board keeps on repeating. And the despicable injustice of the warden's corrupt regime increases further the audience's desire to get Andy out.

Norton invites Tommy for a smoke in an out-of-the-way place in the yard, and has a chat with him, just to make sure it's true. He claps Tommy's shoulder, then stubs out his cigarette. His blank, shark-like eyes lift to the nearby control tower, and he gives an imperceptible nod before he walks away. Tommy's gaze follows the warden's up to the watchtower. There is a muzzle flash from Hadley's rifle. Four bullets are driven into Tommy's chest.

There will be no appeal, no retrial. By virtue of his own actions in helping the warden, Andy has sealed himself up in Shawshank until his dying day. He cannot even give up helping the corrupt warden, as the latter threatens to 'cast him down among the sodomites', brick up the library and burn all the books if he stops work.

The injustice crowds in on us from every angle. Shawshank, an institution that is, after all, supposed to deliver justice, generates an increasing injustice. It redoubles the audience's desire for Andy to be out of there.

It also creates a growing desire in the audience to wreak justice on the warden, Norton. This moral universe is the wrong way up. The prison officers, the ones who are meant to be upholding justice, are in fact the criminals, the ego-driven bullies and cheats, living in freedom. The convicts are the sharing, co-operative, righteous men, imprisoned. The audience wishes to tip the scales the other way.

Throughout all these events Andy Dufresne hasn't exhibited any desire to escape. If anything, in his mulish way, his desire is apparently to make the best of his imprisonment in Shawshank – to endure.

Andy's best friend and the narrator of this film, Red, himself exhibits the bare minimum of a desire to get out. The decades, as they've passed, have been punctuated by Red's visits to the parole board and every time Red says the right things, makes the right noises, but the answer comes down in a single word stamped on his application: 'Denied.' That word is a punctuation mark that not only describes the result of Red's application for parole, it also describes how the audience feels: they are frustrated because they are denied any hope of Andy's even showing a desire to escape, at all, and instead have to watch the opposite: his strategy of endurance. This frustration increases the audience's wish for both Andy and Red to escape, or get out somehow, and for their persecutors to be brought to justice.

It is an irony that has been strengthened throughout the film: Andy's apparent lack of desire works to further inflame the audience's desire on his behalf.

After all these setbacks, Andy now begins to show more than just a lack of a desire to escape; it looks as if he is going the same way as Brooks. He has made a strange comment to Red. 'Get busy living. Or get busy dying,' he says. He's going to commit suicide.

'Have to keep an eye on him,' advises Red, to the others.

'That's fine during the day, but during the night he's got that cell all to himself.'

'Oh Lord.' Heywood is suddenly worried.

'What?'

'Andy came down to the loading dock today. He asked me for a length of rope.'

'Rope?'

'Six feet long.'

'And you gave it to him.'

'Sure I did. Why wouldn't I?'

'Jesus. Heywood.'

'How was I supposed to know?'

'Remember Brooks Hatlen?'

'No. Andy'd never do that. Never.'

'Every man has his breaking point,' says Red thoughtfully.

After lights-out, Andy reaches under his pillow for the rope. He looks determined. The screen cross-fades to Red, wakeful, illuminated by a flash of lightning. A roll of thunder sounds outside the prison walls.

The next morning, it is roll call as usual. The prisoners stand outside their cells.

There is an empty space where Andy should be standing. 'Man missing on Tier Two!' calls the guard.

But – Andy's cell is empty. He is not hanging from the ceiling, but there is no sign of his escape, either. The bars on the window are intact, the walls are solid, the cell door was locked all night. There is no way anyone could have got out. Andy has vanished.

In a furious mood, the warden goes to see Andy's cell for himself. He rants and raves in the empty cell. 'Man up and vanished like a fart in the wind. Nothing left but some damned rocks on the window sill.' Norton scoops up a handful of tiny stones and then addresses the poster of Rita Hayworth. '[T]hat cupcake on the wall … Let's ask her. Maybe she knows. What say you there, fussy britches? Feel like talking? Ahh. I guess not. Why should she be any different?'

Norton warns Red, 'This is a conspiracy. That's what this is. One big.' He throws a stone at Red. 'Damn.' Another stone at Red. 'Conspiracy.' And a third one. 'Everyone's in on it. Including her.' He throws a stone at the poster of Rita Hayworth.

The stone goes through the poster.

The governor's expression stiffens. His eye sharpens. He steps up to the poster and pokes a finger into the hole made by the stone. He pushes harder – his hand goes in, and his whole arm. With a flurry he tears the poster away from the wall.

It is a tunnel. Andy has escaped.

A tide of emotion sweeps over the audience. Their desire for Andy to escape, which has, so many times, to such a degree, been intensified by the terrible injustices visited on him by the sisters and by Norton, and by positioning him in the shoes of the pitiful Brooks, and furthermore by the scenario involving Tommy that proved Andy was always innocent of murder, joins together now with Andy's suddenly *evident* desire, during all these years, to escape. It is the virulence of Andy's desire that startles us, and this virulence depends for its effect on all the work the writer has done to keep it *hidden*, until now. These elements combine to make for a rush of feeling, of love and admiration for him, and approval.

The revelation is not only that Andy has wished all along to escape, but at the same time, due to the careful work of the writer, the quality of that desire is made clear. The audience clambers backwards over the story in order to measure the persistent strength and intelligence of Andy's willpower.

The same persistence that saw him write a letter every day for fifteen years to the prison authorities meant he could chip away at the prison wall with the rock hammer.

When he asked Red to get the poster of Rita Hayworth, he arrived in the middle of the film that starred the actress herself but had no eyes for the screen; instead he climbed over everyone's legs to reach Red and put in an order for the poster. He didn't have time to watch the film, as the other prisoners so avidly did. He was too busy scraping away at the wall.

For over twenty years he hid the rock hammer in that cut-out he made in that Bible, and he kept going; and alongside digging the hole in the wall he hand-carved a chess set out of stone. If the chess set was, previously, the audience's measurement of Andy's spending twenty years in a prison cell, how much more impressive it is now that the audience can see that the chess set was a mere sideshow in order to distract everyone from the digging of the tunnel. He did both.

The intricate methods Andy used to purloin the clothes, the shoes and the money he needed to get started in the outside world are evidence of the intelligence with which he applied himself to his desire – he ingratiated himself with the guards for this sole purpose.

The ceaseless fightback that he exhibited against the 'sisters' is the same as he demonstrated against the injustice of his imprisonment.

Andy Dufresne wasn't institutionalised. He was about as far away from 'becoming' Brooks as it was possible to get. The quality of his willpower, suddenly revealed as muscular, intelligent and ever-present, inspires our awe, and our love. Andy's is a singular, vigorous, hidden desire.

If it were an action-adventure film, the story might have ended there, but it is a legal drama and the story has to answer its genre, as well as tie up the character of Red in particular. We are only two-thirds of the way through. The rest of the film reveals not only how Andy escaped, but how, at the same time, he has wreaked justice on the warden, a justice that the audience so badly want to see performed.

As a final grace note Andy not only escapes, and not only causes the warden's suicide, and not only puts the other prison officers in jail, but when his friend Red finally gets that 'Approved' stamp on his parole application and is let out, and follows Brooks to the same halfway house (with the same job, bagging up in the Foodway store), Andy saves him from Brooks's fate. In the middle of a bucolic, peaceful landscape, hidden behind a stone in the wall, is enough money for Red to go and join Andy on the Mexican beach where Andy works on his dreamed-of fishing boat. The two old friends are together again. In effect, they saved each other.

The audience's powerful feeling of love for both Andy and for Red is mixed up, somewhere hidden out of sight, with an equally powerful inclination to embrace the writers (Stephen King for the book and Frank Darabont for the screenplay), that they should have managed to create such a thing as this film, as well as pride that we are of the same species. Like all great art, it is the human race putting its very best foot forward. And we have taken part in it thanks to the writers' skill, because they've arranged for us, in the poetry of their events, to join up our desire with the desire of the characters on the screen for a better and more just life.

Hidden (unconscious) desire in *Secrets and Lies*

Schopenhauer described desire, or willpower, as –

> the innermost, the kernel of every individual thing ... it appears in every blind operation of a force of nature: it also appears in deliberative human action; these differ from each other only in the grade of their appearing, not in the essence of what appears. (135)

The writing of a character's hidden (unconscious) desire seeks to portray dramatically the kernel within that kernel within the individual character. Delving into the surreal world of the unconscious, Jean-Pierre Cauvin (1982) described desire as 'the energizing principle of the unconscious' and it is perhaps in this deep, hidden place that is found the closest, most tight connection between the art of story and the raw instinct that is our desire or willpower.

In a wholly different way from that used by the writers of *The Shawshank Redemption*, Mike Leigh's *Palme D'Or* winner, *Secrets and Lies*, hides the desire of its protagonist not from the audience, but instead from the character herself. It is an unconscious desire that can be observed rising to the surface, over the first half of the film, to become a conscious one.

Middle-aged factory worker Cynthia Purley (Brenda Blethyn) operates a machine that makes the cuts in pieces of cardboard so they can be folded into boxes. Every day, after eight hours performing this mind-numbing task, she returns to the scrappy, untidy, terraced house that she shares with her daughter, twenty-year-old Roxanne (Claire Rushbrook). The relationship between the two is complicated: Cynthia on the one hand wants her daughter to go out and have fun, find a man ('You want to get yourself a bloke,'), but in the same breath reminds her that her own life was blighted by a man getting her pregnant – 'and then I was saddled with you', she complains.

Roxanne bites back with violent intensity, 'Well you should have thought about that before you dropped your knickers.'

From the outset the audience understands that Cynthia's mother died when Cynthia was ten years old and she became responsible for the upbringing of her brother and sister; and then, still not much more than a child herself, she was a single mum looking after Roxanne.

Unlike Cynthia, the audience is privileged with the viewpoint of a young black female optometrist called Hortense (Marianne Jean-Baptiste). Hortense was adopted at birth; and she has the singular, vigorous, and evident desire to find her birth mother, who is Cynthia Purley. The audience feels the mechanical grip of the story as Hortense progresses through various bureaucratic offices and makes her way towards that terraced house where, unsuspecting, lives her birth mother, Cynthia.

Not only was Cynthia at an early age a single mum to Roxanne, but even before that, when she was just fifteen, she had a baby who was taken away from her and given up for adoption.

The combination of the two separate viewpoints – that of Hortense, and of Cynthia – allows the audience to identify and understand Cynthia's *hidden* desire, a desire that is so thoroughly repressed by Cynthia that it becomes an unconscious one: to have returned to her the baby that was taken from her arms at birth when she was just fifteen years old.

The audience experiences the poignancy of that unconscious desire when they witness the middle-aged Cynthia, dressed in her nightie, looking into the mirror and smearing moisturising cream onto her face, an action that becomes a performance of maternal longing as the strength of her unconscious desire briefly overtakes her and she smears the cream around her mouth and then grips and lifts her breasts.

The viewpoint cuts sharply to her lost daughter, Hortense, civilised, calm and hopeful, sitting on her bed and looking through the papers that will tell her where she came from, and about her birth mother, Cynthia. The juxtaposition of these two scenes stirs in the audience the knowledge of Cynthia's psychology: her maternal, sexual desire is to replace and feed the baby taken from her breast.

We are already getting a sense of how the relationship between Cynthia and her grown-up daughter Roxanne is affected by Cynthia's repressed desire. Roxanne's conception and birth, we might guess, was a response to the earlier baby being taken.

The grief and sadness that reposes in Cynthia is again made evident when her younger brother, Maurice (Timothy Spall), whom she nurtured, too, as her child, comes to visit. Together they go up to a disused spare bedroom, where a jumble of old stuff from their shared past is stored, forgotten. Cynthia quite suddenly descends into tears and begs, 'Give us a cuddle, Maurice. Please, sweetheart?' She holds onto him, but his reluctance to return the embrace is poignant. She chastises him for never coming to visit. 'Why have you left it so bloody long?'

'It is work, and tha ... '

'There's nothing wrong with your dialling finger.'

'You can ring me.'

'You're always too busy, ain't yer … ' Her next line, 'You're the only one I've got, Maurice,' comes to the audience laden with dramatic irony, given their knowledge that it is not true. Even as she blurts out this line, Cynthia's missing daughter, Hortense, is plucking up the courage to lift the phone and call her. Thus is Cynthia's hidden desire for her missing child, which she has suppressed for so long, given the extra power of dramatic irony. The audience is certain that this unconscious desire is about to be brought to the surface because we've already witnessed the first phone call to arrive at the house from Hortense, which was answered by Roxanne. The latter hears nothing but silence from the other end of the line and dismisses the call as probably from 'one of them perverts'.

Cynthia's unconscious desire to restore to herself her lost baby is then powerfully dramatised in one of the most extraordinary scenes in modern British cinema in terms of its writing, performance and direction. It occurs at around one hour into the film. In her neglected back garden Cynthia lies back in a white plastic sun lounger while loosely holding a drink in her hands. Her daughter Roxanne sits alongside, scuffing through a newspaper.

'Ain't you seeing him tonight, then?' asks Cynthia, about Roxanne's boyfriend. To start with, the dialogue is banal.

'I'm having an early night,' replies Roxanne.

'Keep me company.' It sounds like a comfortable wish of Cynthia's, but Roxanne dashes her hopes. 'I've got a hangover.'

The tension escalates a notch. 'You should stop in more often,' Cynthia advises her daughter, and then asks, 'You are looking after yourself with him, ain't you, sweetheart?' It sounds kindly, but our previous experience of the relationship between the two women means we can sense danger.

'What d'you mean?'

'You know, taking care.'

Roxanne's discomfort shows in the slight movement of her shoulders, as if she's shrugging off an unwelcome hand.

Cynthia presses on. 'I don't want to ask you nothing personal darling, but … ' Cynthia's eyes blink repeatedly as she trespasses on her daughter's privacy. 'You taking the pill?'

Roxanne shouts, 'That is personal.'

Cynthia can't help herself. 'Why don't you bring him round?'

'Leave it out.'

'I'd like to meet him. I wouldn't know him if he stood up in me soup.'

'Don't hold yer breath.'

The camera's eye moves closer to the two women. 'You don't want to leave it up to him, darling,' says Cynthia, 'men are all the same.'

Roxanne tries to stop her. 'Mum!'

'I hope he uses a whassersname … condoms.'

'Mind your own business.'

'They can leak! You wanna be careful.' For all the accusations, recriminations and warnings that Cynthia flings at her daughter, she is in fact aiming them at herself. She had Roxanne when she was twenty-one and brought her up on her own. Her motherly kindness is poignantly glimpsed here and there, but merely slips out of the cracks between her own suffering, her own lack.

Roxanne sees the truth. 'You're jealous, in't yer?'

'Where is he tonight, anyway?'

'I dunno.'

'Most likely out givin' someone else one. That's how I got caught with you … running out of the pill. You could have a coil fitted.'

The anger is boiling in Roxanne. She only pretends to read the newspaper, now. She flinches as her mother's lines arrive, one after the other. Yet she still does the decent thing: with a warning look, she tries to shut down the conversation. 'Change the record.'

'Dr Mullholland. Make an appointment. You'd suit the sponge.'

'Keep your voice down!'

'I got a Dutch cap floatin' around somewhere upstairs – you could have that … ' Cynthia's desire to stop her daughter from falling pregnant is attached to the machinery, the equipment, which should have been used to stop herself from ever having become pregnant. Her desire to have returned to her the baby that was taken away is mixed up with wishing never to have been pregnant in the first place.

Roxanne leaps to her feet and is gone.

Cynthia carries on, regardless, ' … run it under the tap, bit of talcum powder … Where you goin?'

'I don't have to listen to this.' Roxanne is already on her way into the house.

'Sweetheart! Sweetheart, darling, I'm only trying to help yer!' Cynthia hurries after her daughter and follows her into her bedroom. Roxanne is sitting in the chair in the corner, hands pressed to her temples, trying to contain her anger. 'Leave me alone!'

'I'm yer mother!'

'Get out of my room!'

Then comes an abrupt turnaround. 'It don't matter if you have a little baby,' says Cynthia, 'I'll look after it.' This line is so very suddenly and deeply affecting because it is sponsored by grief; we recognise it as evidence of Cynthia's long-repressed desire to have her baby back. This recognition mixes with the fact that it is an act of kindness, of generosity towards her daughter, in any event, which doubles the emotion that is carried by the line.

Roxanne is battling her mother's demons for her. 'I ain't getting pregnant!'

'I'll give up my job.' This plaintive request from Cynthia for Roxanne, her own daughter, to provide her with a baby to replace the one that was taken from her is poignant in the extreme. Cynthia's subconscious desire is playing on the surface of events.

'It is nothing to do with you.'

Cynthia turns – and then all the weight of repression that has forced her desire to be buried for all these years comes forcefully down and steers her once again towards cruelty and rudeness. 'Yes it bloody is! I'm not having you dropping it at my door!'

A moment ago, Roxanne's future baby was longed for as a replacement for the one that was taken, but now it is just so much rubbish that might be thrown out for Cynthia to deal with. The forces of repression are powerful enough that she will hurt her own daughter that much.

Roxanne reels under the blow. 'Jesus Christ!' She is on her feet and on her way out already.

It wasn't Cynthia talking – not the real Cynthia that we know is underneath the hurt and suffering. She pleads with her adult daughter and clings to her arm to stop her from going, 'I'm sorry darlin', I don't mean ... '

Roxanne flings her off. 'Get off! You make me sick, you stupid bitch!' Roxanne storms from the house while Cynthia is thrown face down on Roxanne's bed. She stays there, sobbing uncontrollably into her daughter's duvet.

Cynthia is controlled by two different desires. One of them is on the surface: she wants to protect her daughter from making the same mistakes as she made, while at the same time wishing for her a full life, with children and a mate. The other, unconscious desire shows its power with that unhealthy greed for her imaginary grandchild, her offer to take over its upbringing, its nurture, the loving of it, in order that it might act as a replacement for the baby that was torn from her arms when she was nothing but a child herself. The simple line of dialogue, uttered with such a heartfelt, pleading cry, 'I'll give up my job,' enchants us with its double meaning, its twin strands of logic: 'I want my missing baby, and I want you to have a baby.' It is no more than a glimpse, but has the full force of our survival instinct – to breed – of which love is the emotional expression.

Like all the best drama, the emotive power of this scene increases with each viewing, as we train ourselves into an understanding of the psychology.

Meanwhile, Cynthia's unconscious desire is steadily brought closer to the surface of events, whether she likes it or not. With dread, and with an awful stirring of sympathy, we observe Hortense pluck up the courage again to call her birth mother.

Barely recovered from her row with Roxanne, Cynthia hears the ringing phone and moves into the hallway to answer it. Unknowing, she talks in a bruised, suffering voice to her lost daughter, the young woman who was once the baby never allowed to her.

'Hello?'

'I'm sorry to trouble you, but I'm trying to locate a Cynthia Purley.'

'Yes?'

'Is that Cynthia Purley?'

'Yes.'

'Cynthia Rose Purley?'

'Yes!'

'Of 76, Quilter Street?'

'Yes,' says Cynthia impatiently. 'What is it you want, darlin'?' And she listens to the silence on the other end of the phone and asks, 'Did you want Roxanne? She's gone out.'

'No ... '

'She ain't in any trouble, is she?'

'No, it is about Elizabeth.'

'Elizabeth? Elizabeth who?'

'Elizabeth Purley.'

'Oh ... oh ... ' Cynthia's expression is strangely affectionate, and relieved. Then she answers, 'She's dead.'

We are busy computing these new names and new relationships. The woman we know as Hortense was obviously christened Elizabeth, and perhaps Cynthia was told that her baby had died – but why, then, is Cynthia's expression so kindly?

'No, she isn't.'

'She is, darlin', I should know.'

'I should know.'

'Look, sweetheart, she's me mother – she went in 1961.' The situation clicks into place. Cynthia still hasn't realised that she's talking to her long-lost daughter. But the most poignant realisation comes with it – Cynthia named her baby daughter, before it was taken away, after her own mother. The emotional value of motherhood is linked from the long-dead past to the living, but hidden, present.

'No, I mean *baby* Elizabeth Purley.'

'Baby Eliz ... ' The look of incomprehension on Cynthia's face, inch by inch, is replaced by one of strange disbelief. 'Who is this?'

'She was born on the twenty-third of July, 1968, at ... sorry about this. Er, yeah, at The Haven, Wells Grange Avenue, Sutton, Surrey. Look, I'm sorry, I know this must be a shock to you ... '

Cynthia's disbelief graduates to fear. She puts down the phone and stumbles from the hallway to the kitchen. She leans over the sink and is physically sick.

The writing of this scene allows us the privilege of observing how deeply repressed in Cynthia is the desire for the return of her baby. The evident answer to Cynthia's unconscious, hidden desire has arrived in the form of an adult stranger's voice – it has made itself heard in a dramatically powerful way. The repressed desire is a sickness that must find its way out.

In her flat, Hortense paces back and forth and calls the number again. In her cluttered, broken-down home Cynthia is washing out her mouth; and her face registers terror at the renewed summons of the phone. She stares at it, pressing a tea towel to her mouth. Slowly she inches towards the instrument, picks it up. 'Listen darlin', what is it you want?'

'Look, I'm really sorry.'

'You mustn't come round here, sweetheart.'

'I didn't want to upset you.'

'You mustn't do that. And you mustn't phone, neither.'

'I just needed to know.'

'Yes but you *can't* come round 'ere,' Cynthia commands emphatically through her tears, 'cos no one knows about you, see?'

In this exchange the audience witnesses Cynthia's continued attempt at repressing her unconscious desire. It is intensely moving.

'Right,' says Hortense drily.

Cynthia's crying deepens. 'Promise me you won't come round 'ere, promise me!' she begs. 'I'm ever so sorry, sweetheart, I'm a little bit upset. Promise me you won't come round.'

The forces at work to repress Cynthia's desire (a desire that is also an instinctive need) seem still to be in control; she is trying hard to put the genie back in the bottle. However the audience has witnessed the emotional power of Cynthia's unconscious desire in that earlier scene when she offers to give up her job to look after an imaginary grandchild, and the audience senses quite rightly that the unconscious desire – to have in her arms again her lost baby – is too powerful. Despite the effort she deploys to repress it, to make it not exist, as if it had never happened, the truth has begun to find its way to the surface.

Sure enough, a moment of curiosity pokes its way through. 'What's your name, anyway?' Cynthia asks.

'Hortense.'

'Hortense?'

'Yeah.'

'Hortense what?'

'Cumberbatch.'

'Clumber-bunch? That's a funny name, isn't it?'

'Yeah, I suppose it is.'

The humour emerges through the suffering. Our experience with narrative tells us that this leavening of humour is a harbinger of things to come.

And so it turns out: in a great rush of chaos and misunderstanding and emotion, the two women meet, and become friends. Cynthia changes in character: she is suddenly wearing a new coat, and she begins to take pride in her house; she comes to life before our eyes. She is suddenly an uncomplicated, loving mother to Roxanne, who is astonished to find steak bought for her supper, and cans of beer.

The unconscious desire transforms into a conscious one: Cynthia wants to bring her lost daughter back into the orbit of her true family – for everyone to know the truth and to accept Hortense as her daughter, and Roxanne's half-sister.

The start of the unconscious desire's transformation into a conscious one, tentative at first but then at full strength, is greeted by us with profound emotion because we have observed the degree of suffering caused in Cynthia by virtue of its being repressed. We see immediate improvement in Cynthia, as a person, and this adds to our certainty that underneath the suffering lies a woman who has earned our respect, our love.

Cynthia's desire is granted and finds its fullest, most emotional expression when the secret finally emerges into the light of day with her announcement, during Roxanne's twenty-first birthday barbecue, that Hortense 'takes after her mother'.

'Does she?'

Cynthia announces, 'You're looking at her.'

Other secrets emerge in sympathy, in an extraordinary scene of ensemble writing and performance.

When a hidden, unconscious desire is written into a character it provokes critical admiration for such characters and their stories as being 'three-dimensional' (see John Yorke's analysis (47–52) of *Thelma and Louise* (Weir 1991)), and deservedly so, but it is a mistake always to aim for three dimensions in the dramatic construction of a character. In the design of a comic or a tragic character it will be important to concentrate on writing only one dimension (cf. page 59).

More pertinent would be the use of the word 'complex' as it is the pattern of the desire, its multi-stranded logic, which gives the sensation of depth, of our knowing this character 'deeply'. The moment that we recognise Cynthia's unconscious desire, our wish for her is different from her conscious wish for herself. Cynthia has buried the secret because it is too painful and is attached to a risk of humiliation; we want the secret to come out. And so there is a difference between what Cynthia wants, and what we can see that she needs. We, the audience, are working on a different system of logic from the character, and that makes for dramatic irony; the writer allows us the luxury of knowing the character better than she knows herself. This distinction between what a character wants on the surface and what, under the surface, the character *needs* and *unconsciously* desires is the model for some of the most rewarding expressions of the desire principle in narrative.[7]

4   Conclusion

The desire principle is used in conjunction with morality (the subject of Chapter 3) in order to engineer the audience's increasing involvement in the desire. Wittgenstein describes how the two, willpower and right-and-wrong, are related – 'What really is the situation of the human will? I will call "will" first and foremost the bearer of good and evil.' (1914–1916/1961, 76e)

Furthermore, a hidden desire, either conscious or unconscious, demands particular skill at logic. In the case of a desire that's hidden from us, the audience, it creates mystery, or surprise, by masking the 'cause' of cause-and-effect. In the case of the unconscious hidden desire, when we are allowed to observe it but the character is blind to it, dramatic irony creates two strands of logic that we watch carefully; the first describes the reasoning that we make of the situation, and the second describes the reasoning of the character who is blind to their own desire. We watch these two strands of logic in order to see how they will eventually join up to make a single, overall version of the truth.

---

[7]For an example of a conscious desire and an unconscious need being written into the same character, watch the two-handed love life of Pat Solotano (Bradley Cooper) in *Silver Linings Playbook* (Russell 2012).

Further still, it will be seen how desire is often prompted, and quickened, by an emotion (Chapter 4).

I haven't spoken about the recruitment to the desire – or not – of the other characters in the story, but these other characters if they are not bystanders will inevitably find themselves either allies or opponents, whether they know it or not; in *Fargo* Jerry recruits his own wife into the scenario, as well as his father-in-law, both of them unknowingly – but poignantly, not his son.

It might be the case that a single desire unifies a plural protagonist, as is the case in the heist movie *Ocean's 11*, or in a number of Brecht's dramas that contain an entire class of people, the proletariat, as a protagonist. The desires of multiple protagonists are woven around each other in 'rope' narratives such as *Crash* and *Magnolia*.

A desire can also be imparted to another character. In *Little Miss Sunshine* (Dayton and Faris 2006) the grandfather, Edwin (Alan Arkin), uses his granddaughter as a surrogate carrier of his hidden desire to sabotage a beauty pageant. The film has a plural protagonist, in that every member of the family commits to the singular, evident, vigorous desire of getting Olive (Abigail Breslin) to the pageant, but it also has multiple protagonists, as each character, in addition to being recruited to the singular desire, also has an individual desire, on their own account.

The 'map of desire' is therefore infinitely variable in effect, in the pattern of its recruitment and the gradient of its contours; but knowledge of the different effects, and why they work, ensures that the energetic flow of the narrative is put in place and the audience carried with it. The word 'plot' incorporates within its meanings that of 'plotting' a route, a series of directions, but the traction to move from the beginning to the end must be transferred to the audience. Whether singular or habitual, vigorous or placid, hidden or evident, to orchestrate skilfully both the desire itself and the audience's *increasing involvement* in that desire is the task facing the screenwriter in his or her attempt to carry the audience magically through the screen, in order to take part in the drama.

2

Logic Junkie

In *Three Uses of the Knife* (2002), dramatist David Mamet describes how important is the art of logic to the human animal.

> It is our nature to elaborate perception into hypotheses and then reduce those hypotheses to information upon which we can act. It is our special adaptive device, equivalent to the bird's flight – our unique survival tool. And drama, music and art are our celebration of that tool, exactly like the woodcock's manic courting flight, the whale's breaching leap. The excess of ability/energy/skill/strength/love is expressed in species-specific ways. In goats it is leaping, in humans it is making art. (65)

This statement is fundamental to the craft of dramatic writing. Mamet identifies logic as an instinct, a species-specific skill that has evolved in the human animal to allow us dominion over our surroundings, and ensure our survival.

Boyd agrees – 'Humans uniquely inhabit "the cognitive niche": we gain most of our advantages from intelligence.' (Boyd, 14) Hegel judges of mankind, 'so much is logic his natural element, indeed his own peculiar *nature*' (Hegel 1969, 23). He defines logic as what separates man from animal – 'it is *thinking* which distinguishes man from the beasts' (23) – whereas the opposite is true: it is thinking, logic, that describes what is most animal about mankind; it is the most highly developed evolutionary trait in our species. Toads jump, and so do humans, but toads are better at it. All animals have cognition; they think, to differing extents; but we are better at thinking. Wittgenstein, also, described our creaturely instinct for logic – 'In what sense is logic something sublime? For there seemed to pertain to logic a peculiar depth – a universal significance.' (Wittgenstein 1953/1976, 42) Plantinga speaks up for the cognitive theorists – 'Some cognitive theorists seem to assume that cognitive play is the primary motivating pleasure in film viewing.' (Plantinga 2009, 39)

Our instinct for logic takes its place among the most unusual and successful evolutionary success stories. In the Philippines, the *Aerodramus* species of swiftlets uses echolocation in the same way as bats in order to hide their nests, which are made of saliva, in the darkest of caves. Australia's Cane Toad is, like us, an indomitably expansive species, and the individuals at the edge of their expansion have the longest legs and are the most energetic, just as the individuals at the forefront of our expansion, our thriving, have the biggest brains. Among the Galapagos Islands, the island of Daphne hosts no less than four different types of finch: each one developed separately from a common ancestor. Like in the Goldilocks story, there is a finch with a small beak for small seeds, two medium-sized finches with medium-sized beaks for middle-sized seeds, and a large-sized finch with a big beak for the big seeds with tough shells. Likewise we have different types of intelligence.

These aforementioned species have developed specific physical qualities and specialist mental skills in order to gain power over the world that surrounds them, and therefore survive, and, moreover, thrive. We, the human animal, have earned for ourselves a more extraordinary level of control over our surroundings, from the use of tools and fire to the harnessing of nuclear power and computer science. Matched with the manual dexterity granted by our opposed thumbs, our instinct for logic has made our thriving, our self-advancement, phenomenal. We learned to use flora and fauna of every kind to feed ourselves, provide shelter, clothing, food, medicine, to give comfort and pleasure and to reduce our work, we learned to trap the wind in our sails and alter the course of water to drive our mills. We worked out how the stars could give directions, how predicting the weather might help our farms. At the same time as looking into deep space we burrowed further into the minutiae of things and began to build machines out of invisibly small particles.

The most startling demonstrations of our instinct for logic must have come during the Industrial Revolution: Faraday watched that strand of copper wire stir and revolve around the magnet in the middle of the glass jar; for the first time gas lamps lit up Pall Mall; Humphrey Davy staggered about in the garden after inhaling carbon monoxide and with great showmanship demonstrated at The Royal Society with potassium flares and crumbs of sodium sizzling on the surface of water. That particular strand of logic has brought us as far as CERN, the European Organization for Nuclear Research, whose scientists have built a twenty-seven-kilometre-long underground particle accelerator in order to smash together subatomic particles travelling at near enough the speed of light.

Our every waking moment is, and has been ever since the suffix 'sapiens' replaced 'erectus' in our species nomenclature, dedicated to the enquiry into (and the engineering of) cause-and-effect, or logic.

It's not just about science; all our art, observation, psychology, all our design, every moment of our behaviour, our every action, is the operation of logic's pulleys and levers, and not the least important is the delicacy of the logic which we use to make continual appraisals of moral issues, the root of all storytelling and the subject of Chapter 3. Boyd describes our fascination with logic as an addiction to *pattern* – 'I suggest that we can view art as a kind of cognitive play, the set of activities designed to engage human *attention* through their appeal to our preference for inferentially rich and therefore *patterned* information' (Boyd, 85). Branigan agrees that narrative fiction is 'a perceptual activity that organises data into a special pattern which represents and explains experience' (Plantinga, 22). This describes exactly my suggestion earlier that writers are concerned not just with logic but with a beautiful *display* of logic.

Logic is only 'learned' so vigorously because it is an instinctive behaviour.

The successful screenwriter will make use of the audience's instinctive need to work with logic, and will generously provide for it, create patterns of irony and mystery, metaphor and symbol, and thereby make a place in the story where the audience can *work*; the audience is therefore not just a visitor in the drama, but takes part.

1   The logic paradigm

The structure of reason, or logic, can be expressed by way of the commonplace phrase 'cause-and-effect'. But there is a word missing from this phrase. It is the most potent word of all, and is a staple of every creative writing class, discussed in every screenwriting manual. It should be positioned in the middle, between the other two. That word is 'change'. Yorke titles his Chapter 1.4 'The Importance of Change' (Yorke, 45) and Bordwell and Thompson define plot as 'a series of changes [arranged] according to a pattern of cause and effect' (Bordwell and Thompson 2001, 60).

Our working out of the world, to create advantage for ourselves, involves us in the constant, moment-by-moment process of measuring change, and working upstream to judge causes, and downstream to forecast effects.

We monitor the changes in how people look, the change in the amount that people love us, or dislike us, the change in the level of humour in the room – and why. We measure any slight change in the measure of excitement, in the measure of fear – and we immediately analyse the reason for it, and the possible outcomes. We measure knowledge, information – who knows what, and why. We measure any change in wealth, and the causes and the outcomes. We measure truth and beauty and the reasons behind their increase or decrease. We are especially concerned at any change in morality, in right and wrong, in ourselves and in those around us, and we set ourselves the task of working out why and what will be the consequences.

We measure the changes in abstract concepts such as love, excitement or illness by virtue of actual, concrete events. We see that a mole on our cheek has grown in size by an almost imperceptible amount; immediately we calculate the possible causes: cells beginning to breed, out of control. We forecast the possible effects: an operation, treatment, death from skin cancer, or recovery and a small scar.

We find a receipt for a motel bedroom in our wife's or husband's pocket: immediately we consider our partner's distracted air, the strange delays and absences. We automatically and quickly bolt together all the possible causes for these changes. We invent a lover, we predict a divorce.

We're wrong. We discover that our partner has skin cancer, and the motel receipt was for a trip to a specialist that was kept secret.

And, if something gives us reliable pleasure, and safety, we cling on to such things that don't change, that stay the same.

The power of this word 'change', sitting in the middle of the cause-change-effect paradigm, is the reason why politicians mention it copiously, and pretend to be in charge of it. Their communications chiefs have coached them that if they can persuade us they control change in a way that's beneficial to us, we will vote for them. We are voting for the excitement of the word itself. At the time of writing (August 2016) Donald Trump is repeating just two words, 'Real change' over and over again.

The logic paradigm can therefore be accurately written as –

cause – change – effect.

A variety of causes assemble which together create pressure for a change of some sort to happen, whether explosively quickly or very slowly, small or large in scale, and that change then does happen, or it doesn't. Either way, it leads to a series of after-effects.[1]

By way of an example, pressure builds along the San Andreas Fault as the Pacific Plate and the North American Plate attempt to move in different directions along the north–south axis in what is termed a right-lateral strike slip. That pressure – the cause – might lead to an earthquake in any of its three different zones, or it might result in just a tremor, or it might lead to nothing at all except for the expectation of an earthquake. To each of these possible change scenarios are attached different after-effects: a dramatically changed landscape, razed buildings and many dead,

---

[1]Our appreciation of logic is only allowed to us, therefore, because of our appreciation of time – the before-and-after. 'Minds exist to predict what will happen next. They mine the present for clues they can refine with help from the past … to anticipate the immediate future and guide action.' (Boyd, 134)

or a few broken tiles, or merely the expectation of an earthquake and a revision of the regulations for new building construction. It is important to realise that among the variety of possible changes is the possibility of no change at all, despite the pressure of the causes.

Screenwriters therefore import this cause-change-effect paradigm and use it as their plaything. Charged with bringing their audiences through the screen and have them take part in the drama, they develop a passionate engagement with the logic paradigm, and an understanding of how it might be manipulated and beautifully displayed. They invigorate logic, interrupt it, make different strands of it, dangle it, rub out one part of it and stay for too long in another part; they create synaptic connections that lace together points of logic in their stories and sponsor in audiences little rushes of comprehension that are sometimes called, by Kant and others, 'cognitions'. Screenwriters use logic as the stuff of their art, like the painter reaches for his brushes and his paints, the musician for his score, his staves and his piano keys (music is a game of logic, which is why it appeals uniquely to the human creature[2]).

They become logic junkies.

2   Dangling the logic in *Glengarry Glen Ross*

In the film adaptation of his 1984 stage play *Glengarry Glen Ross* (Foley 1992), the Pulitzer- and Tony-prize-winning dramatist David Mamet builds one moment of change after another, and each possible moment of change is dangled (that is to say, the likelihood of the change happening is teased back and forth) with exquisite skill. It is as if he is playing with his character, and his audience, using a ball on the end of a piece of string. The change moves towards the audience, appears more likely; we clutch at it, think we've got it, but then it moves out of reach again.[3]

---

[2]'Musical themes are in a certain sense propositions. Knowledge of the nature of logic will for this reason lead to knowledge of the nature of music.' (Wittgenstein, 1914–1916/1961, 40e)

[3]Bordwell and Thompson describe it as 'dangling causes' (2011, 115) but it is more accurate to describe it as dangling the possibility of change.

Twenty-three minutes into the film, Shelley 'The Machine' Levene (Jack Lemmon), one of the older members of the sales team, is riled because the premium leads, the ones that will convert more easily into closed sales and commission, have been withheld from the salesforce, to be given only to the top two closers this week.

The rest of them will be fired.

It is a carrot-and-stick situation that has been forcefully laid out by Blake (Alec Baldwin), the top salesman sent from Mitch and Murray's office downtown, who wears a wristwatch that's worth more than a man's salary.

Shelley holds the duff leads in one hand and smacks them with the other. What can anyone do with leads like these? He is going to appeal to Williamson, the office manager, and try to get his hands on the premium leads. It is dark outside, and the rain is falling against the windows. The office manager is heading home.

Thus David Mamet has already made sure that we understand, firstly, the reasons for the possible change (Blake's carrot-and-stick scenario), and, secondly, what is the change that is the subject of this scene (Shelley Levene might or might not get his hands on those premium leads), as well as the possible after-effects: if Shelley has the premium leads he stands to make money and head up the leader board, whereas if he doesn't, he'll lose his job.

Our accurate comprehension of every part of the logic paradigm allows us to formulate a pattern of inductive reasoning, a more everyday version of what logicians call a 'truth table', whereby a collection of logically connected statements form a relationship with truth and untruth.

Williamson is about to go home: he switches off the lights and locks the sash windows. Shelley is still in shirt and braces, and he will either persuade Williamson to give him the premium leads, or not. 'I've got a bit of a problem here, John,' he says, while holding up a brace of ordinary white cards, the two old leads he's just failed with.

Williamson is impatient. 'I'm closing up the office … I gotta go home, grab one hour with my kids, come back here and see if any of you have closed, take a contract to the bank … '

In this first beat within the scene, the audience glimpses only the possibility of a small change on the way to the bigger one – will Shelley be able to get Williamson's attention, even?

Shelley alternately assumes a friendly manner, 'Come across the street to have a drink with me … just five minutes … ' and then an angry one, 'How about one minute?' He talks over Williamson's blather and asks that question more forcefully, 'How about one minute, huh?'

After a short pause comes Williamson's reply, 'What is it?'

The ball-on-the-string has been dangled closer to the audience. Williamson is now listening.

(The orchestration of this scene will, in fact, follow the prescription for salesmen written out earlier on the chalk board by Blake, describing the various stages, the various small changes, that a salesman should engineer in his 'client' in order to close a sale – Attention, Interest, Decision, Action.)

The small change has been allowed: Shelley has Williamson's attention. It is a step-change in the right direction. The next step, following the guide to salesmanship, is for Shelley to gain Williamson's interest.

Williamson has asked a question, 'What is it?' and Shelley's reply is crucial. He tells the simple truth, 'I can't close these leads.'

'Then move on.' Williamson turns away.

It didn't work. Shelley has not gained Williamson's interest; moreover he has lost his attention. The ball-on-a-string has been moved away from us with that decisive turn of the office manager's shoulder and the curt piece of advice. We measure this effect, and we alter our reckoning of the logic of the situation. We work with our inferences, adjust our truth table. We have reconfigured the likelihood of the change happening, and adjusted our expectations as to the effects. And therein lies the drama's narrative power. We feel like we are 'inside' the story because our measurement of the logic has had to be adjusted and therefore we have work to do, mental work of the sort that it is our primary instinct to perform: a small alteration in the logic. It means that our place in the story is one that we instinctively feel is required of us – we need to be here, to work this out. We are involved.

Shelley has been forced to take a step backwards; he's once again trying to gain the manager's attention. The expressions on his face change quickly from anger to friendliness, 'Hey, hey, don't jump out of your manager bag … ' He chases Williamson around the office, trying to prove to him, with tales of past glories, that he's a top closer. For Williamson, this old salesman is like a wasp buzzing around his head while he's trying to leave the office: he clears up the milk carton; he puts back the glass jug on the coffee machine; he throws away the dregs; he takes his coat from the rack. Meanwhile he gives small moments of attention to Shelley, before ignoring him. Shelley labours on, talking furiously.

Williamson has his coat and brolly. He's on the way out. He just has this one file to put away.

A frustrated Shelley lets his anger get the better of him. He pokes Williamson's shoulder, hard. 'Hey, look at me.'

Williamson freezes. A moment of animal intensity passes between the two men. It was a wrong move, and with that small bullying action Shelley has taken a step even further backwards from accomplishing the change. These small moments when Williamson appears to offer some hope of giving Shelley his attention will now disappear. Shelley let his desperation show. It was unattractive. Williamson shrugs on his jacket, his coat. We feel the possibility of the change offered at the beginning of the scene slip away, become less likely. More likely are the negative effects: Shelley Levene's poverty, his losing his job.

A passing train throws a confusion of light and sound over the scene, Williamson says, 'I can't do it, Shelley,' and leaves the office. The ball-on-a-string is further away than ever.

But it is not over. Out on the street, under the pouring rain, Shelley ducks under Williamson's brolly and says something that's going to swing the ball-on-a-string suddenly much closer. 'I'll give you ten per cent.'

The director, actors, and editor know that a pause is needed here, to allow the audience to register that the change is swinging towards us again, suddenly.

'Of what?' asks Williamson. The ball-on-a-string is close enough to touch. Shelley has gained Williamson's attention and, furthermore, his interest. The audience recalibrate their position within the logic of the situation, and welcome the increased possibility of the change, and forecast the effects. It is as if the story depends on the audience for its existence.

'Of my end. What I close, you're in for ten per cent.'

After a pause Williamson counters, 'Twenty per cent.'

The ball-on-a-string is poised, motionless. The change is on the point of being allowed, but still it might swing away.

'All right.' Shelley agrees to the twenty per cent. The change is certain …

'And fifty bucks a lead.' Williamson's greed threatens the situation. The step forwards that we've just made might be reversed. The ball-on-a-string has been jerked out of our grasp, just as we thought we had actually caught hold of it. It is the *movement* of the ball-on-the-string that counts – the teasing back-and-forth, the constant adjustment of our inferences in order to identify anew the accuracy of the logic.

Williamson has asked for twenty per cent, which is double what Shelley offered, plus that extra fifty bucks per lead. It takes a moment or two for Shelley to decide whether or not to accept, even as he stands there in the rain and Williamson climbs into the car. But Shelley's got everything to lose and he gives in. Twenty per cent, OK, plus the fifty bucks per lead. Shelley makes his way around to the passenger side of the car in order to climb in and make a plan.

The door is locked.

Shelley's woebegone face looks in through the side window and he taps on the glass.

For a moment it seems that Williamson isn't going to let him in. Each tiny moment, both in Mamet's writing and in James Foley's direction, teases us back and forth on the question of whether or not the writer is going to allow or disallow this small change on the way to the bigger change: will Shelley get his hands on the premium leads or not?

Williamson lets him in.

Shelley, drenched in rain, slumps into the passenger seat and for a while tries to claw back to ten per cent, his original offer, but he has to accept the deal. He's energetic. 'OK, now let's go.' He wants two of the premium leads to work on, right now, tonight.

Williamson says patiently, 'I've got to go back to the office to get them.'

'Yeah, go on, let's go, huh? This is what I was saying, John, all you need, a little boost, and you turn the [losing] streak around, am I right? Good, huh? Huh?' He's smiling broadly. He thinks the change has been allowed to him, but we recognise we are in the hands of a master of narrative and we are ready for the ball-on-a-string to be pulled out of our hands.

Williamson's eyebrow lifts just a fraction.

'What?' asks Shelley. 'What?'

'Two leads, a hundred bucks.'

'*Now?*'

'Now, yes … '

'Shit, John.'

'I wish I could.'

'You fuckin' asshole. I don't have it ….'

The small changes that we've earned (along the way towards the bigger change) are now cancelled out; it seems like the ball-on-a-string is wildly out of reach. The smaller arcs of back-and-forth have been eclipsed by this bigger event. It's impossible, now, surely? As in music, it is the relationship between the repetition and the variation that we find enchanting. This is Boyd's *pattern*.

But then Shelley is muttering and digging in his pocket. He has got the money after all. The change looms closer; it's possible, again. He pulls out a few crumpled notes.

He only has thirty dollars – not enough even for one lead.

Williamson holds firm. Shelley's threats, his imploring, have no effect on the stone-faced office manager. He won't even give Shelley any more of the old leads.

The change is denied. Williamson drives off. Shelley is left standing in the rain. We feel an enormous draft of pity. Christine Gledhill (quoted in Macdonald) references a wonderful name for it, 'heart-reading' (Macdonald, 147), as she notes actor-director Henry Edwards's realisation of 'the difficulties that confront the scenario-writer when he sets out to tell a story in the language of actions' (Macdonald, 147).

For seven minutes of screen time we have seen the possibility of the change dangled in front of Shelley's nose, making it seem, at one moment, closer to happening, and then, in the next moment, further away. We've sensed the movements back and forth with a variety of small and large swings, and, along with Shelley Levene, we've constantly adjusted our thinking according to the pressure of events, the likelihood of the change happening. This pattern has been created by the writer in order to invigorate our instinct to work within the logic paradigm.

Written on the page, with just those three words linked by dashes, it appears as if each section of the cause-change-effect paradigm bears equal weight, is of equal importance; however, the very nature of change means it often happens in an instant (a decision that goes one way or another, an event that happens or doesn't happen). Therefore, it can be seen that the writer must spend the majority of the page length, most of the invention and most of the dialogue, on either side of these pivotal moments of change.

In the foregoing example, David Mamet's work was to make the situation clearly understood: the causes and the effects (Blake's carrot-and-stick scenario). After this first responsibility has been answered, the page length has been given over to the dangling of the logic, the increases and decreases in the apparent likelihood of the change happening. This requires invention, and constitutes almost the entire length of the scene. It is where the virtuosity of the writing lies. The moment in which the change is categorically denied is the work of an instant and is easily written: Williamson's silence; Shelley Levene's climbing from the car, slamming shut the door and being left in the rain.

The after-effects, of course, make themselves felt immediately (we have already forecast them) but as far as the writer is concerned they are the groundwork for subsequent scenes. In this case, Shelley has to try and make a sale using a low-quality lead, and, as it happens, fails also to implement that change.

If the moment of possible change for Shelley Levene, getting hold of those premium leads, is a unit of change within the drama, it is part of a bigger change, making any deal at all, that is also going to be denied to him. The scene dangles a small change; the acts dangle a bigger version of the same change; the screenplay itself dangles a larger version of the same change. *Glengarry Glen Ross* is the story of Shelley's failure; it is, as the cast apparently described the production, the 'death of a fucking salesman'.

In *Fargo*, the central desire of Jerry Lundegaard is to get hold of enough money and, on the way through the drama, each movement, each drift of action, small or large, either accelerates or obstructs a number of smaller changes that together make up the possibility of the larger change. That change is denied, and as a consequence he is ruined.

In *There Will Be Blood* (Anderson 2007), the central desire of Daniel Plainview (Daniel Day-Lewis) is to get hold of enough money, and that change is allowed to him by the writers, over and over again, but it is never enough, and as a consequence, although he becomes as rich as Croesus, he also is ruined.

If one counts as accurate that description by Don Paterson, mentioned in the Introduction, of a poem as 'a machine for remembering itself' then a dramatic script is, similarly, a machine made out of logic that remembers itself – each of the three elements in the logic paradigm continually adjusts to the others, remembers the others, in a beautiful display or pattern. The screenwriter will construct the poetry of events.

There is a further, serious challenge that faces the screenwriter in the manufacture of this logic-machine. All the design, all the stitching together of scenes and of moments within scenes, has to be done invisibly. The technique should disappear and it should be as if 'real life' is happening – but it will be a version of 'real life' that insists its audience takes part, because it captures their instinct for logic-work.

It is one thing to realise that to make a virtuoso display of logic is central to the art of drama; to write that drama is another; but to write it invisibly well, gracefully, can only come with practice. It takes psychological insight, and imaginative powers of invention, to orchestrate circumstances, characters and their desires and make this little machine that works by creating patterns of repetition and variation inside the logic paradigm – within any given scene, within any given act or movement, within any drama – and to make it appear as if it were happening artlessly, without design.

The art of 'dangling' the logic is only the first of many displays of logic that account for dramatic techniques. It will be seen now that *all* techniques for dramatic writing should be understood as variations in the available displays of logic: dramatic irony, mystery, dialogue, choice, parallelism, metaphor and symbol, but perhaps most important of all, and therefore coming first, is character.

3   The logic paradigm applied to character

There are three ways in which the cause-change-effect paradigm intersects with the notion of character; and all powerfully dramatic portrayals of character in films (not to mention other forms of fictional narrative) are written using one of these three models.

The first model describes how a character undergoes fundamental change from one thing to another, in the way that, for example, in

Breaking Bad (Gilligan 2008) Walter White (Bryan Cranston) turns from being a mild-mannered chemistry teacher to a violent drug lord.

The second model describes how the *perception* of a character can change (either the audience's perception, or another character's perception, or both). For instance, in the Bollywood classic *Sholay* (Sippy 1975) our perception of Jai (Amitabh Bachchan) changes radically, although he himself doesn't change at all.

The third model describes how a character does not change, not in reality, nor in our perception, nor in the perception of other characters. This model is usually attached, in its simplest version, to TV detectives and suchlike, but its most skilful use is seen in the construction of comic and tragic characters, where the dramatist's concern is to foreground one particular trait of character, such as greed, stupidity or arrogance, and then demonstrate just how ingrained this trait is, in the character, by increasing the pressure of the causes that should make the character change. The results are either tragic or comic. Two successful recent examples in cinemas are the satirical comedy of manners, *Borat* (Charles 2006), written and performed by Sacha Baron Cohen, and the tragedy *There Will Be Blood.*

Real change in character

The creator and writer of *Breaking Bad*, Vince Gilligan, said in an interview with Andrew Romano published in *Newsweek* –

> Television is historically good at keeping its characters in a self-imposed stasis so that shows can go on for years or even decades … when I realized this, the logical next step was to think, how can I do a show in which the fundamental drive is toward change. (Romano 2011)

He added that his goal with Walter White was to turn him 'from Mr Chips into Scarface'.

Over a period of sixty-two television episodes, Walter White changes from being a mild-mannered and peaceable teacher of chemistry to being a calculating, murderous, wealthy drugs lord. Significant stepping stones along the way can be defined as the first time he makes and sells a batch of drugs, the first time he kills a man, the first time he kills a man in cold blood, and the first time he himself takes control of a network of dealers. These step-changes portray a character 'breaking bad' – but he is always placed next to characters who have already, some time ago, broken worse, as it were, and thus he remains our protagonist. The writers arrange for him to change irretrievably from one thing to another, and they also arrange for us to witness his obstinate refusal to stop this transformation, and it causes his destruction. Our pleasure is in assessing the play of events that, combined with his refusal to stop changing, cause both his downfall and his enrichment. We bolt together the irony contained within this core of logic in the story, that in trying to save his family he loses his family, and thus we take part in this compelling, sixty-two-hour tragedy.

In *Wings of Desire* Damiel changes from being immortal to being mortal. In *Secrets and Lies* Cynthia Purley changes from being repressed to being open. In *The King's Speech* (Hooper 2010) George, Prince of Wales, changes from a prince who can't talk to a king who, when war is declared, manages to address the nation over the radio. In *The Artist* (Hazanavicius 2011) George Valentin changes from being a star of the silent movies to an abject failure when talkies are introduced. In *The Lord of the Rings: The Fellowship of the Ring* (Jackson 2001) the character of Gollum (Andy Serkis) is inhabited by two people and changes back and forth frequently from his poisonous side to his obsequious side, sometimes in the same sentence. In *My Fair Lady* (Cukor 1964), Eliza Doolittle changes from an uncouth, foul-mouthed wretch to a well-mannered lady. The writing of the logic paradigm in these examples concentrates on the causes and the effects of the change that occurs in the character.

Change of perception in character

In *Sholay*, the Bollywood classic whose popularity has endured since 1975, the character of Jai (Amitabh Bachchan) doesn't actually change, but our perception of him changes dramatically in the closing minutes of the film. His brother in arms, Veeru (Dharmendra), shares our experience of the revelation.

In the film's opening scene, the two scoundrels Jai and Veeru – thieves and bandits, and best friends – are suggested by the stern-faced retired policeman, Thakur Baldev Singh (Sanjeev Kumar), as the best people to help the town fight back against the local warlord, Gabbar Singh (Amjad Khan), who is terrorising the area. It seems like a wrong choice to hire people who are dishonest thieves, replies his lieutenant.

No, replies Thakur – and he then relates an episode from the past when he himself had managed to capture and manacle the two notorious thieves, and was taking them by train to face justice when the train was attacked by outlaws. There were too many of the outlaws, and the two friends, hands tied behind their backs, urgently requested to be let go so they could help in the fight. After all, their own lives were at risk, too. They were let go, and they fought with extraordinary courage and invention. They saved the train from being taken. When the battle was done, when the last attacker had been shot and had fallen, a particular situation arose: their captor, a much younger Thakur, was gravely wounded and fell unconscious into their arms. They could make their escape – but should they kill him, first? The two friends couldn't decide, and so Jai tossed a coin for it. He displays such a playful amorality, such carelessness, in deciding whether or not to cold-bloodedly shoot a man dead on the toss of a coin.

The coin lands on 'heads'. They didn't shoot, but left him alive.

Thakur never forgot the bravado of those two thieves, and their inventiveness in the fight against the bandits, and their leaving him to live. On account of their extraordinary skills they must be hired for the task of destroying the warlord, even though both men are carelessly amoral.

The two friends are found and are brought to the village. But should they agree to take on this dangerous challenge and save the village? They don't consider the moral imperative – whether or not it is the right thing to do. Instead, bravado prevails: once again, Jai tosses a coin.

Towards the end of the film, a coin is used once more. Jai has rescued Veeru from the warlord's camp, and they are both wounded and attempting to make their escape. One of them must take the horse and the girl and gallop for help; the other must lie on his belly and shoot for all he's worth in order to hold up the pursuing attackers, otherwise they will all perish. But whoever stays behind will surely be overrun and shot dead. Both men try to make the sacrifice.

It can only be decided on the toss of a coin.

It comes down heads. Jai will have to stay; Veeru must gallop for help as fast as he can.

Veeru drags the girl up behind him and spurs on the horse. He gallops full tilt, but by the time he's reached the village, rounded up enough reinforcements and come back, it is too late. His friend Jai lies in the dust, shot dead. Veeru throws himself down next to his friend, raising a cloud of dust. He holds Jai in his arms.

A coin rolls from Jai's lifeless hand. Veeru picks up the coin, and sees on the one side the figure of a head. He turns it over – another head.

It is a double-sided coin.

In one moment, the audience's (and Veeru's) understanding of Jai's character is transformed. The audience run back over the script and the new logic snaps into place.

In that opening scene, when the two friends wanted to decide whether or not to kill Thakur, in tossing the coin Jai had *chosen* not to shoot him.

When faced with the decision whether or not to save the village, in tossing the coin Jai had *chosen* deliberately to make the morally correct choice and attempt to save the town.

And by making sure he was the one to stay behind and face the gunfire, he'd chosen to save his friend's life at the expense of his own.

Jai is not a casually amoral man, as the audience had previously thought. He is deeply moral.

An important point about this coin sequence is that it works even after its first viewing. An audience might have seen variations of that two-headed coin trick played before, but they can even view this example of its use again and again, and still the narrative pleasure arrives at that moment. On first viewing, the audience experience (with delight, and at one stroke) a change in their perception of the character of Jai, which works as the substitution of one pattern of logic, or cause-and-effect (look how amoral he is, deciding people's fate on the toss of a coin) with exactly the opposite pattern of logic (no, look how moral he is, how modest and how brave he is, using a double-sided coin in order to put the interests of other people before his own, without appearing to do so). On subsequent viewings, the audience's pleasure comes instead from dramatic irony – the twin strands of logic run alongside each other; the audience understands Jai better than anyone else in the film, better even than his best friend Veeru, until that point when the coin rolls from his hand and Veeru's reading of the logic matches that of the audience.

There is a similar, coin-related pleasure in *No Country for Old Men* (Coen and Coen 2007) but it is set the other way: Anton Chigurh (Javier Bardem) is a hitman who decides whether or not to kill people on the toss of a coin, irrespective of the effect on him, even, or on the situation in which he finds himself. It casts him as amoral, of course, as opposed to Jai's coin revealing him to be moral, but in terms of dramatic technique it works in the same way: it is an entertaining, unusual display of logic (attached to morality, the subject of Chapter 3).

Examples abound of this form of dramatic character, that is to say the form that engineers a change in the audience's perception of any given character, and/or an alteration in the other characters' perceptions of the character. In *The Shawshank Redemption* our perception of Andy Dufresne's character profoundly alters when the warden pushes his arm through that poster and discovers the escape tunnel. In *Fargo*, our perception of Mike Yanagita changes when we find out, during that phone conversation, that he was never married, after all. In *King Kong* (Jackson 2005) our perception of the creature changes as he becomes fully human in our eyes. In *Tootsie* (Pollack 1982) the other characters' perceptions of Michael Dorsey change radically when he secretly dresses as a woman. In *Rain Man* (Levinson 1988) Charlie Babbitt's (and our) perception of his autistic brother, Raymond, changes radically as the pair are forced to share a car journey across the United States. There are countless examples also in works of prose fiction that have been sourced for films and television. Jane Austen's novel *Pride and Prejudice* (1813) engineers a change in our perception of the character of Darcy; in F. Scott Fitzgerald's *The Great Gatsby* (1925) the narrative is designed to alter radically our perception of Jay Gatsby. In Ford Madox Ford's *The Good Soldier* (1915) multiple alterations in our perceptions of the four main characters are arranged by way of the narrator's carrying us backwards and forwards in time, and from place to place.

The challenge that faces the writer, in this playing with the cause-change-effect paradigm made evident through character, is in the hiding of that one aspect of the character that is going to appear in a changed light either to the audience or to other characters or to both, and subsequently the revealing of it in a way that's at once satisfying and credible. In any event our pleasure comes from swapping our allegiance from the old pattern of logic to the new one. The more points of comprehension that can be laced together between the original strand and the one that replaces it, the more beautiful the display of pattern, and the greater our satisfaction and our admiration of the writer's craft.

No change at all in character

The third way in which the cause-change-effect paradigm affects the design of a dramatic character is when a character doesn't change at all. Leaving aside the more prosaic examples of TV detectives such as Poirot and other characters in continuing TV series, a more sophisticated kind of model leans heavily – the more heavily the better – on the 'cause' part of the cause-change-effect paradigm, because, tragically or comically (and in either case astonishingly), no change occurs in the character despite the pressure, the increasing weight of these causes that are leaning on them, that should make them change. It is an interruption, a block in the normal flow of logic. The causes build up, press harder, but to no avail; the writer will continue to accelerate the character's blind, stubborn streak. There will be no change. Either it is pitiful, or it is funny.

In *Borat*, a satirical comedy of manners, we visit the eponymous hero, a television presenter in Kazakhstan played by the film's writer, Sacha Baron Cohen. For the purposes of the film, Borat's evident, habitual, vigorous desire will be to travel across America, employed by the 'Ministry of Information' to bring back 'Cultural Learnings of America for Make Benefit Glorious Nation of Kazakhstan'.

The film starts as Borat strolls towards his home town with a pack of villagers walking alongside him. He cheerfully points out a youth languishing in charge of a donkey and cart, 'That is Urkin, the town rapist. Naughty naughty!' He walks through the town's kindergarten, where children languish with machine guns in their laps. The town's mechanic, wielding an arc welder, waves a greeting. He is also the town's abortionist. Borat gestures to the camera to come towards him. 'This my house. Entry, please.' His neighbour is 'pain in my assholes.' Borat introduces a blonde girl, 'This is Natalia,' he says and leans down to kiss her extravagantly and sexually. He stops and takes her hand proudly. 'She's my sister. She is number four prostitute in all of Kazakhstan.' The girl holds up a gold cup.

Borat walks on, and introduces a woman who looks like she's in her 80s. 'This my mother. She is oldest woman in whole of Cusek. She is forty-three.'

Satirical jibes arrive in quick succession accompanied by jolly folk music. It is a discomfiting critique of the country's manners and morals, and it angered Kazakhstan's government sufficiently for them to ban the film, even though the target of the film's satire is America. The writer and performer of *Borat*, Sacha Baron Cohen, is cementing in our minds the manners and customs of his protagonist in his home country. That it is funny, also, is a logic-game: wit and jokes are games of logic, little startling twists, exaggerations and embarrassments, all playing delightfully on what is wrong with Borat, and with Kazakhstan.

Borat is sent on his journey with a flurry of celebrations. He embraces the men of the village and kisses them on both cheeks. He is packed into the rear seat of an old green motor car that lurches forward, a child wrestling with the steering wheel. The camera angle widens to reveal that the car is towed by a flyblown old horse.

Borat takes a jet and lands in America, carrying a jar of gypsy tears to protect him from AIDS.

He *should* change his manners, now, change his behaviour, given the change of circumstances around him. Any normal person would.

He doesn't. The writer's work is to demonstrate to what extent Borat doesn't change. Baron Cohen is improvising scenes with real people as his unwitting co-stars, but the comic structure is the same as in Molière's comedies: the script leans on the 'cause' part of the paradigm, but will block any progress towards 'change'. With Molière it is a single trait of character – meanness, or misanthropy – whereas with Borat it is his manners that are unchanging.

We've seen previously that it is Borat's custom, in his home town, to greet any man with a kiss on both cheeks. He doesn't change his habits for New York City, although he ought to. On a crowded subway train he introduces himself to the other male passengers, 'Hello, my name is Borat,' and tries to kiss them.

'Hey, what's your name?' Borat cheerfully asks a fellow passenger on the subway.

'My name is mind your own fucking business,' answers the New Yorker.

It adds to the riskiness of the comedy that Sacha Baron Cohen is playing this stunt for real, on members of the public rather than actors. New Yorkers are scared of him, or they are angry, insulted – often all three at once. For the audience it is satirically funny and at the same time heart-stopping. 'You're fuckin with the wrong one, man,' says a man wearing a bandana as he rises to his feet. Borat returns to his seat and picks up his suitcase. It falls open and live chickens escape. There is pandemonium on the subway train; Borat chases his chickens.

Borat's progress through New York is always funny, but takes turns in being frightening and unbearably touching. When the receptionist at Borat's hotel announces in a slow, careful voice the exact price of the room in dollars and cents, Borat spits in his palm, holds out his hand and offers to shake on two thirds of that price. When the receptionist takes Borat into the elevator, Borat unzips his bag. 'Very nice room,' he murmurs, and starts to unpack. 'Not in the room yet, sir,' advises the receptionist. 'Hold on, might want to repack your things,' he adds kindly, 'we are going to be moving again shortly.'

'I will not move to a smaller room,' complains Borat, standing in the elevator, crowded in with the man who is operating the buttons. It's a line of comic genius.

'Sir, this is your floor and I'm going to take you to your room.'

'This is not my room?' queries Borat.

'This is the elevator,' explains the porter/receptionist.

Borat washes his underwear in the nearest river, just like he would do at home. In his hometown it would be customary for him to perform his toilet anywhere convenient. In America, he can see that, all around him, people's habits are different; he should learn, as we would, that no one here performs their toilet in the flower border fronting a major international hotel. He must change his habits. The causes, the reasons that he should and must change, lean ever more heavily, because the effects of not changing are so excruciatingly uncomfortable. But still Baron Cohen maintains the interruption, the blockage in the logic paradigm, that doesn't allow the 'change', as should be the natural order of things. Borat, trousers around his knees, squats among the greenery adjacent to the long, rich, glossy sign that reads in bold silver letters, 'The Trump International Hotel and Tower'.

'This has been most happiest days of my lifes,' he says, looking around at New York's neon streets, as darkness falls.

An essential component in the building of this type of comedy is that Borat himself is blind to the fact that he should, according to the normal rules of logic, change his behaviour. If his character were to be *knowingly* transgressing America's manners and customs and moral values, it would be merely uncomfortable, and funny only to a small minority of its audience. Our narrative pleasure comes from processing two streams of logic at the same time: how Borat behaves, and why; and how Americans behave, and why. The gap between the two is where the comedy lies, and if Borat himself sees that difference, the gap is occupied by Borat and not by us, whereupon the gap narrows sharply to exclude us, the story's innocence is lost, and we no longer have our privileged, insightful position.

We watch with increasing, hilarious disbelief as Baron Cohen refuses to allow Borat the ability to understand that he should change. Meanwhile the reasons that he should do so become increasingly, weightily pressing. No dinner guest should excuse himself to go to the toilet and then bring his own faeces down to the dinner table in a plastic bag. No one should try and win the heart of the flower of America's womanhood by putting a sack over her head and carrying her off through a shopping mall. The scene in which Borat sings his own version of the American national anthem to an audience at a rodeo is a deadly critique of America, so funny that it literally halts or swallows the audience's laughter with its gravity.

The other generic narrative space where, in the design of character, the no-change model thrives is tragedy, which is built to the same pattern as comedy but is slanted differently in order to elicit a different but related emotion, the flip side of humour: sorrow, and pity. In *There Will Be Blood*, the character of Daniel Plainview starts out by exhibiting a defining characteristic – ambition. The film opens with fourteen wordless minutes of Daniel, alone, at the bottom of a deep hole in the ground, striking at a rock face with a pickaxe. He has worked for so long, already, that he's equally adept at handling the tool right-handed or left-handed. So many hours have passed that he's blunted the pickaxe and must sharpen it with a file. Up at ground level, he crouches, alone in a desolate landscape, in front of a flickering camp fire. His tent is a canvas sheet flapping nearby. He is grubby from head to foot, and cradles a cup of coffee in his hands. All he's got is this hole in the ground. He is dirt poor.

The fourteen minutes continue: he lays an explosive charge at the bottom of the shaft, climbs to the top, but then struggles to haul up the bucket full of tools; when the charge goes off, he might have lost them all in the explosion. He climbs back down, but one rung of the ladder comes away in his hand and he falls to the bottom of the shaft. Darkness closes in, and when he wakes a terrible gasp escapes his lips. Even with his broken leg, the first thing he does is look among the rocks loosened by the blast, spit on them and rub the surface to see if there is any glint of gold. There is; he pockets the pebble of ore and, with that broken leg trailing uselessly, drags himself to the surface.

The fourteen-minute sequence gives us, relentlessly, without dialogue, a portrait of Daniel's determination, his Will.i.am, to dig out a morsel of gold. It is a habitual, vigorous, evident desire for money.

Because he is alone, and because he is as poor as the dust and rock in which he digs, Daniel's ambition to make money registers in us, the audience, as admirable. It is his defining virtue.

It is oil that he finds, not gold.

He becomes rich. Everything changes – clothes, food, drink, motor cars. He is in demand. Circumstances have changed. He is no longer alone, in a hole. He is up on the surface, in among other people, with enough money to give him power.

But Daniel Plainview still wields a metaphorical pickaxe. He scrabbles for money with even more vigour and determination, and with even more power now that he is wealthy; but his desire for money, to succeed, means that others must fail. It looks like greed, now; what was a virtue under that previous pattern of logic (he was poor and alone), has now become, after the change in circumstances (he's rich and surrounded by other people), a vice. Underneath, inescapably, is exactly the same, unchanged man. The audience watch with increasing disbelief as he refuses to change, even though the reasons that he should do so become more pressing – he stands to lose more with each error of judgement. He loses everything; he destroys himself, even as his pile of money grows bigger.

As with comedy, it is important that the character is blind to the flaw in his own character, so that we are allowed the privilege of knowing the character better than he knows himself. It makes for dramatic irony at the same time as it renders the protagonist's suffering unmerited – it is unfair that what was once a virtue turns into a vice. It also makes the end inevitable, because we cannot choose but to be subject to our own character, and so there is that dread of knowing a man's destruction before he does.

'Your home is a miracle,' says Eli Sunday (Paul Dano), when he turns up at Daniel's mansion at the end of the film. 'God bless it.' He means that it is a huge house full of extraordinary treasures, but we know Daniel's home is a barren desert, occupied by just him and a manservant.

In this final scene, set in the bowling alley (in order to carry a sporting metaphor) in the basement of this enormous, inhuman mansion, Daniel crushes Eli's skull with multiple blows from a bowling pin, having rubbed it in for him that he, Daniel Plainview, has taken everything from Eli – 'If you have a milkshake, and I have a milkshake, and I have a straw – there it is,' – and he holds up a finger – 'there's the straw, you see, … and my straw reaches acrroooossss the room, and starts to drink your milkshake, I – drink – your – milkshake!'

The body of Eli lies on the bowling lane, his blood a thickening pool. Daniel sits next to him.

The manservant comes down to the bowling alley in a dressing gown, presumably alerted by the noise of the murder. He asks quietly. 'Mr Daniel?'

Daniel is out of breath, sitting in the next bowling lane along from the one occupied by Eli's body. 'I'm finished,' he says, in a tone that denotes the manservant may come in and clean up. But the audience read the obvious, alternative meaning: he's finished. The duality in the logic of this sentence makes for a perfect end to the story.

4   Creating strands of logic – dramatic irony

Screenwriting makes ever more strenuous demands on writers to capture larger audiences for longer periods of time, over months and years, and thus dramatic irony has become of such importance that a screenplay or teleplay could be described as a farm required to grow it as a crop.

Dramatic irony is usually defined as the technique by which a dramatist allows the audience to know something that one or more characters in the story don't know. It has a sensual effect: the audience feel royally privileged; they are included in the story by virtue of the fact that one or more of the story's characters have been excluded from knowing a piece of information that is in their possession. Above and beyond this sensual effect of privilege, dramatic irony exerts narrative power because (and this would make for a better definition) it creates two or more strands of logic that run alongside each other. Often it is a lie or a secret that separates them, or it will be a misunderstanding, or simple ignorance. The 'knowing' characters (including the audience) therefore organise their actions and reactions according to one strand of logic, while the 'unknowing' characters, subject to the same play of events, organise their actions and reactions according to a different strand of logic. The delight for the audience is to watch how the writer arranges for the two (or more) strands of logic to 'talk' to each other, to create a pattern, almost coming together, just touching, or even tangling, but then separating again. It gives the story a complicated music, and makes it intensely involving for the human brain – 'cognitive play stimulates our brains more than does routine processing of the environment. It offers what biologists call a supernormal stimulus … a rush of patterned information that our minds particularly crave' (Boyd, 94). Because dramatic irony provides this supernormal stimulus, 'the lie' and 'the secret' become commonplace ingredients in storytelling, whereas if, in real life, we are caught up in a lie or a secret, it is discomfiting. It is not the lie or the secret, as such, that compels us to work, to take our place in the story, it is the discernment of the logic pattern, and our delight at how the two or more strands of logic play alongside each other.

Also, dramatic irony elicits narrative tension: we are curious to see how the unknowing characters might come to find out whatever it is that they don't know, and what will happen as a result. TV series frequently have an entrenched, long-running dramatic irony as a major component in their design.[4]

Creating strands of logic – dramatic irony in *The Truman Show*

In *The Truman Show* (Weir 1998), the writer Andrew Niccol engineers a powerful dramatic irony from the outset. The film opens with a middle-aged man wearing the trademark back-slanted cap of a younger man, talking directly into the camera – talking to the audience. 'We've become bored with actors giving us phoney emotions … While the world he inhabits is, in some respects, counterfeit, there's nothing fake about Truman himself. No scripts, no cue cards, it isn't always Shakespeare but it is genuine.' This man is Christof (Ed Harris), creator and executive producer of The Truman Show. Christof's lifelong project has been to choose a man, from before he was even born, to be the unwitting star of a reality television show.

The man in question is Truman (Jim Carrey), and he has no idea that everyone else around him – his mother, father, wife, friends, his neighbours, his work colleagues, every passer-by in the street – is an actor. The whole town is a set. The sky overhead is a painted screen. The sea is an enormous tank of water.

On day ten thousand nine hundred and nine of The Truman Show (which makes Truman twenty-nine years old) the camera descends onto

---

[4]*Breaking Bad* owes its narrative power to the fact that Walter White's wife, his son, plus his brother-in-law and sister-in-law don't know that he has become a manufacturer of crystal meth. The writers slowly allow his brother-in-law's family to find out, and his wife, but never his son.

the set to find the perfectly realised world of an American seaside town, Seahaven, with everything in its proper place. Truman galvanises himself with a motivational speech in front of the bathroom mirror. His wife calls that he's going to be late for work. He steps outside the front door and greets the neighbours over the road: a perfect dad, a perfect mum and their child. Another neighbour's dog, Pluto, jumps up at him, as always, and Truman hates that.

A global TV audience, tens of millions of people, are watching this TV show from their sofas, or leaning on bars, or while they are in the bath. They, along with us, the film's audience, are privileged with the information that Truman is television's most famous 'reality' star. The sheer number of people who know, so many millions of them around the world, the show's audience and the film's audience, when set against the singular person who doesn't know, Truman himself, plus the import of his lack of knowledge on his life and on the lives of the actors and production crew and the show's audience surrounding him, constitutes an enormous weight of dramatic irony. It makes for a miles-wide gap between the strand of logic that Truman lives by and the one that the other characters and his two audiences live by, while occupying the very same events. Moment by moment he is right up against the truth, as close as can be. The gap, the huge difference between his understanding and ours, is filled with our pity for him.

He opens his car door, as usual, ready to drive to work.

Out of the blue, a stage light drops out of what Truman thinks is the sky and shatters on the road. He's startled – as are the audience. It is a mistake, and might give Truman a clue as to what's happening. The two strands of logic suddenly come closer: the audience hold their breath and watch with rapt attention to see if the membrane between the two strands of logic will be ruptured. The audience know that the 'sky' is a painted carapace that sits like an enormous dome on top of the set. The stage light is there, shattered on the ground, and Truman sees it: the glass sprinkled on the pavement, the housing all buckled. But he can't comprehend what it means. He carefully approaches. He nudges it, pats it. He picks it up and reads the lettering that we can see on a piece of tape stuck to the side: 'Sirius 9 canis … ' The audience understand that it is a technical description of the light's position mimicking a star in the 'sky'.

He looks up at the unbroken, cloudless blue, puzzlement on his expression.

The vast resources of the TV show swing into action: a few minutes later, as Truman drives down an immaculate residential road populated with immaculately casual 'residents', the car radio informs him that 'an aircraft in trouble began shedding parts as it flew over … '

Writer Andrew Niccol brought the different strands of logic closer, but then separated them. He will do so repeatedly, in a series of set pieces that, one after another, increase the length of time during which the two strands of logic remain close together, and even become entangled, before finally joining together.

Years previously, an actor was employed to play Truman's father. He died (i.e. was written out of the show) when Truman was still a child. Now this same actor, decades older, suddenly reappears on the street, dressed this time as a homeless man. The audience's strand of logic tells them that the actor must have got himself hired as an extra; the casting directors will have changed, over the years, and they didn't recognise him. Truman, operating on his strand of logic, sees his dead father come back to life, in front of his eyes.

The show's security team swoops and the 'homeless man' is lifted off his feet and carried into a bus, while every manner of object – motor car, cyclist, a team of runners – is put in Truman's way in order to stop his anguished pursuit of his 'dead' father. His 'friends' and 'relations' conspire to persuade Truman that it was a psychological trick, a ghostly imagining.

The dramatic irony is even more vigorously agitated when the film goes back in time, to when Truman was at university, and he swapped intense looks with a fellow student, Lauren Garland (Natascha McElhone), which threatens the marriage that the show's producers are arranging for him with Meryl Burbank (Laura Linney). Lauren wants to alert Truman to his position as the unwitting, lifelong star of The Truman Show and manages to meet him in the library and escape with him, running fast, hand in hand, over the deserted car park to the beach.

The two threads of logic not only touch, but wind around each other. According to Truman's logic, he invited a girl for a pizza, and finds himself more urgently taken up on his offer than he expected. Here, now, on this wide open beach, he happily jokes about it, 'This is my favourite pizza place. Tony! One large, extra plankton.' According to her logic, she has broken all the rules and knows she will be sacked; and she knows she has only a minute or two to say what she's come here to say. She spares a brief smile at his joke but hurries on, 'We have so little time. They are going to be here any minute.'

'Who are?'

'They don't want me talking to you.'

'Then don't talk,' he replies and kisses her. She responds, and we sense the valuable time, just a minute or two, draining away, and we recognise in that kiss her real love and pity for Truman, before the sound of an engine grows louder and she breaks off. 'They're here.' Eyes wide with determination, even as the car bucks down the sand dunes towards them, she tells him, 'Truman, listen to me. Everyone knows everything you do ... Everyone's pretending, Truman ... do you understand ... my name's not Lauren, it is Sylvia ... '

The two strands of logic are closer, they are tangled together, but they are about to be separated again by the film's writer, Andrew Niccol.

A man jumps from the car and pretends to be Lauren's father.

Lauren is frightened, agitated. 'I've never even seen him before,' she pleads as she is dragged away by her 'father'. She picks up a handful of sand and shows it to a bewildered Truman. 'This, it is fake, it is all for you ... '

'I don't understand ... '

'It is a set, it is a show ... ' Even as Lauren's 'father' puts her in the car she tries to warn Truman, 'He's going to lie to you.'

Sure enough, the 'father' says, 'Schizophrenia ... ' and pushes Truman further away. 'You're not the first,' he repeats. 'She brings all her boy-friends down here.' The two strands of logic, having become entangled, now begin to separate again.

The dramatic irony is magnified by the fact that this happened so many years ago, and, therefore, not only did the strands of logic separate, but the film's audience are privileged to know the strands are going to remain separate, the lie maintained, for many years to come.

Lauren manages to call to him from the car window, 'Come and find me ... ' and the father's final words, thrown casually from the side window as he reverses the car, are telling. 'We are moving to Fiji.' These words provide an extra piece of logic-work for us to perform, because here, we now understand, is the cause of Truman's evident, vigorous, singular desire in the film, which he's held from this very moment, for almost ten years, to abandon Seahaven and go to 'Fiji' and find 'Lauren'. He loves the person he knows as Lauren. She left a cardigan behind on the beach; we recognise it as the one that he keeps in his trunk full of precious memories in the basement of his home. The badge stuck in its lapel asks poignantly, 'How's it going to end?' There is a rush of comprehension, a series of 'cognitions', as we lace together the points of logic that the writer has arranged for us to find.

We have no sooner recovered from this entangling of the twin strands of logic than we are carried to the next occasion on which they touch and wrap around each other even more strongly.

The car radio goes wrong. Instead of his usual radio station, Truman overhears the production team's radio messages orchestrating his progress. 'He's making a turn down Lancaster Square … ' Truman looks out of his side window and the sign slides past – Lancaster Square.

There is a vicious attack of feedback over the radio, and the whole town, every pedestrian, every policeman, stops and holds a hand to his or her ear, before the show's producers, once again, attempt to reinstate the lie.

This time, we watch, enthralled, as it doesn't quite work. Truman has finally cottoned on; he is suspicious of his 'reality'. He holds up the traffic, he dives into a different building, he glimpses a refreshment table 'backstage' before the set is hurriedly re-made, even as he is hauled away. When he is finally at home, and his wife is doing her best to persuade him that he's had a mental breakdown, and his mother is showing him the family photograph album in order to reinforce the grip of his fake life, we understand from his manner that he knows something is wrong. The strands of logic have begun to join together. His reading of the logic is becoming the same as that of the surrounding characters, as well as his two audiences.

When his wife tries to persuade him of the virtues of a brand of hot chocolate as part of the show's product placement strategy, Truman sees through her fake tone. He takes her hostage using a combined peeler, grater and dicer that she'd previously tried to advertise and it is only the arrival of his best friend, Marlon (Noah Emmerich), that saves the situation.

Truman's world slowly becomes as one with ours. The story ends with his sailing to the edge of the tank of water, opening a door in the 'horizon', and leaving the show. His vigorous, evident, singular desire to escape from his imprisonment has been achieved. His character has undergone an actual change, from innocent and unknowing to experienced, knowing.

In real life, the majority of us feel deeply uncomfortable living in, or around, a lie; we are allergic to un-truth even as, in big ways or small, we tell lies, but in a fictional story we are gripped because it is not real, it is not our lives, and it gives us this rich pattern of logic to work with. And it doesn't have to be a lie; dramatic irony can be forged using a simple lack of knowledge, or a misunderstanding.

The pleasure and excitement that the exercise of logic gives to us in the real world is described by Colin McGinn in *Logical Properties: Identity, Existence, Predication, Necessity, Truth* (2000) when we are 'grasping the unique (and remarkable) way that truth operates: it performs the miraculous feat of taking us from language and thought, on the one hand, to the world of objects and properties, on the other' (12). In the world of the film narrative, the journey is in the other direction: from the 'objects and properties' arranged for us by screenwriters towards 'thought and language' – i.e. towards the judgements and the inferences that we make and re-make using the internal voice in which we talk to ourselves when we are immersed in a film's story. McGinn celebrates this feeling that logic gives us – 'No other concept has this power: truth is the adhesive that binds mind and world, to put it metaphorically and portentously.' (12)

Creating strands of logic – suspense

Dramatic irony has a more sophisticated older sister – suspense. However there is an ongoing argument about what constitutes suspense; as late as 1996 Fredrickson observed that, 'One of the problems concerning the internal and external validity of suspense research arises from the fact that a tight definition of suspense is still missing.' (Vorderer et al., 338)

A tight definition of suspense can be offered and it's worth looking briefly at the arguments in order to describe a reasonable basis for it. The arguments can be separated into two camps, one based on uncertainty, the other on certainty.

Suspense, as a general term, implies the sense of an audience waiting anxiously – suspended – for how things are going to turn out, which might otherwise be described as narrative tension. This narrative tension might be elicited either by uncertainty, that is to say, by not knowing what is going to happen and at the same time feeling more or less intense curiosity about the outcome; alternatively, it can be elicited by certainty, by the certain knowledge of what is going to happen, and if that event is negative then dread is aroused; if it is positive, it is anticipation.

Suspense on the 'uncertainty' side of the argument is defined by McKee as a circumstance where 'the audience and characters know the same information' (351), i.e. without dramatic irony as an ingredient, and furthermore Carroll says, 'uncertainty is a necessary condition for suspense. When uncertainty is removed from a situation, suspense evaporates' (2001, 255). Bordwell and Thompson agree – 'Normally we say that suspense demands an uncertainty about how things will turn out' (2011, 97). This 'uncertainty' argument is the one I would propose to reject as not qualifying for suspense, although it should still be described as narrative tension. In fact, with its reliance on questioning and on curiosity, it amounts to mystery writing, described on page 88 below.

On the 'certainty' side of the argument Hitchcock gives us his often-quoted definition of suspense during a 1970 interview with the American Film Institute. He described suspense in metaphorical terms; he said it was like a ticking bomb hidden under the table –

Four people are sitting around a table. Talking about baseball. Five minutes of it. Very dull. Suddenly, a bomb goes off. Blows the people to smithereens. What do the audience have? Ten seconds of shock. Now take the same scene. And *tell* the audience there is a bomb under that table. And it will go off in five minutes. The whole emotion of the audience is totally different. Because you've given them that information. That in five minutes' time, that bomb will go off. Now the conversation about baseball becomes very vital. Because they're saying to you, 'Don't be ridiculous, stop talking about baseball, there's a bomb under there.' You've got the audience working. (American Film Institute 1970)

Hitchcock's metaphor thus describes dramatic irony as *the* central ingredient of suspense. The audience have certain knowledge of the bomb, but the people around the table *don't* know (they are talking about baseball). Furthermore the audience have certain knowledge of precisely when the bomb will go off. These three ingredients, encapsulated in Hitchcock's metaphor, together make up a tight definition of suspense: the 'bomb' itself, the 'ticking' part (a time element, in this case five minutes), and the dramatic irony, the fact that it is 'hidden' from one or more characters.

Given this tighter definition of suspense, it becomes a rarer commodity, and a different, more tricky proposition in terms of writing technique. It's the difference between writing that a young girl with supernatural powers is going to her high school prom, and something awful is going to happen to her but we don't know what, in which case we'd feel the tension of uncertainty and the mystery of what will happen (narrative tension), and, on the other hand, writing suspense: giving to the audience absolute certainty of what will happen. A bucket of blood is prepared, the ropes and pulleys are set up, the bucket of blood is precariously lodged, out of sight, directly above the 'x' on the stage where the young girl must stand when she is voted Prom Queen – and that is the suspense in the final scene of *Carrie* (De Palma 1976). It is the writing of dramatic irony, not mystery, but with the added power of the certain, explosive event, and the ticking clock. When Carrie stands on that 'x', the rope will be pulled, the blood will fall on her.

Hitchcock himself later said that he had come to learn that in the construction of suspense the bomb should never go off, but *Carrie* points to that not being true. However, the fact that the bomb might not go off – it might even be set ticking again later on – does not mean that the writer is not creating certainty: the technique demands absolute certain knowledge in the audience during the period in which suspense is in play. The power of its effect lies in the remorseless progress through measured time towards a certain, known fate, and if that fate suddenly doesn't happen, the suspense ends in just the same way as if it does happen, if the bomb does go off. It is the after-effects, the rest of the story, that will be manifestly different.

As soon as the name 'Hitchcock' and the word 'suspense' are put next to each other an assumption is made that an audience is about to be made to feel afraid – but suspense can be brought to bear within any genre, and the 'bomb' can either be a change for the worse (which evokes dread), or for the better (which creates anticipation). In Hitchcock's adaptation of du Maurier's *Rebecca* (1940) there is a suspense sequence that contains one after the other in a scenario that is designed to evoke feelings of love rather than danger.

In *Rebecca* the nameless heroine (Joan Fontaine) is a young woman who, after the death of her parents, works as a companion to the ghastly Edythe Van Hopper (Florence Bates), a harridan with a swivelling eye who bosses the younger woman's manners and behaviour while at the same time, due to the writer's dexterity with ironic humour, reveals herself to be a bully who is blind to her own awful character. However, this nameless young woman, who painfully tries to please Edythe Van Hopper in a plush hotel in Monte Carlo, has caught the eye of the handsome but troubled Maxim de Winter (Laurence Olivier), wealthy owner of Manderlay, a beautiful country house in Cornwall. Mrs Van Hopper has fallen ill and lies in bed eating chocolates in order to take away the taste of her medicine. She is attended by a nurse, so the nameless young woman can take advantage of Maxim's offers to take her dancing, or to play tennis, or to drive along the romantic coastline and to wait while she sketches. This idyll is going to end soon because Mrs Van Hopper is recovering and will need looking after again. Dramatic irony is already in play: Mrs Van Hopper knows nothing about her companion's romantic success. She operates according to one strand of logic, while the nameless young woman operates according to a different logic.

Maxim takes the nameless young woman for a drive in the open car along a winding clifftop road; she is happier than she's ever been and she says she wants to bottle the happiness and keep it. Maxim warns that such bottles might contain demons, and spoils her optimistic mood. She changes from being carefree to being anxious, and Maxim idly instructs her to 'stop biting your nails'. She loses confidence and begs him to tell her why he is bothering with her, when she isn't a young woman wearing a black satin dress and a string of pearls, aged thirty-six. Maxim abruptly brings the car to a halt and makes her promise never to wear black satin, or a string of pearls, and never to be thirty-six. He explains that he invites her on these jaunts because he wants her company, and because, more than all the bright lights of Monte Carlo, she helps him to blot out the past. He kisses the tip of one finger and touches it lightly against her forehead. With this gesture, her expression melts into one of surprised adoration and pleasure. She is in love with Maxim; she is happy, and there is a chance that he too, in his way, loves her. With Max's gesture and his words at the front of her mind she returns, gaily humming, to the company of Mrs Van Hopper. Maxim has delivered a large spray of red roses with the accompanying message, 'Thank you for yesterday.' Nothing will spoil her mood.

The 'bomb' is now planted. Mrs Van Hopper squawks from her habitual position, in bed: 'For the love of Pete, come here!' The nameless young woman dashes through to Mrs Van Hopper's bedroom. 'What do you think,' says the harridan. 'My daughter's engaged to be married.'[5]

'Oh really, how nice!'

'We must leave for New York at once ... '

The camera finds the nameless young woman's face, and we can see the impact of this news on her falling expression. If she has to leave, then she will be torn away from her budding romance just at the time when it should be given a chance to bloom. Three strands of logic – hers, Mrs Van Hopper's and Maxim's – are heading for this explosion.

The 'bomb' will definitely go off; there is a set time for it to explode. 'Get reservations on the Aquitania,' Mrs Van Hopper bosses her, 'and we'll take the 12.30 train for Cherbourg. Hurry up and get the maid to help with the packing. We've got no time to waste. ... Go on and don't dawdle!' she shouts even before the girl has time to move one step. This inclusion of an exact time adds urgency to the situation and makes the 'explosion' inevitable. Without time being marked in such a way (whether

---

[5] In du Maurier's novel, the reason the pair immediately have to leave is because of a nephew's sickness in New York. The writer of the adaptation settled on the idea of the marriage engagement because it provides a more potent irony: the young woman will have to give up her own romantic pleasure in order to be forced to witness someone else's – that of Mrs Van Hopper's daughter.

a short time ahead or many weeks or years), in other words without it being clear at what moment the bomb will explode, the suspense will lose this quality of powerful inevitability.

The third ingredient in the suspense form is the most important – dramatic irony. The prospect of the love affair being ruined is hidden from Maxim de Winter, and the love affair is entirely hidden from Mrs Van Hopper.

The nameless young woman therefore operates along her own strand of logic, no longer shared with Max, while Max, blissfully unaware, operates according to another, and Mrs Van Hopper attempts to work her way along her own strand of logic: she must get to the railway station, catch that train and board the liner to America. All three parties live through the same events, but act according to the demands of differing strands of logic, more or less well-informed.

Once again, it is when the script brings these different strands close enough almost to touch, and then moves them further apart, that we become most involved. As with 'dangling the logic' (cf. page 52), it is the movement that creates the chance for us to re-compute our measurement of probabilities, which gives us this intense involvement in the characters' desires.

The nameless young woman hurries to try and get in touch with Max and tell him what's happened. She hides in her bedroom, ear to the phone, and relays for our benefit the replies given to her by the hotel's receptionist. 'Oh, he's gone out riding? He won't be back 'til noon?'

There is a ticking clock: the pendulum swings back and forth, the *tick, tock* is loud and insistent. The hands show five minutes to twelve, and Mrs Van Hopper is out of bed, dressed and ready to go, pacing back and forth. A trunk stands there, packed and labelled; the nameless young woman wears a hat, her coat is over her arm and her handbag is clutched tight. 'I'll go and see if there's anything left in my room.' She tells the lie in order to be able to call Maxim again and see if he has returned from his ride.

In her bedroom, the anxiety clears from her expression as she learns from the receptionist that Maxim is, in fact, in the hotel. 'Could you put me through, please?' Two out of the three strands of logic are quickly moving closer together; as soon as she manages to talk to him, surely, they will occlude, turn into one strand, and there will be a change of circumstances: either her hopes for the romance will be made, or broken. The causes begin to cluster around the moment of possible change. She listens intently to the insistent ringing of the phone in Maxim's room. One small action, his answering the phone, is all that's required.

It is here that Carroll's words spring to mind, ' … uncertainty is a necessary condition for suspense. When uncertainty is removed from a situation, suspense evaporates' (255). If feels like uncertainty here, but it is in fact a dangling of the possibility of change within a certain knowledge of what will happen, and most importantly, the tighter definition of suspense requires the *lack* of knowledge of some of the characters. If the dramatic irony were removed the suspense would disappear; and if the *certainty* of what is going to happen were to be degraded or removed, the suspense would disappear. The audience is watching a character struggle against a certain fate. She might just win, but that is immaterial. It is the relationship with the logic paradigm that gives us the tight definition. Suspense is dramatic irony with extra effect.

Mrs Van Hopper wonders what's keeping her companion and imperiously marches towards the bedroom. The door handle rattles; Mrs Van Hopper is about to come in and, just as she does so, for a short moment all three different strands of logic are actually touching: Mrs Van Hopper's, the nameless young woman's, and, via the phone extension, Maxim de Winter's.

The nameless young woman hurriedly drops the phone into its cradle and casts around, looking for an excuse. 'I was looking for my book … I suppose I've packed it.' The strands of logic begin to move further apart. 'Well come on! The car's waiting at the door.' Mrs Van Hopper and her companion leave the room.

The camera's eye immediately closes on the phone. Sure enough, in the empty room, it rings.

Hitchcock makes sure we can hear every breath taken by the nameless young woman as she carves any spare second she can in order to find Maxim de Winter. When she is told that he went up to his room, the concierge telephones on her behalf, and again an invention is required that will allow the writer to bring the different threads of logic – the unknowing and the knowing – as close as possible. The phone rings in

Max's room, and yes, he is in there – but he's in the shower and further-more he is loudly singing. The phone rings on, unheard.

The concierge reports, 'I'm sorry Ma'am, he's not picking up'.

Mrs Van Hopper waits impatiently in the car with the luggage.

The nameless young woman hears from a waiter that Max just ordered breakfast to be carried up to his room; she hurries up the stairs. She knocks on the door – twice. The water from the shower has stopped running and Max hears her. 'Come in.'

She walks into his bedroom.

At this point, we understand that two out of three separate strands of logic are about to join together. The suspense begins to leak out of the sides of the story.

None the less we can sense the nameless young woman's trepidation; her every hesitant, uncertain breath is a punctuation note of sound as she timidly walks across Max's room. She can't see him, but, through the wall of the bathroom, she tells him the news. She is going to New York – right now. There is nothing she can do about it.

The suspense has gone, but it is replaced with a different type of nar-rative tension: what will Max do, when he hears she is about to be taken from under his nose? He will be faced with a choice, where the differ-ent causes gather into a nexus and one of several effects might emerge on the other side. We know that he's troubled, haunted. Yet he has, after all, asked her out on several occasions. He placed that fingertip on her forehead – but that was hardly a passionate gesture. This situation, now, demands all or nothing. We are at the very moment where a change might or might not be effected in the nameless young woman's desire for Maxim.

'Which would you prefer,' he asks, 'New York or Manderley?'

There is a pause. Her humility means she answers, 'You mean you want a secretary or something?' The writer is teasing us – dangling the moment of change.

Max's next line bursts all the anxiety and delivers it – 'I'm asking you to marry me, you little fool.'

An audience will often laugh at this point in the film, which is a release of nervous energy. The comical, downward spiral of the music perfectly describes the diminished tension.

Her life is transformed, and we know that this change, delivered to us on a tidal wave of suspense, and visualised for us by Hitchcock (who started his film career in the silent era) as a wonderful alteration in the expression on Joan Fontaine's face, will have powerful after-effects, not least because we already know that the country house, Manderley, will, for some reason as yet unknown, burn to the ground.

As described earlier, suspense is generally associated with something about to happen that is bad, frightening, but the form can equally well be used to foretell an event that is happy, good, in which case the suspense model works in the same way, but the feeling attached to it changes from dread to anticipation. An example of this immediately follows the scene described above, from *Rebecca*.

There has been a moment of celebration while the newly engaged couple sit down to the breakfast delivered to Max's room ... but suddenly they remember Mrs Van Hopper, still waiting downstairs in the car. She must be told. The delivery of this news will be a pleasure for the audience, since she's a harridan and deserves to be punished. Thus two elements of suspense are there: dramatic irony (Mrs Van Hopper doesn't know about the engagement), and the 'bomb' (as soon as Mrs Van Hopper sees them together, she will lose the companion whom she's so enjoyed bullying, all this time). The 'ticking' part, however, isn't immediately evident. In the previous scene there was the device of the train leaving, which created urgency and allowed for, literally, a ticking clock and thus pinpoint accuracy as to the point when that particular bomb would go off, and a sense of the story's inevitable march towards that moment. No such inventions are available on this occasion; a ticking clock would be wrong, heavy handed, as would be Mrs Van Hopper's feet marking each stair as she climbs to meet them. Instead Hitchcock does what he often does:[6] he uses a metaphor to represent time's remorseless progress. The audience know at what point the bomb will go off: as soon as Mrs Van Hopper on the one hand, and Max de

---

[6]In *The Birds* (1963) for instance, in the sequence when Melanie Daniels waits outside the children's playground, Hitchcock uses the singing of a 'round' to mark the insistence of time's progress, and a cigarette burning down.

Winter and the nameless young woman on the other hand, stand and face each other. It remains to give the sense of time steadily and inevitably progressing towards this point. Hitchcock now betrays his past work, before silent film even, as a stage director, because, arm in arm in their hotel room, Max and his new fiancée stroll in a circle, which marks out the shape of a clock for us. It is highly contrived, 'staged', but none the less has its effect: we can feel Mrs Van Hopper's willing progress up the stairs, as she gladly and proudly answers this astonishing invitation to come to the hotel bedroom of no less a personage than Maxim de Winter.

When she comes in, once again early film-making betrays its debt to the stage: the nameless young woman takes a step back and suddenly becomes invisible, while Mrs Van Hopper, obsequiously pleased to be invited to Maxim de Winter's room, is all smiles and explains her lack of manners in not informing him of her departure. 'It was so rude of me,' she says to him, 'not to let you know, but a cable came this morning announcing that my daughter is engaged to be married … '

'That's rather a coincidence Mrs Van Hopper,' replies Maxim. 'I asked you up here in order to tell you of my engagement.'

'You don't mean it,' says Mrs Van Hopper, delighted to be in his confidence. 'Well how perfectly wonderful. How romantic. Who is the lucky lady?'

Maxim gestures behind her, and Mrs Van Hopper turns around.

The explosion is written on the face of the actress: Mrs Van Hopper's smile falls, like so much dust and debris.

Suspense adds extra muscle to an episode of dramatic irony: the 'bomb' bolts onto the end of it as a moment of specific and dynamic change, either for the better or for the worse, while the 'ticking clock' induces a sense of inevitability that makes certain our feelings either of dread, or of anticipation.

It is famously effective on repeated viewings, as is dramatic irony. There are various reasons that work to help this – Bordwell and Thompson mention a 'firewall' (2011, 99) between past viewings and the current one,[7]

---

[7]See pages 96–102 of *Minding Movies* (2011) for a detailed look at this phenomenon.

but to add another, if the power of the effect is in the pattern, the pattern is always there regardless of how many times you experience it.

Suspense is not the same as foreshadowing; it is not the same as crisis, or danger. As with the art of 'dangling the logic paradigm' (cf. page 52), Hitchcock's suspense demands complete knowledge of the situation by the audience, which the writer must somehow impart. Within this definition it is not suspenseful (for example) to have a character walk down a corridor with several closed doors along its length, behind one of which *might* be something nasty, accompanied by a dangerous tone of music. Suspense would require us to know exactly what the nasty thing is, and behind which door it is, and for the inevitability to be measured either by the doors or by the footsteps – but most importantly it would require one or more of the characters not to know that it is there. The powerfully intensifying factor in Hitchcock's form of suspense is dramatic irony and its multiple streams of logic. It is rare because it's difficult to write.

Creating strands of logic – the twist

In pulling off a twist or a surprise, a screenwriter doesn't operate like a magician; the skill is almost opposite, and for good reason. In pulling a rabbit out of a hat, the magician obscures the logic of how the rabbit got into the hat in the first place, because this is the difficult thing to do. We look into the hat, it's tipped upside down, we can even stick our hand in there and feel for it. There is no way the rabbit could be in there. But – there it is. The logic of how it got in there is hidden, and remains hidden, on penalty of expulsion from The Magic Circle. The difficult part, for the magician, is always to hide the logic.

For the screenwriter, it is easy to hide the logic, because the writer is in charge of everything that the audience sees. To simply reveal a surprise or a twist, having hidden the logic, is the equivalent of the magician asking the audience to close their eyes, or the use of trick camerawork in the act of a TV illusionist. It will create similar disappointment. The writer is therefore charged with creating two strands of logic, both of which are visible, and, at the moment when the twist is revealed, the audience merely switches from one strand of logic to another, *which was always there, noticed by the audience but disregarded until now.* An example of how this difficult feat is performed is offered by the South Korean film, *Mother* (Bong Joon-ho 2009), described in Chapter 4, page 164.

5   Interrupting the logic paradigm – mystery

If dramatic irony, suspense and the twist all depend, for their beautiful display, on creating and orchestrating multiple strands of logic, then mystery makes use of the opposite technique: it chops up the logic and excludes the audience, prevents the audience's view of one part or another of the cause-change-effect paradigm. It usually (but not always) makes evident the third, 'effect' part of the paradigm while deliberately obscuring either or both of the first two parts, the 'cause' part and/or the 'change' part. Screenwriters who use the mystery technique will offer to their audience something, an 'effect' perhaps, that can't be explained, and thus will invoke the audience's hunger to complete the logic paradigm. The audience searches upstream, to look for the causes, and finds an empty space. Therefore we feel curiosity; mystery plays on our creaturely instinct to find the missing pieces of the paradigm, and we search within the world of the story in order to find them. The audience's quest is to discover; the dramatist's task is to lead the audience through this pattern of speculative hypothesis and synthesis, to lay the trail of this logic-game, until the audience arrives at the truth of the situation, and always with the impression that they have found out for themselves, on their own account, which is a necessary act of generosity on the part of screenwriters. It is as if the audience is placed, like Hansel and Gretel, in a dark wood, and without, at first, the white pebbles that will allow them to find their way out. Carefully the mystery writer has to position pieces of information, the white pebbles that must be picked up by the audience, but without the writer's hand being evident. If that darkness can finally be lifted at a stroke, in one dramatic moment, then so much the better.

For the logic-junkie mystery screenwriter, 'the question is only: *How will the understanding know itself?*' (Kant 1963, 4)

Interrupting the logic paradigm – mystery in *Amour*

Amour (2012), written and directed by Michael Haneke, opens inside a Paris apartment at the moment when its doors are burst open by a group of helmeted firemen, accompanied by the police. They quickly come in; it is clear they are not expecting violence but they are asking questions: 'Fire Department. Is anyone home?' and 'What's the date on the mail?' The answer is, 'The ninth'. Immediately the writers are making clear to us there are things the story knows that we don't know, but at the same time they are giving us the means to work stuff out. The 'effect' part of the logic paradigm is in front of us: the emergency services are breaking down doors. We search for the causes, and for the change. What's happened and why? The fact they are asking about the dates on the mail has to mean the inhabitants haven't been seen for some time. The story thus demonstrates there is something we don't know at the same time as putting down one or two small clues that allow us to think that we ourselves are working out the answers as to what that might be. If the dialogue had said, 'How long is it that they haven't been seen?' then a certain irritation would have infected our reaction, and we would have called it bad writing. The writer would have occupied the place where we, the audience, are meant to be, he would have failed to allow us the means to think we've worked out something for ourselves.

One of the fire officers holds a hand to his nose: it is another clue. There's a dead body in this apartment: the smell is either from a gas supply left on, or the smell of death. The interior doors are locked shut and the gaps between the doors are sealed with tape: with these 'effects' we can work backwards along the logic paradigm and arrive at the conclusion that not only will there be a dead body in the apartment, but it will be a murder or a suicide, perhaps caused by gas. This invokes new, bigger questions: who is dead and why were they killed, or why did they kill themselves?

The landlord, or perhaps the concierge to the building, gives us the line, 'They had a nurse' and these words allow us a further small inference: because of the use of the third person plural, 'they', we can judge more than one person is involved; and the pair of them were old ('had a nurse'), and perhaps ill, and so they have died. We suspect a suicide pact. As before, if the line had been, 'A married couple, very old and pretty sick,' we would have been prevented from performing our instinctive logic-work.

And then we see the dead body: an old lady, beautifully dressed, a halo of flowers on the pillow around her head, lying on the bed, hands gracefully together, resting on her stomach. The writer has given us the means to forecast an image such as this, and therefore we congratulate ourselves: we have been successful. Having been excluded from the story we have worked our way back in. We have bolted together (apparently by virtue of our own cleverness, but in fact due to the writer's generosity) one strand of cause-change-effect: she became too old, too ill, and she and her husband have opted for a merciful, loving release for her.

A further question is immediately aroused: what about *him*, where is he?

And there are other questions: what was the illness, what were the circumstances that led to such a decision?

But most persistent is this question: the concierge had said 'they' and the positioning of the flowers around her head means he (we presume it is a 'he') attended to the woman's body after her death. So – where is he, what happened to him? What has been the effect on him, the husband?

The answer to this question will be denied to us for the length of the film.

We will go back in time, we will meet him and her, and we will find out some of the causes that contributed to her death – her age and illness – and we will witness the change, her deathbed scene, but the effect on him will remain obstinately missing. We will not want to leave the story until we find out.

In this way, by depriving the audience of sections of the logic paradigm, a feeling of curiosity creates the involvement of the audience simply by excluding them, leaving them out of the story.

The title appears, *Amour*. It is a title that we know already because we've bought the cinema ticket or the DVD or the download, but it reinforces our judgement that this was a mercy killing.

The next thing we see is a large audience in a grand old-fashioned auditorium settling down in expectation of a performance of some kind (it is the only time the film leaves the setting of their apartment). Our practice at narrative tells us that we've seen the end of the story and now we've jumped back to the beginning; we scan the rows of faces, looking for hers, alive and well, and we also look out for him, for her companion or partner – we presume that he will be her husband.

The writer instead introduces a significant player in the drama: music itself. The performance is a concert of Schubert's Impromptu Opus 90 No. 1. To watch so many hundreds of faces intently listening to the same music that we are listening to imprints the music on us – and we will come to learn that both husband and wife were music teachers before their retirement.

During the next scene, music is made concrete by way of the person who performed it. During the interval a young man (the pianist Alexandre Tharaud who was cast in the part of Anne's former pupil, and whom we see, later in the film, paying her a visit) is talking to friends who have come to see him play. He sees someone out of the corner of his eye and he breaks off the conversation to go and greet them affectionately.

Her profile is immediately recognisable from her deathbed. But she is alive and well, so it is confirmed to us that we have gone back to the beginning of the story. Her name is Anne (Emmanuelle Riva).

At last, there he is – her husband, Georges (Jean-Louis Trintignant), the one who was missing from the last scene, which was set some time in the future from where we are now. He has a handsome, sensitive face to match the gracefulness of hers. What happened to him?

Both dramatic irony and its opposite technique, mystery, are now invoked. For the dramatic irony, we are privileged to know (unlike Anne or Georges) that before the story ends Anne will lie on her deathbed, garlanded by flowers. At the same time the story knows, but excludes us from knowing, what part Georges had to play in Anne's death, and what effect it will have on him. The dramatic irony and the mystery are overarching structures that hold the weight of the drama. Both are made out of the writer's manipulation of the logic paradigm. The dramatic irony arouses pity and dread; the mystery arouses curiosity. Only when we find out what happens to Georges at the end will we have the story and its meaning in our grasp. This mystery – keeping us demonstrably out of the story, excluded instead of included – has a powerful motor effect in a film that has a low-key, habitual, placid and evident desire: that husband and wife might continue to share their love for one another. The more we grow to care for them, the more we feel pity for her undignified illness, and the more we need to know what happened to Georges. The question grows bigger even as we become more certain that we know the answer already, given the character of Georges – that he too will die, alongside her, in that apartment.

Philippe Rouyer, who ghosted Haneke's autobiography, was interviewed in 2012 by TF1 to make an introduction to the film, and he points out that Haneke 'succeeds not only in surprising us, but leaving us with our questioning. Questioning is really the crux of Haneke's films' (Rouyer 2012).

That questioning is partially answered near the end of the film, after an hour and three-quarters, during which the audience has observed Anne's slow descent into a mental vacuum. Finally, Georges leans over Anne as she sleeps, and he draws towards him a pillow. With a sudden movement he drops it over her face and bears down with all his weight; meanwhile to obscure the sight of what he's doing he buries his face in the pillow.

Her legs kick feebly, give a final twitch, and lie still.

It is an act of love.

Slowly, Georges makes the preparations that will result in the scene that we were privileged to see at the opening of the film. He brings back to the apartment the flowers that we know will garland her pillow. If they were to be arranged in a vase he would trim a mere half an inch from the stems. Instead he nips off each flowering head. Enriched by our prior knowledge, we marry up cause and effect: we've seen where they will end up, arranged carefully in a halo around Anne's head. Similarly, when he reaches into her wardrobe, we lace together the points of logic provided by the writer in order to afford us this small rush of comprehension: that was her best dress, the one she's going to wear on her deathbed. These are the small bursts of comprehension – 'cognitions'.

The cause, the reason behind every one of Georges's actions, is love – the title of this film.

The dramatic irony is invigorated by the writer's use of specific details that allow us to make such cognitions, and furthermore, as far as the mystery is concerned, the questioning remains: what will be the effect on Georges? At the beginning of the film, our questioning was about the causes, and about the change – what happened and why? By now we have come to understand the causes and the change, but this one 'effect' part of the paradigm is still missing. A deliberate *lack* of telling is one of the elements that has kept us glued to this story.

Georges looks increasingly dishevelled, thin and unable to cope. The audience is virtually certain he will take his own life. They demand from the story that ending, but it remains to be seen how their expectation will be answered.

The audience's expertise in narrative will lead us to think we are going to revisit the scene showed to us at the outset of the film in which the fire brigade and the police break down the doors to the apartment. For almost the entire duration of the film (the only exception being a concert at the beginning) the action of the film has been located inside this apartment; it doesn't seem possible to leave it now. The audience is close to the point in time when that scene will happen. Anne is dead; she is dressed in that blue dress; flowers garland her pillow.

For a moment the audience thinks Georges, also, is dead because he lies on the bunk bed that he's made up in the kitchen of the apartment and he's in the same position as her: fully dressed with his hands gracefully folded over his stomach. Did he switch on the gas and allow himself to be asphyxiated? Or has he simply not eaten, and merely lowered himself into his own death? But then he blinks; and there is the sound of someone else in the apartment: domestic noises of washing-up. He rises to his feet, staggers a little, sits down. He is not dead, after all, not yet. He tries again and, weakly, shuffles around the corner. The noise is made by Anne, who is haunting him with her presence. She appears to him, a ghost, perfectly well, the same as when she attended the concert.

The questioning arises more strongly in the collective mind of the audience. What's happening?

Anne asks if Georges is ready to leave, if he is going to put on a pair of shoes? She has finished the washing-up; she is ready to go. He seems a little frightened of her ghostly presence. He puts on his shoes; and helps her into her coat. When she's standing at the door, she asks him if he isn't going to wear a coat, himself. He reaches out, unhooks his coat and with some difficulty shrugs into it. He follows her and together they leave the apartment. With an air of finality, the door closes.

Somewhere along these few minutes of quiet, peaceful narrative, trained as we are by previous imaginary or dream sequences that carry a metaphorical weight, we come to realise, in witnessing his departure from the apartment, that we are watching his death.[8] Not only is she a ghostly imagining, but so is he. He departed this world, not long after she did. That sight of him fully dressed, hands folded gracefully over his stomach, was, in the end, his final position; they both passed out of the apartment and the door closed on both of them, together.

6   Dialogue and logic

Film narrative has two modes of expression: action and dialogue. Cherry Potter asks screenwriters to become actors, and thus develop accurate empathy with their characters in order to write good dialogue. She suggests that writers should convey psychological subtext in their dialogue, and gives ten further functions of dialogue, such as, 'To reveal something about the speaker ... To give the audience information ... To reflect the speaker's mood or emotional state' (238).

Yorke details his priorities for dialogue – 'The three most important functions of dialogue – characterisation, exposition and subtext – are all ... products of character desire. Dialogue, then, is both born out of and is an essential component of structure' (149). He describes other important functions – 'Dialogue plays an essential part in the creation of a character's façade' (150) – and he gives a prescription for what it should sound like – 'Good dialogue doesn't resemble conversation – it represents the illusion of conversation, subservient to the demands of characterisation and structure' (150) and 'Dialogue must make every character individual.' (151)

---

[8]Metaphor is of course a logic-game, in which we enjoy the strange aptitude for one thing to stand in for another and therefore refresh our view of it. See Cherry Potter's Chapter 3, 'Metaphors and Archetypes' (2001, 48), and McKee's section 'Image Systems' (400–408) and, for another logic-game, Bordwell and Thompson's 'parallelism' (2001, 53).

Robert McKee advises us, 'Dialogue is not conversation' and 'what is said and done is not what is thought and felt' (388). As does Yorke, McKee describes what dialogue in films should sound like – 'Screen dialogue, therefore, must have the swing of everyday talk but content well above normal' (389) – and he describes an important difference between screen and theatre dialogue when he describes theatre as eighty per cent auditory and twenty per cent visual, with cinema the other way around, eighty per cent visual and twenty per cent auditory.

All writers of fiction, whether screenwriters or playwrights or novelists, look closely at the difference between dialogue in real life and dialogue that is effective in a drama.

Dialogue becomes effective for use in drama when it enjoys a fruitful relationship with logic. (And it is appropriate to mention at the outset that the number one culprit in the writing of poor dialogue can be described as the clumsy deployment of logic in dialogue: when the writer uses dialogue to simply explain logic, which makes for a short cut to exposition.)

Interrupting the logic paradigm – mystery expressed in dialogue

In John Ajvide Lindqvist's adaptation of his own novel, *Let The Right One In* (Alfredson 2008), the first line of dialogue (or more accurately, monologue, since twelve-year-old Oskar is talking to himself) is 'Squeal like a pig. So, squeal.' It is a striking line, a command that arouses the audience's curiosity, their questioning, more effectively because they don't at first see, even, who it is that says it. A boy, Oskar (Kåre Hedebrant) appears as a ghostly reflection in the window of his bedroom and, ominously, carries a knife. Alone in the room, he thrusts the knife forwards and repeats a slight variation of the line, 'Squeal. Squeal like a pig.' The action with the knife and the location of the boy, semi-naked in his bedroom, allows the audience to infer that this is a rehearsal. The line of dialogue and the action attached to it is the result of something that's happened previously in Oskar's life and we try and complete the logic paradigm. What caused this behaviour? Either this boy has enemies, is being bullied, or he himself is the aggressor.

It is no accident that the line also carries an image (pig) as well as a sound (squeal). Like any writing, we depend on our five senses to connect with it. The action with the knife also implies an action (stabbing someone) that works to create the cognition – a rehearsal.

Later, the audience come to learn that Oskar is being bullied at school, and will observe Oskar once again as he rehearses the stabbing of his tormentors with the knife that he keeps under his mattress. On this occasion, he will rehearse outdoors, by the snow-covered play structure at the front of his apartment block; and he pretends that a tree is a bully, and he stabs the tree. This is the audience's reward – because it was one of their answers to the earlier, mysterious line of dialogue. They can congratulate themselves that their logic-work was correct.

No sooner is one question answered, than the next mystery, the next question, is provided by the dialogue. While Oskar practises with the tree, he is observed by his new neighbour, twelve-year-old Eli (Lina Leandersson). One of the first things she says to him is, 'Just so you know, I can't be your friend.' It is an odd thing to say. The question leaps to mind – why not? If we have prior knowledge of the film, one answer arrives almost at the same time as the question; otherwise it will be a while later. She's a vampire, and therefore she is a danger to him, and if she likes him, shouldn't be his friend. The questioning, the mystery, is aroused by the dialogue; our work is to answer it.

Dialogue that creates 'cognitions'

After his first rehearsal with the knife in his bedroom, the audience next sees Oskar in his school classroom. This morning the class is furnished with a visit from a local police officer. Dressed in uniform, complete with baton, the police officer strolls between the rows of desks. 'The police have ways to determine foul play,' he says in a comforting voice. 'Do you remember that fire in Angby? A house burned down and a body was found inside. We knew that the fire had been set to conceal the fact that the person had been murdered beforehand. So, how could they know that?'

After a pause, Oskar puts up his hand and replies, 'There was no smoke in the lungs of the person who died.'

The police officer, in a surprised tone of voice, makes it clear that he wasn't expecting to hear the answer. 'That's correct,' he says. 'Did you figure that out, right now?'

'No, I read a lot.'

'What kind of books would that be?' His question means that the audience, of course, make up their own ideas as to what kind of books those must be: Oskar will read books about true crime, about murders.

'Just books,' says Oskar – and the line thus leaves us with our judgement, our work, intact. The not-writing of the answer generously allows us to keep for ourselves the cognition.

This section of dialogue allows us to come to a judgement about Oskar's character. It is part of the logic-work the writer is performing in order to build the credibility of Oskar's reaction to the murderous vampire girl, Eli, his new neighbour. He will fall in love with her, and eventually he will become her guardian and lifelong companion, and he will, after the film ends, go on to perform murders on her behalf in order to keep her fed. This dialogue sequence allows *us* to make a judgement about Oskar's character that will cement the credibility of his later actions; and in order to create that workplace for the audience it is important for the writer not to occupy it. If the writer had attempted to do the work on behalf of the audience, he might have written a scene between the mother and the son in which the mother would tear into Oskar's bedroom, snatch a book from his hands and say, 'I don't want you reading about real-life murders anymore.' Oskar would reply, 'But Mum, I love reading about real-life murders.' She in turn would reply, 'You really are a macabre little boy.'

What is not written, what is not done, is therefore the essential flip side of what *is* done, what speech *is* written, in order to create the informative dichotomy, the cognitions, the rushes of comprehension, that give to the audience the narrative luxury of a piece of logic-work;[9] it is what makes this dialogue 'good'.

---

[9]In his chapter 'Do Androids Prove Theorems?' Michael Harris describes how it is – 'The successful author of fiction engages the reader: the reader becomes both capable of and responsible for the reality effect, whatever it may be.' (Doxiadis and Mazur 2012, 139)

Creating strands of logic – dramatic irony expressed in dialogue

Hakan, the middle-aged man who is Eli's companion and helpmeet, has already murdered one person on her behalf since arriving in the town. In the Sun Palace, the local café that is the habitual drinking place of some residents of Oskar's apartment block, a group of neighbours gathers as usual and the discussion centres on the death penalty, which might be given to the murderer who strung up a young man in nearby woods and drained the blood from his neck.

One of the neighbours notices a newcomer sitting by himself over by the window, drinking a glass of milk. It is the murderer, Hakan.

'Never seen the guy before,' says the blonde woman.

The unshaven man tells the others, 'That guy over there just moved into my neighbourhood. He has a kid.'

'They're in Janne's old place.'

'Should I ask him to join us?'

'Sure.'

'He might pay for a round.'

'In that case, he's welcome even if he has cancer.'

The unshaven neighbour goes over and sits opposite Hakan. The fact that we know who Hakan is, and the unshaven neighbour doesn't, means that dramatic irony is in play, and that dramatic irony is invigorated, emphatically expressed, in the choice of vocabulary used by the writer in the dialogue. 'Bad news?' asks the neighbour. Hakan is bad news, indeed, but the neighbour is merely making a joke about Hakan's bill arriving, and Hakan having to pay it.

Hakan's refusal to reply speaks volumes. In effect he is saying, 'Leave me alone.'

The neighbour provides an answer to what he imagines Hakan might have said. 'Yeah, life stinks ….'

This exchange – the multiple ironies, the missing dialogue, our reaching to be able to understand what's happening, creates for the audience a kind of multi-tasking in the playground of logic: cognitions and mysteries and dramatic ironies all at the same time.

'You just moved into number fifteen, right?' persists the neighbour. The audience listen in awe at the grave mistake the neighbour doesn't know he's making. 'You don't have to sit here all alone, join us and have a laugh.'

It's that 'have a laugh' that is so rich in dramatic irony, expressed via dialogue.

Creating strands of logic – subtext expressed in dialogue

Later in the film, the murderer, Hakan, is in the apartment that he shares with Eli, the vampire. He is assembling his murder kit: the large-bladed knife, the container that will hold the blood, the funnel that will capture the blood that runs from the victim's throat and guide it into the container. He is about to go out and kill a second victim. Eli watches him from the doorway, leaning against the doorframe.

Facing away from her, Hakan asks, 'Could you do one thing for me?'

It seems like a reasonable request. After all, he does so much for her.

She doesn't answer, but takes one step into the room.

He asks, 'Could you not see that boy tonight? Please?'

The line carries a freight of meaning underneath its surface. It is our task to work it out. In the subtext, he is also saying to her, I am jealous, I love you.

Hakan is in late middle age; Eli is of an unknown age, but in terms of her physique, around twelve. And yet we already know she is a timeless creature who never grows old, as he has.

Hakan is declaring that he is a victim of his love for her; and her pity for him is evident in the hand she lifts, slowly, just to touch his face.

This subtext is not the truth hiding underneath a lie, which would be dialogue as an expression of dramatic irony; instead it is an additional message – sometimes even opposite in meaning – carried underneath the dialogue but none the less made evident by the choice and arrangement of the words and the manner in which they are expressed, and the situation that surrounds the words. The audience congratulates itself on its powers of perception, but it is the writer who has arranged it for us.

As before, the skill is to 'not-write' at the same time as to write. If Hakan were to explain his jealousy and proclaim his love for Eli – a love that he has probably held for her since he was Oskar's age – the opportunity to deliver a subtext would have been taken away, and therefore the audience's workplace in the story, their involvement, would have been removed.

One way for screenwriters to develop a subtext running underneath dialogue is not to ask in the first instance what the characters will say to each other, but instead to determine what it is they are *doing* to each other. The subtext to most conversations will be about either recruitment of the other individual(s), or the opposite – an attempt to avoid or get past them, or at the least to put up with them, to pass time in their company. If the screenwriter can establish what a character's motives are, then make the dialogue about something else that sits easily to hand, the gap between what they are saying to each other and what they are doing to each other will become apparent. In the foregoing example Hakan is meekly cornering Eli to try and keep her, because he is jealous, but the dialogue is about Eli not going out on the very evening that Hakan does have to go out – on her behalf.

In this sense, just as the engineering of the poetry of events demands that screenwriters pay as much attention to what *events* they leave out as to which they include, so the writing of dialogue, also, demands the same two-handed approach: writing and not-writing. To write a screenplay is therefore not like driving a car, in which the writer presses down on the 'writing' pedal in order to make the story go forwards; it is more like controlling a light aircraft, in which the pilot has both feet, left and right, on the rudder pedals, and is constantly using both pedals at all times, the 'writing' pedal and the 'not-writing' pedal, to keep the drama in flight.

7   Tying a knot in the logic – choice

Moments of choice, wherein a character's decision will send them down either one narrative route or another, to encounter one set of effects or another, are rich in dramatic pleasure if the choice is held up, delayed, because it is a difficult choice to make (and this means it usually intersects with morality). Therefore the logic paradigm is tangled, held fast, in a knot that's been tied by the writer.

In *Sophie's Choice* (1982), directed and written by Alan Pakula from William Styron's novel, three such choices are arranged in increasing order of intensity, in a series of flashbacks. The first choice faced by Sophie (Meryl Streep), in her past life, is whether or not to help Jewish children escape from an emerging Nazi pogrom. The writing makes clear that she is choosing between the persecution of her own two children, if she is found out, or the persecution of hundreds of other children, if she does nothing. It is her lover, Jozef (Neddim Prohic) who is asking for her help, and it's an agonising decision: she chooses her own children.

She faces this first choice at around one hour and seventeen minutes into the film. History rolls forward, and, an hour and forty-three minutes into the film, another flashback shows her now as a prisoner in Auschwitz, but her Aryan looks have allowed her to be hired as a secretary to an SS doctor (Karlheinz Hackl) who is performing experiments in the camp. The resistance movement in the camp have asked her to use her position to steal a radio, and given the doctor's attraction to her, she faces the same choice as before: to help others, or to look after her own interests. She chooses to look after her own interests. She forgets about the radio and instead begs the SS doctor to save her son, to have him taken out of the camp where he is interned and where he will certainly die if he remains. However, on her way back down the stairs she happens to see the radio and does try to steal it, but is prevented from doing so in a most unusual and moving scene.

Two hours and ten minutes into the film, she faces a third choice, the worst of all, when the flashback shows her initial entry into Auschwitz, when she had both her children, daughter and son, and she is spotted by Rudolf Hoess (Günther Maria Halmer). He gives her a sadistic ultimatum: she must choose which one of her two children will be taken away and killed, or both of them will go. The scene hangs on this impossible choice. Under terrible duress she chooses her daughter to be taken from her arms. It is a political fable and the message is clear: choose not to help the suffering of others, and that suffering will be visited on you. She cannot live with the choices she made.

8   The logic of the timeline – syuzhet and fabula

It will be evident from the foregoing sections in this chapter that in order to generate the effects as described attention must be paid to the order in which events appear in front of an audience. This will often involve a difference between the *fabula* (the chronological timeline) and the *syuzhet* (the order in which the events appear in front of the audience).[10]

Any difference between the two that might be required is usually created by skilful use of point-of-view and the breaking of the 'unities' of time, place or action.

In *Sophie's Choice* the three episodes of choice are played out of sequence, the second one (chronologically) coming last (in the story) because it is the worst, the most difficult choice to make, and it carries the moral message of the film.

In *Rebecca* the story starts in the notional 'present day' with a mansion long since burnt to the ground, it then travels back to the past to see how Maxim proposed to his new wife, jumps forward to their return to Manderlay, only to go even further back in time and find out what happened to Maxim's first wife, before the story is allowed to travel forwards again to the trial and to the burning down of the mansion.

Let the Right One In simply rolls forward in time over a period of some weeks, but along the way it makes sure that we understand the back story of both the main characters, not by creating flashbacks but by allowing us to fill in the history without resource to scene-making.

The Truman Show delivers past knowledge, on the other hand, with a flashback to the time when Truman met Lauren.

Borat simply shows us the eponymous hero's journey across America without breaking the timeline.

Screenwriters will suffer headaches in the construction of a 'syuzhet' that selects, out of a 'fabula', the right events and places them in the right

---

[10]The terms 'syuzhet' and 'fabula' originate from the Russian formalists Vladimir Propp and Viktor Shklovsky. Various theorists – Derrida, Bakhtin and others – have written about the two words, but their ideas are not pertinent to the screenwriter.

order, to make a structure that delivers the sort of narrative 'stickiness' that the design aims for, while creating an audience's unwavering belief in the story.

9   Conclusion

Other books on screenplay writing propose three 'cells' of dramatic structure, usually called conflict, crisis and resolution, or words to that effect. Syd Field, in his Academy of Screenwriting, has a 'paradigm' that he identifies as 'setup', 'confrontation' and 'resolution' (Field 2013). Lajos Egri's Chapter 10 is titled 'Crisis, Climax, Resolution' (Egri 1942/2004). Yorke has a 'Change Paradigm' (47) and makes it part of his explanation of the five-act structure and the importance of a 'there-and-return' narrative complete with a mid-point. But such words as 'conflict' and 'crisis' lead screenwriters to think they must have arguments, they must have shouting and secrets and so on. And the dreaded word 'setup' implies (although Field will be the first to advise against it) that screenwriters should entertain the one thing that kills dramatic writing: explanation of logic, of circumstances, in dialogue.

The logic paradigm, cause-change-effect, is not an invention or a theory, it is an observation of how logic works, and it has only remained for this chapter to describe how, in drama, various opportunities for logic-work can be offered to an audience who will seize on such opportunities and, unwittingly in collusion with the screenwriter, make for themselves a workplace in the story.

Apostolos Doxiadis, a novelist and at the same time a logician and mathematician, reads from Joseph Gold's *Story Species* (2002) and concludes 'A "story-species" we may be, but not in the sense in which seagulls are a "flight-species"' (Doxiadis and Mazur 2012, 292). The opposite is true: our compulsive working with logic in stories is akin to the seagull's very necessary grooming of its flight feathers. Boyd points out that 'all fictions offer intense doses of pattern' (211) and he ascribes to fiction the same purpose as that of childhood play – '... we happily succumb to the training in social cognition that pretend play and fiction reliably yield' (191).

Anne Ubersfeld agrees –

The spectator, by analysing the signs of the performance, can become the master of social and mental processes, and the pleasure he takes in that process is the same one that is engendered by any intellectual activity that succeeds: the pleasure of understanding is always the pleasure not only of receiving but of doing. (2003, 241)

Stephen Davies, in 'The Artful Species: Aesthetics, Art and Evolution' (2012) even goes so far to suggest that screenwriters (as 'artists') might be at the forefront of the human race's evolutionary development:

If there are connections between ... art and evolution, what evolutionary roles could aesthetics or art play? ... they might be adaptations, that is, transmissible capacities that increased the fitness of those who displayed them so that their possessors parented more extensive and far-reaching lineages. (73)

The logic paradigm can be used in the writing of drama in ways that are endlessly flexible, like music. Film scripts can be composed using as many or as few acts and scenes as is appropriate for the material, its length and its proposed distribution method, but every moment of every act will play with the logic paradigm.

It takes sustained practice to be able to create for an audience beautifully designed opportunities for logic-work. Hegel recommended –

It is only after profounder acquaintance ... that logic ceases to be for (the) subjective spirit a merely abstract universal and reveals itself as the universal which embraces within itself the wealth of the particular .... Thus the value of logic is only appreciated when it is preceded by experience ... it then displays itself to mind as the universal truth, not as a *particular* knowledge *alongside* other matters and realities, but as the essential being of all these latter. (58)

The recognition of logic as a primary instinct in the human animal, not a learned behaviour but a practised instrument, the practice being the hard work of writing displays of logic, will allow the screenwriter to understand why certain dramatic techniques are effective, and thus how to write them.

There is a heavy, deliberate nod given from the screenwriter John Ajvide Lindqvist to all other screenwriters who might be watching his film, *Let the Right One In* (Alfredson 2008), when he gives to his immortal vampire, Eli, only one set of possessions that she always carries with her in her endless journey through time: it is a collection of logic puzzles.

3

The Line in the Sand

In 1871 James Crichton-Browne wrote to Charles Darwin from a lunatic asylum in Yorkshire –

My dear Sir,

I have been watching the Idiots under my care, and making various experiments upon them but have not been able to produce a genuine blush in any one of them. In several the face becomes red and engorged when food is placed before them and when rage is excited, but no amount or kind of scoldings produces a similar result even in those of the higher ⟨and⟩ more intelligent ⟨cl⟩ass.

In the period when he was researching for *The Expression of the Emotions in Man and Animals* (1872) Charles Darwin swapped correspondence with a multitude of people in different parts of the world looking for the human blush. The blush was of particular interest because it is a physiological, animal reaction; it cannot be cultivated or repressed. It is a behaviour in our species that could only be attributed to instinct, our fundamental nature, the raw creature, *homo sapiens*. Blood rushes to the surface of the skin to denote a particular reaction – anger, or shame.

Darwin searched the world over for the human blush. During that same year, 1871, he wrote to the English sculptor Thomas Woolner –

My dear Mr. Woolner

I dare say you often meet and know well painters. Could you persuade some trustworthy men to observe young and inexperienced girls who serve as models, and who at first blush much, how low down the body the blush extends. Several eminent surgeons have been observing for me, and with a single exception have never seen a blush extend beneath (and rarely so far down) as the upper 2/3 of the breasts.

Moreau says a celebrated French painter once saw a new model blushing all over her body. So that I want much to hear what the experience is of cautious and careful English artists: I always distrust memory. Can you aid me?

Over a period of many years he received replies from all parts of the globe, not only from those he wrote to but from others, briefed, in turn, by his correspondents using a questionnaire provided by Darwin. A typical example came back from The Royal Botanical Gardens in Calcutta –

4. ⟨I c⟩an best illustrate this from observation upon a Sikkim Lepcha whom I have had in the Botanic Gardens here for a few months back. On his arrival I got from him the native Lepcha names of many Sikkim plants which we have in the Gardens, which at once affixed. A month or so later I told him that he must again re-name them all for me, further cautioning him to be careful as I had already notes of all that he had given me previously. When brought to the plants, he examined them and after some little hesitation named one incorrectly. I accused him of falsehood and told him the name he had previously given the plant; he looked confused held down his head and slightly averted his face, while a very faint discoloration of his cheeks, ears and neck was observable. (Scott 1868)

Darwin would find that blushing could be found in all peoples, however primitive or advanced, in all parts of the world. It was a sign of shame, when we have done wrong, or of anger, when wrong is done to us; and these two feelings thus define morality as an instinct.

Social anthropologists such as Christopher Boehm (2012) have searched for the method by which morality evolved as an instinctive behaviour in the human species, as well as the ways in which different societies have made use of morality to create tribal unity and force. To find out exactly what *is* right-and-wrong, what are its roots, they studied Late Pleistocene-era Appropriate (LPA) societies, deemed to be living in the same way, in the 1950s and 1960s when first contact was made, as our ancestors did a hundred and twenty-five thousand years ago. One such LPA tribe is the Ituri Pygmy, observed closely in the 1950s by Colin Turnbull who lived for extended periods of time as part of the tribe, accepted by them and fluent in their language.

Hunter-gatherer tribes such as the Ituri Pygmies hunt for game in small bands of families, and for such groups their intra-group co-operation and therefore egalitarianism had always been a matter of survival. Just as wolves and other predator species co-operate in order to bring down prey, the Ituri have co-operated successfully and intricately, using the same methods, for over a hundred and twenty-five thousand years. And they bring to it all their powers of language and thinking. 'Because other agents – prey, predators, and especially human friends and foes – make the most dramatic difference to our chances and choices day by day, our understanding of other minds has evolved into our richest natural mental capacity.' (Boyd, 281)

An early *homo sapiens* living two hundred and fifty thousand years ago was not only a hungry, selfish creature who cared primarily about her own surviving/thriving, but more than eating to keep her own strength she built her genetic future: she not only fed herself but pushed food into the mouth of her son and daughter, especially when she was starving she favoured her children. As a consequence her brood thrived more than her sister's, because her sister didn't give to her offspring with the same generosity. With her care for her offspring thus genetically rewarded, she created the increased thriving of her children's children who in their turn were generously treated, and who in turn gave selflessly to their offspring. This nepotism, the love and nurture of children, was rewarded biologically in both parents and children with the production of oxytocin, especially in the mother (see below for how far back in time this mechanism can be traced). This chemical reward system was blindly rewarded by evolution and thus refined, increased, as it passed down the generations, cemented into the genetic writing of her species, described now as an emotion – love. She therefore moved her concern from solely 'herself' to the first small 'us' – her children, and those others who share in the love for her children, her family. Her concern for her family allowed her family to out-thrive others who did not possess this feeling of solidarity and of child-love.

She moved from selfishness to nepotism. The members within her family group co-operated with one another and they reaped the benefits.

She began to eat meat, and she, and more often her sons, would hunt and kill larger prey. Now she would benefit from the co-operation not only of her family but of other family groups because other families contained skilled individual hunters and if they co-operated, just like wolves or lions, they could increase the amount of meat available, as well as the stability of the supply. But they had to share the meat, and so, when it came to dealing with the rewards of co-operative behaviour, they immediately had to watch out for the bullies, thieves, the cheats and the free-riders who would, from this moment forwards and for the rest of time, try to ruin co-operation by allowing free rein to those selfish instincts that we all possess, still and ever since way back when, and which have to be continuously and vigorously kept in check if the mechanics of co-operation, of sharing, are going to work.

It wasn't until the early twenty-first century and the 'vampire economist' Paul Zak's experiments on Columbia students that we found out that the same hormone that cements the female's pleasure in child nurture, in breast-feeding, oxytocin, also rushes in immediately to reward ordinary trust and co-operation between, and among, males and females. In *The Moral Molecule* (2012), Zak describes how he performed multiple trials among many different groups of students using the Trust Game, a well-used game of strategy that measures the level of trust shown by anonymous individuals when sharing money for mutual profit, but the difference with Zak's programme was that he took blood tests and measured oxytocin levels *immediately* before and just as quickly after his subjects made their decisions on whether or not to co-operate with other members of the group. The results were startling – oxytocin rushed into the bloodstream, either on giving human trust or on receiving it, and just as quickly it diminished – oxytocin acted as a finely tuned and immediate system of reward for co-operative behaviours on both sides of the transaction, on giving and on receiving. The same chemical reward is also attached to gift-giving: it is as pleasurable to give as to receive. Zak's control experiment showed that the same oxytocin-rewards were not available if it was a computer that 'trusted' the individual. It was only the human hand, the human action, even if it was delivered via a computer terminal, that delivered the reward of oxytocin.

Thus sharing, 'moral' behaviour is rewarded sensually, biologically. Zak was looking at the end result of the evolution of our moral sensibility. He was excited by his results, but not surprised. 'For social species, if moral behaviour is more adaptive than ruthless behaviour, then it only made sense that there would be a biological basis for it. And where would it be more likely to originate than in reproduction, where all bonds and attachments begin.' (25)

In a chapter titled 'Lobsters in Love' (it could be a new comedy blockbuster) Zak draws his readers even further back along the evolutionary timescale. He describes how lobsters are territorial, aggressive, heavily armoured and weaponised and inclined to eat each other in captivity, yet they have –

> a courtship ritual that's like an old French film. It all begins when the female sprays a seductive perfume into the male's grotto, then scuttles inside to slip out of her shell ... But for a lobster, leaving the shell behind means being utterly vulnerable until a new one grows back. Which suggests a huge leap of faith. The female must trust her life entirely to the male she's chosen, a creature she would ordinarily treat as a competitor, if not an outright threat. The chemical signal that allows her to suspend her wariness just long enough for the tryst, and for the growth of a new shell, is an ancient precursor of oxytocin. (28)

In his 'vampire version' of the Trust Game Zak thus proved that 'the most basic, physiological mechanism for all our moral impulses dates back to a time long before animals ever ventured onto dry land. And it all began with sex' (28).

The hunter-gatherer and her family, rewarded by oxytocin and having expanded the circle of virtue beyond her own family to include others, will now move about in the forest in a group or band made up of perhaps a dozen different families. She has furthered the interests of her progeny with her oxytocin-fuelled bonding with her offspring; and she now is building the success of her group by virtue of the sharing and co-operation within her band – still fuelled by oxytocin but at smaller levels.

The 'circle of good' has expanded. Now there is 'her', and 'us' (her family), and 'her group' (the band of families who co-operate) and she has moved from nepotism to the first, weakest circle of altruism, defined as reciprocal altruism.

> Co-operation spreads wider, beyond kin, through reciprocal altruism, the 'you-scratch-my-back-and-I'll-scratch-yours' principle, helping now in return for similar help later. This trait requires the ability to remember individuals (the person to repay) and what they have done for us (the reason for repayment), the probability of repeat encounters (a reason not to fail to repay) in a non-dispersing population (an occasion to repay), and a relatively long life (time to repay). (Boyd, 292)

This is the 'Golden Rule', the principle that underpins all religious doctrines – 'Do unto others as you would have done unto you' – and it is entirely instinctive.

The more the group fosters co-operation, the more successful the group will become. This success depends on keeping watch for the enemy of co-operation – selfish behaviour, the human ego: the greedy acquisition of more than a fair share. Thus, apart from the daily excitement of hunting, as well as eating and sleeping, most important to the hunter-gatherer's group will be to monitor the selfishly motivated actions performed by certain individuals who might so easily wreck the co-operative effort, and around the campfire it will be the group's continual work to gossip, talk about others either with approval or disapproval, and therefore arrive at the truth, and a code of ethics, and a system of good practice, which rewards the good with approval and greater sharing, or punishes the offenders in such a way as to mend co-operation as quickly as possible ('pro-social punishment'). If oxytocin is a sensual reward for co-operation, testosterone is the hormone that provokes punishment for selfish, unco-operative (unfair) behaviour. 'Even in primate societies perceived violations of the social code are the single most common cause of aggression' (Boyd, 306). But testosterone threatens to break co-operation, rather than mend it. Forgiveness is of paramount importance in rebuilding co-operation and maintaining recruitment to the group, and forgiveness is rewarded by oxytocin on both sides of the argument.

Gossip makes and breaks the reputations of individuals, and searches for truth to make appraisals, judgements, to enable rewards and punishments. A moral code is established by good practice, by ritual, but it is maintained and policed by gossip, by naming and shaming and other punishments, hence the evolutionary signal: the unique human blush.

Gossip, when it is effective enough, enjoyable enough, is repeated, and if it is repeated often enough it evolves into stories, and stories are exaggerated for effect, so they will last longer and earn greater attention, and consequently they become myth, they become untrue, fantastical – but they never lose that same purpose: the cultivation of our moral instinct, which is essential to our thriving.

It is a matter of life and death. Other groups who are more skilled in co-operation, and who therefore might also be larger, will threaten a smaller group. Part of the work of morality, therefore, becomes the identifying and signalling of one's group, with costume, ritual, tattoos, and language.

The more effective the group's co-operation among themselves, the more they will be secure against attacks from other 'out-group' bands, therefore on both counts – internal cohesion and defence against the external groups – the group must be aware, every moment of every day, of the enemies within, the characters who for whatever reason, at this very moment, threaten the effectiveness of co-operation. Co-operation was then, and still is now, a continual, internal battle in the mind of each individual between the benefits to the self of egoism, of putting the self first, and on the other hand of the benefits of co-operation within the group, which requires the suppression of the many and powerful egotistical impulses that offer themselves as constant temptations. This is the battle between right and wrong, complete with its reactive agents, reward and punishment.

Evolution, over countless millennia, has blindly rewarded the moral instinct as the method by which co-operation is achieved in the human species. Other ultra-social species such as ants evolved their ultra-co-operative behaviour with the use of pheromones and know nothing of right and wrong; we were carried forwards with the wave of evolution catching instead at our morality, and the chief vehicle for our moral instinct, the one that carries that instinct on the air almost as if it were a pheromone, is a sound, rather than a scent. That sound is language, more specifically, gossip, and gossip's naturally evolved successor, story. This 'evolutionary – Darwinian – approach' (Boyd, 2) to storytelling describes why we are, as Gottschall titles his 2013 book, *The Storytelling Animal*.

The characters who mitigate against co-operation – the selfish, egotistical characters – have been defined by social anthropologists as belonging to four different types: the bully, the cheat, the thief and the free-rider.

They are the story archetypes, staple characters in all our stories, then and now.

1   The free-rider

Reality TV seeks out the same audience as drama – every man, woman and child – and it's no accident that reality TV formats trade in the same dramatic principles as does fiction. Reality TV looks for the ways in which it can most violently invigorate our moral instincts and therefore create narrative 'stickiness', the power to attract and keep audiences.

Judge Rinder (2014–2016), the UK's answer to *Judge Judy*, recently (May 2016) offered a classic example of a free-rider. In the dock were two adversaries at loggerheads over the sum of sixteen hundred pounds spent on a weekend away in a small-town seaside resort. The plaintiff was a slender young man wearing bubblegum-pink lipstick, luminous eye-shadow, a closely fitted, snow-white shirt buttoned all the way to the neck and skinny jeans. His hair was artfully cut and dyed in two colours: mostly straw-blonde, but with a swatch of chestnut brown at the front. I shall call him the Hairdresser. He was claiming half of the cost of the weekend, eight hundred pounds, from his former lover, who stood on the opposite side of the courtroom. This latter was respectably dressed in a tie and a dark suit; he was overweight and the arms of his spectacles pressed into the flesh on either side of his face as if they had been fitted when he was a smaller size. His weight implied greed and laziness, yet his demeanour was calm and sensible. Let him be called the Free-rider.

Judge Rinder, with his close-cropped blonde hair, his affected voice and arrogant manner, began his investigation into the circumstances. The Hairdresser described how he came into a sum of money, and immediately decided to spend it on a weekend away with his lover, who wasn't in a position to pay for his share. They made a verbal agreement between them: the Hairdresser would pay for everything, but when the Free-rider would become, at a later date, in a more fortunate financial position, he would pay back the Hairdresser his share of the expenses.

Judge Rinder was impatient to ask if there was anything written down concerning this agreement? An exchange of emails, texts? No, both men agreed, it was only a conversation.

The audience reads this situation in a very exact way. If there had been a written agreement then it would have counted as proof. But since there was only a verbal conversation, any proposed truth was open to interpretation and disagreement, and it would become more interesting because the audience would be required to work harder. The minds of the audience were enchanted by the former co-operation between these two, who now stood as unco-operative enemies.

Go on, said Judge Rinder.

The Hairdresser continued his tale. They had arrived on a Friday night and booked into a hotel. How much did the hotel cost? asked Judge Rinder. Thirty pounds. In the audience's mind's eye this was an exceptionally cheap hotel in a second class, off-season resort. Our judgement of the Hairdresser went down a notch. He had hardly spoiled his lover, in terms of the hotel. The Free-rider began to look like a victim, with his sensible haircut and his agreeable expression.

The pair had gone out for a drink and had returned and spent the night in the hotel, but unfortunately, the next morning, the guests in neighbouring rooms had complained about the excessive noise. The management of the hotel had told the pair they were no longer welcome. They were kicked out.

The situation became like a playground for the audience's moral sensibility. The Hairdresser and the Free-rider who stood on opposite sides of the courtroom as enemies, were once so vigorously co-operating with each other as to lead to these complaints of excessive noise. But still, they were *both* unfair in disturbing the sleep of others, which might be judged a form of bullying. Furthermore there was the Free-rider's crime in not paying up according to their agreement. And that sadness, that they were once in love, which was essentially sympathetic to the two men, might have been occluded by the audience's moral disapproval of the couple's selfish behaviour in keeping their neighbours awake, or indeed if a portion of the audience was homophobic, any potential sympathy would have been completely covered over by their disgust. Each member of the audience would have reached out to find particular moral handles by which to steer their judgement on this situation, and they would have done so instantly, as quickly as an ant will read the pheromone trail of its neighbour. However, for good drama to maintain and increase its hold on its audience, the situation had to change; new handles would have to be found if the audience were to take delight in wrestling with the story.

'And so you had to move to a new hotel,' guessed Judge Rinder.

'Yes.'

'And how much did that hotel cost?'

The Hairdresser paused. 'Twelve pounds.'

Judge Rinder's expression was a mask of dismay. The impossible cheapness of this hotel! Rinder himself wouldn't have climbed into any hotel bed that cost less than three hundred pounds. The Free-rider shifted his weight uneasily. He looked less like a greedy hanger-on and more like a long-suffering sex-slave belonging to the ebulliently camp and cheapskate Hairdresser.

Judge Rinder was totting up the maths. 'Thirty plus twelve equals forty-two pounds. For both of you. For two nights.' He was emphatic in his disapproval. 'That is the total bill for your hotel accommodation. Which leaves fifteen hundred and fifty eight pounds that you spent, in addition to your hotel, is that correct?'

The Hairdresser pursed his bubblegum lips. 'Yes.'

'So what on earth did you spend that amount of money *on*?' Judge Rinder leaned forward, curious. 'Fifteen hundred pounds in two days.

What was it, expensive meals, on jewellery, on gifts for your partner?' He nodded at the Free-rider.

The Hairdresser was curiously hesitant, and gave a mealy-mouthed glance at his former lover, who remained silent.

'What was it?' insists Judge Rinder. 'Drugs?'

The Hairdresser shook his head.

'Just going out, together?'

The Hairdresser pouted. 'I guess so.'

Judge Rinder saw the truth and shared a critical look between the pair. 'Did you spend it on alcohol? Drinking?'

'Yes,' replied the Free-rider, sensibly.

The ashamed Hairdresser added, 'I suppose, yes, we must have.'

Suddenly, the Free-rider's excess weight made sense. He was a drinker. Judge Rinder was round-eyed with shock. 'Fifteen hundred pounds in one weekend, on drink,' he repeats, stupefied. 'You spent that amount.'

The Hairdresser had the good manners to look ashamed but at the same time he was insolent. 'Yes.'

The Free-rider then spoke the most important words in the quietest voice. 'But not on *me*,' he said.

'I beg your pardon?' Judge Rinder latched onto this swerve in the moral play of events. And here the audience's instinct for morality was joined together with the instinct for logic, because one line of dialogue had just demanded that we re-work the truth-table, the logic paradigm.

'He didn't spend that amount of money on me,' repeated the Free-rider.

'Well who did he spend it on?'

The Free-rider was not aggressive or accusing. 'On everyone else. On the whole bar, the whole room. He bought everyone drinks. All night … '

'One couple,' interrupted the Hairdresser. 'I did buy some drinks for another couple that were there.'

The audience's antennae were looking for truth, for manners, for an authoritative demeanour, and found it in the Free-rider, not in the Hairdresser. With those four words, 'But not on me,' the Free-rider was no longer a free-rider, but someone against whom an unfair charge had been laid. He was the victim of a bully.

'Why didn't you stop him?' asked Judge Rinder.

'I tried.' The Free-rider shook his head. 'But he wouldn't listen.'

The two men were far in advance of hunter-gatherer tribes of the Late Pleistocene Era, but Judge Rinder's audience were looking at an example of the same old gossip – events, appraisals of truthfulness, judgements, provocations either to reward or to punish – that has continued to alert us, for hundreds of thousands of years, to our instinct for moral reckoning. There couldn't have been a more flamboyant portrayal of egoism than the Hairdresser's. However it was interesting to see that the Hairdresser's instinct to share, once his critical inhibitions had been repressed by alcohol, had overwhelmed him, and with his reaching out for the trust and co-operation of strangers in that bar he would have enjoyed the same rush of oxytocin as the lobster feels in his den when his mate loses her shell and trusts him to protect her, as when Zak's students in America played their trust games, and no doubt the Hairdresser might have expected, with his copious generosity to those strangers, to have recruited allies to his band, however briefly, just as the LPA tribe, with their meat sharing, were 'quickly and actively buying a few allies' (Boehm, 138). When the alcohol had dissipated from his system and the weekend was over, his egoism surfaced again and led him to complain blindly and unfairly, in the pain of having spent so much money during his alcohol-inspired fit of reciprocal altruism. This was his attempt selfishly, unfairly, to wrest some of it back from his unfortunate lover.

Judge Rinder quickly dismissed the Hairdresser's complaint. With a bang of his gavel he brought proceedings to a close. The Free-rider was no longer a Free-rider; instead the Hairdresser was a Bully.

Outside the courtroom the two men faced each other. The judgement had shamed the Bully, who could have been blushing at this point, and the audience would have been ready for an apology from him. The apology/forgiveness scenario is an oxytocin-inducing mechanism that soothes away conflict and rewards the group with continued co-operation; it maintains the numbers of the group and, with a hoped-for learning of the moral code, will educate the egoist without excluding him. The audience, because they are involved in the story, can look forward to a similar rush of oxytocin as would be given to the Hairdresser at the moment of his apology, and to the ex-lover, in his moment of forgiveness.

Unfortunately the Hairdresser wasn't able to escape from his egoism. He wiped the chestnut hair back from his forehead, slumped on one leg and drew a squiggle in the air that described, top-to-toe, his ex-lover's unattractiveness. 'Look at you,' he said meanly. 'Just look at you.' And he flounced off, their co-operation broken.

2   The bully

The audience first sees a child's hand carrying a turquoise mug as it reaches between bars to stretch as far as it can and pour a cupful of water onto a single, weedy pot plant. The hand belongs to Zahra Naderi, a twelve-year-old girl, and after a while we see her face, behind those same bars, looking vacant, but benevolent. Soon we will meet her sister, Massoumeh Naderi, also behind bars. Next we see their father, Ghorbanali Naderi, who walks the streets carrying a block of ice in one hand and a sheaf of hot bread in the other while he cries out, in a grating voice, to attract customers. He wears a green hat and thickly lensed glasses.

He doesn't look like a bully. He is a poor man, scratching a living for his family.

There is a handwritten letter, now, with a pen writing across the page from right to left in Farsi. It's addressed to the Director of the Welfare Department, and it details the concerns of neighbours regarding 'a man, a blind woman, and two twelve-year-old girls' who live at 10, Sajadi Avenue, on the road to Saveh. 'The two girls have never been out of the house. Their door is locked. They cannot speak. They haven't had a bath in years. All the neighbours complain about the situation, but no one dares intervene. So we, the undersigned, request you to take urgent action.' There are twelve signatures. A moment later there are thirteen, then sixteen.

The moral line is scratched deeply into the sand, immediately, and the film's call on the audience's moral sensibility draws them into the story. The wrongful actions of the father in imprisoning his daughters causes our desire to join up with the neighbours' desire – to free the girls; and so the engine of the narrative is in place within the first two minutes. Our moral instinct urges us to want to give to the daughters, to share with them everything we have, while our instinct to punish the parents is tempered by their apparent poverty, and by the fact that the mother is blind.

This is the opening sequence of Samira Makhmalbaf's first feature film, *The Apple* (1997), made when she was seventeen years old, with her father credited as writer and editor although no doubt she played a hand at both those ends of the production process also.

A social worker turns up at 10, Sajadi Avenue, demanding to see the girls, Zahra and Massoumeh. She has with her the letter signed by all the neighbours. A crowd of children gather around the solid green metal door that opens from the street into their yard. The poor man, the street-seller, the girls' father, opens the green metal door and complains about this campaign against him. With his woollen hat and his one freezing cold hand and the other burning hot, he has locked up his daughters for all their lives, twelve years long. Here is our bully, except that he doesn't look like a bully. From the outset he exhibits a humble, non-aggressive stance.

He lets the social worker into the courtyard. On the other side of the courtyard is a pair of iron gates, locked shut, that guards the entrance to the house. We've seen the iron gates before, when we first saw Zahra's hand reaching through them to water the pot plant.

The girls themselves are being prevented from growing.

Inside the house, behind the locked gates, we glimpse the mother, who is covered from head to foot in a lightweight patterned fabric. She pinches the cloth shut in front of her face. Not an inch of her can be seen except her hand. The soundtrack mumbles and skitters, as if she is a ghost, or a monster. Is *she* the bully?

Suddenly the two sisters, Zahra and Massoumeh, are outside, in the sunlight, sitting on a bench and surrounded by neighbours. The crowd has sprung them. Recording devices are waving in front of the girls' faces. They are being interviewed. 'How old are you?' asks the unseen interviewer. Zahra's smiling face leans forward. She touches the end of the recording device with her tongue. Neither of the sisters can talk except in groans, like animals, but they seem to understand each other.

A neighbour is interviewed. 'For years now, they have been living like prisoners,' she says.

The father, Ghorbanali, is interviewed. He is almost blind as well, with his thick glasses. 'It's my fault, I'm not saying it isn't,' he says. The audience measures his contrition, his admission of guilt, and starts to forgive him.

In the analysis of our moral instinct, this is an important moment. Our inclination to forgive Ghorbanali rewards us with a small dose of oxytocin, because 'mirror neurons'[1] ensure that observing a situation is the same as experiencing it for ourselves, which is the mechanism that creates empathy, so crucial to co-operation.

> We can trace empathy from the initial surge in oxytocin, to the release of dopamine and serotonin that makes the experience both pleasurable and something you want to repeat, to the social engagement that emerges as a result. The neuroscience explains not only the Golden Rule but also the Confucian concept of ren (benevolence) and the Buddhist concepts of metta (loving kindness) and karuna (compassion) … empathy, in effect, creates a physiological version of The Golden Rule. (Zak 2012, 61)

We begin to forgive Ghorbanali, the father, because this isn't the behaviour of a typical bully. It steers us more towards blaming the mother, the blind woman, Soghra – she even has the name of a monster.

The situation is on the way to being mended. Not only are the sisters outside the yard, outside the influence of their parents, but now they are in a school. They have been washed, and their hair is cut. They are wearing clean clothes. They look around them at the other children in benign wonder.

Their heads are uncovered.

Shapes are drawn on a piece of paper, and the sisters are asked to copy the shapes. A triangle is drawn; the pencil is put into Massoumeh's hand so she can draw the same shape. Her hand holds the pencil with difficulty; the pencil moves across the paper randomly; it's nothing like a triangle.

However the mother, Soghra, is coming to get them. She still holds shut the printed fabric in front of her face, so nothing of her can be seen.

---

[1]See Gottschall, pages 59–62, for his description of mirror neurons and storytelling.

Her trunk is thick, her gait rolls her from foot to foot. The soundtrack creates uncertainty, fear – our fear, but also her fear. She is blind.

She is next to her children. 'Why don't you come home?' asks her grating, tuneless voice from somewhere inside that fabric. Her hands – the only part of her the audience will ever see – move over her daughters' heads. 'Where's your headscarf?'

The voice of a nearby adult answers, 'We took it off to wash her hair.'

'Give me my children,' says Soghra. The line is chilling. The mother's hands move to cover the daughter's head, once more. 'Don't cry,' she commands. The hand arranges the cloth closer. Zahra's face is now obscured.

'They're her children,' says an onlooker.

The father promises not to lock the iron gates anymore. 'I promise,' he insists. 'And I'll take the children to the public baths.'

The sisters are taken back through that solid green metal gate set into the wall; they are led across the courtyard, and through the gates that let into their house. They are back in prison.

It is with dread that the audience sees the father lock the gates. That one twist of the key breaks the promise he earlier made, and he fails our moral code. He might not be the chief bully – perhaps his wife Soghra is – but he is none the less a bully, and, moreover, now he is a cheat.

Our powers of reasoning, our logic-work, are at the same time engaged with respect to the mother. She is a monster, but she is also a victim of her religion, and we reach further upstream, and perhaps some of us, depending on our own moral code, on the identity of our own group, begin to think that Islam, the religion itself, taken to extremes, is the bully. This new judgement is strengthened when we observe Soghra, a pillar of dark fabric, swaying gently in her own downstairs quarters, and her voice comes, 'Help me, husband, I am scared.'

The film asks us to forgive the bully because she herself has been bullied. It is the forgiveness, this quality of understanding, which sponsors this film's exceptional humanity. We no sooner apportion blame, moral disapproval, to a character's actions, than we are asked to re-assess, to forgive. These varying judgements arouse in the audience first of all the instinct for punishment, which releases testosterone, until the film-makers' request for the audience's forgiveness, for their understanding, releases its opposite, oxytocin.

The father might have locked that gate when he promised not to, but now he is teaching the daughters how to cook, how to wash clothes, and they obviously love him. And his song while he is stirring the pot over the stove, 'God, I am weary of this life,' is unbearably moving.

At the same time as our moral sensibility is being exercised in this way, our appetite for logic-work is answered by our reckoning of these changing judgements, the dramatising of the argument: should these girls be locked up or not? The desire of the audience – to release the girls from their imprisonment – is closely allied to the film's plural protagonist: the neighbours, represented by the social worker whom they have summoned.

The social worker turns up again to check whether or not the father has kept his promise to unlock the prison gates. She stands at the green metal door that fronts the street but receives no answer from the bell-push. The father must be out. The neighbour's boy (and how different he is from the girls – the same age, but he is respectful, personable, clean, eloquent, a son to be proud of) fetches a ladder and climbs on top of the wall. He can tell the social worker that the sisters are there, banging spoons against their prison bars, their smiles benign, optimistic.

It is important to the moral architecture of this film that the sisters, Zahra and Massoumeh, are not unhappy. They often exhibit signs of love for their father, if not their mother, and they love each other. If their imprisonment, their suffering, had been written on their faces, instead of their innocence, we should not feel so inclined to watch this film because it would have been too punishing an experience, and we could not have accorded forgiveness to their parents. The sisters' innocence and optimism allows their suffering to be uplifting, cathartic.

The boy sits on the wall, lifts up the ladder and lowers it on the other side. He climbs down into the yard and lets the social worker in through the green metal door. She crosses the yard and sits next to the prison gate. She talks through the bars to Zahra and Massoumeh. 'Anything you want?' she asks.

'Apple,' comes the reply.

The social worker doesn't have an apple, but she has brought gifts for the girls. She gives to each one a mirror and a comb.

When the father returns, an argument begins. 'You promised not to lock them up,' points out the social worker.

The father answers, 'If I don't lock the door, boys climb over the wall. Their ball falls in our yard and they want it back, so they climb over the wall … If anyone touched them [the sisters], I'd be dishonoured.'

An adherence to Islam bullies the mind of the simpleton, blind mother, as well as the weak, impoverished father, who in their turn bully the innocent children. In their flawed but well-meaning humanity, they all earn our forgiveness.

The social worker tries to find a way forward. 'Leave the children in the yard, ask the neighbour to keep an eye on them. We spoke about this. You promised.'

She takes the key from the father and opens the prison gates; she lets Zahra and Massoumeh into the yard, and furthermore she pushes them through the green metal gate – outside, into the street.

At the same time, in a stroke of narrative genius, she takes the father by the elbow and leads him, pushes him, inside the house, behind the iron gates. 'Let's see how you like it,' she says, and locks him in.

Now he peers out from behind those same prison bars.

Our instinct for pro-social punishment, a type of punishment that is going to mend the situation, restore co-operation rather than create more damage, is answered by the social worker's action, and at the same time it combines with a display of logic, in the shape of this delicious irony, to increase at a stroke our involvement in the narrative.

Meanwhile, outside the green metal gate, Zahra and Massoumeh run down the empty street. They have spent most of their life sitting or lying, and their gait is lame, clumsy, as if they are disabled. They have their mirrors and combs gifted to them by the social worker. They find a hose and pour the water in a stream over the mirrors, looking at their own reflections.

But then they run back, and find their father locked into the same cage where they have lived all their lives. Zahra holds their father's hand through the bars and they try to go back inside. He points out to the social worker, 'See, they lock themselves in.' The social worker shoos the girls away again, 'Go out and make some friends.' They run back out into the street.

An ice-cream seller, a boy much younger than they are, carries his polystyrene box and calls for customers. Massoumeh takes an ice-cream, but she doesn't have any money, has no knowledge of money.

The boy takes her by the lapels and orders her, 'Pay for the ice-cream.' She is smiling; she doesn't understand her crime.

Our forgiveness rushes in, again, as we understand and judge the moral forces at work.

From an open window above the street a neighbour has heard the racket and wants to find out what's going on. She sees it is the girls, Zahra and Massoumeh, and she calls out, 'I'll pay,' and notes fall from her window like confetti – enough to buy the ice-cream. 'That's for you,' she says.

The ice-cream seller takes the money, but he also gives Massoumeh another ice-cream, his own, 'I'll give you mine.'

She in turn gives to him the mirror and the comb.

'Thank-you,' he says.

This excess of sharing between them, their rush to co-operate, their generosity, after its long absence, is intensely moving.

The ice-cream seller combs his hair.

Meanwhile, the social worker sits in the yard outside the prison bars, and the father, from inside, offers her a cup of water. 'It's hot in the sun,' he says. We love the humanity of this film-maker, the way she finds, and shows, the generosity of her characters. We feel a rush of elevation, a pleasure in the right-thinking human animal, made evident in the film-maker herself, a young woman, Samira Makhmalbaf.

A ball drops out of the sky and bounces into the yard. We are quick to rush back, against the flow of the story, to remember this was the reason for the sisters' imprisonment – boys sometimes want their ball back, and they might touch the girls and bring them, and the parents, dishonour. 'I told you,' says the father, as the ball rolls to a halt in the yard. 'I have to lock the door.' The bell sounds – the boys after their ball, no doubt – but no one answers, so the boy climbs up onto the wall. The social worker gives him back his ball. There's not a glimpse of dishonour. The social worker then makes the speech that delivers the film's key argument, 'The problem is that they're girls. If they were boys, they'd go out with you. And they would even climb walls.'

Pity, in its full force, rushes into this tiny outside yard where the social worker waits patiently with the imprisoned father.

The father has a book that he shows to the social worker. It is called 'Advice to Fathers'. 'Here,' he says, 'read what it says about girls.' The book's advice is that 'a girl is like a flower. If the sun shines on her, she will fade.'

The film shows us that the opposite is true. Zahra and Massoumeh are out in the sunny streets, and for the first time in their lives they are thriving. Zahra is leaping in the air, trying to reach an apple that a boy is dangling on a piece of string from an upstairs window. He makes sure she doesn't get it, but then he comes down to the street and leads the sisters to the apple store, where a pile of apples waits for them. However, they don't have any money, so the boy takes them back to the yard, to their locked-in father, to ask for some. The boy explains to the father something about his daughters, 'They take everything from everyone else.'

The girls don't know how to share, how to co-operate. The father explains that he has never given them money, not since one of them swallowed a coin by accident. The boy advises him to give them notes instead. The father gives to each of his daughters a hundred-tomans note, and then he gives the same amount to the boy, and this extra generosity, the step beyond nepotism, earns our moral approval. When Zahra gives her money back to her father, pushing the note through the bars behind which, up until now, he has imprisoned her for her whole life, that moral approval is laced with irony and emotion.

Meanwhile the social worker visits one neighbour after another to ask to borrow a hacksaw. When she gets one, she takes it back and tells the father, 'You may need to get out.' She passes the hacksaw through the bars. The father will, for the duration of the rest of this film, patiently try to saw through the prison bars, and of course if the bars are sawn through the gates will be impossible to lock, and so the mother, Soghra, utters, in her monster-like voice, terrible commands, 'You bastard, don't saw those bars.' And then she gives way, 'All right, I'll let the children play in the yard.' We know already not to trust her. She is in charge, and blind, she is herself locked in, and she is terrified of letting her daughters go out.

Meanwhile the two daughters are roaming far and wide, and each has two apples, one in either hand. Plainly they have already visited the apple store.

They bump into two girls playing hopscotch, and now there comes a dramatisation of the very essence of the psychological shape of this film's moral structure. Zahra, enchanted by the physical and verbal confidence of her new playmate, a girl of her own age, in one moment offers her the apple to share, while the next moment she bumps the apple against the girl's face, a small act of bullying that is only comprehensible when one knows and understands the bullying that these two daughters have themselves suffered, which now infects the next outward circle of acquaintance.

The new friend is startled, and withdraws.

'Sorry.' Zahra, blushing, manages to say the word in her strange groaning voice.

'I forgive you,' says her new friend, and trusts her again, only to be bumped in the face, this time slightly harder, by Zahra's apple. 'Sara, let's not play with them,' says the new friend to the other girl.

Zahra more urgently presses the apple on her as a gift, and says, 'Kiss,' and tries to embrace her, but it's going to be harder work, now, to win back this new friend's trust. When Zahra hits *again* with the apple, for the third time, a bit harder even, it is heartbreaking. The trust is broken by the automatic but miniature acts of bullying which are so ingrained into this twelve-year-old's life. We see how the bullying is contagious: an extreme form of religion bullies a frightened, blind mother and an impoverished father, who in turn bully their daughters, who now can't help but hurt their new friends, while at the same time wanting not to.

It is deeply moving when, finally, the repeated forgiveness of the other girls towards their strange new friends leads them all to be lying on their backs in a row, staring up into the sky, the apples precisely shared out – four girls, four apples – and they're chomping away together. It is only *right* so to do.

Meanwhile their father saws away at the bars with his hacksaw. A neighbour shows him a newspaper article about his 'chaining up' his daughters. He is in tears. 'They dishonoured me,' he says of his neighbours. He has always been worried at the precise difference between 'chained up' and 'locked up', and on such fine distinctions morality is argued. 'Locked up' the father can accept as the unfortunate truth, he did lock up his daughters, and he might blush with shame at having done so, but he has never *chained* them up, a worse crime, so the accusation in the press is wrong, unfair, and instead he will blush with anger.

With his sawing through the metal bars, slowly, and thus trying to get out, the irony of his situation is ever more deeply described.

The closing sequence of the film sees the two daughters return to the yard once again. Their movements are more graceful, their speech seems to have improved, their smiles are more open. They return with friends, the two sisters with whom they shared the apples, young girls of their own age who plainly haven't been bullied; they have been living within a more generous form of Islam.

As if this were a fairy tale, the social worker gives to Zahra, the daughter, the key that will unlock the gates behind which her father is imprisoned. The social worker offers the following promise: if Zahra can unlock the gates by herself, she can set her father free.

Zahra smiles her other-worldly smile and is pleased, after a while, to be able to insert the key correctly in the lock just as she has seen her father do. Likewise, as she has seen her father do, she turns the key, but doesn't immediately succeed in opening the mechanism. Her father waits, glumly, behind the prison gates while his daughter continues to twist and turn the key, and her optimistic smile, her appreciation of the task given to her, begins to pall. The lock won't turn; she twists harder, in both directions. It won't open. Her expression begins to deteriorate. She wants to let her father out but can't; and her forgiveness of him is added to the failure to turn the lock to make a terribly poignant irony. She is in tears, trying to open this gate behind which she herself was trapped for so many years.

Finally the key turns, the iron gates open. The assembled children – Zahra and Massoumeh and their two friends – lead the father out of the yard and into the street. They want to take him to visit the watch-seller. They need more money.

The yard is now empty; moreover both the iron gates and the green metal door that lets onto the street stand open.

Soghra, the mother, is the only person left. Pinching the fabric shut across her face, the blind, invisible monster sways from side to side. She can't see that the iron gates are open, and the green metal door also, but she can sense it – because there is no one there. 'Zahra dear, where have you gone?' No answer comes. She moves into the yard, but still there is silence. She has been closely surrounded by her husband and daughters for all these years; now she is alone. She moves into the street. That same boy is at the upstairs window, dangling an apple on a string. Soghra stands blindly, a pillar of fabric, only her hands visible. She can't see the apple tempting her from above. From her hiding place she fruitlessly offers a series of commands to a pair of daughters who aren't there.

The film has managed to reclaim the apple as a common fruit of the earth with all the value that implies (the Quran version of the Adam and Eve story describes it as a 'forbidden tree' rather than a specific fruit).

This film, *The Apple*, instead of the Bible, should occupy the bedside cabinets of every motel in Britain and America (countries that have often bullied the Arab and Persian worlds), as a fable (written, directed and edited by a co-operative family) that propagates the values of every religion, the so-called Golden Rule of moral philosophy: 'Do unto others what you would have done unto you'.

3   The cheat

The boundary between in-group co-operation and co-operation between groups is richly observed in Colin Turnbull's *The Forest People* (1962). His text gives us an example of mass cheating that an audience or reader might approve of, and also of an individual cheat whom we disapprove of, and who suffers the pro-social punishment of the group.

Turnbull's account is non-fiction, but the writer of drama will always examine closely real life; drama isn't a separate construction from reality but a distillation of its most powerfully adhesive patterns, adhesive in the sense that it secures and intensifies the attention of the audience; it is the writer's task to 'direct others' attention with unmatched precision' (Boyd, 102).

The Forest People is an anthropological study of an LPA hunter-gatherer tribe that has taken its place in the history of our understanding of morality; and the two episodes he describes are good candidates for adaptation into films.

Early on in *The Forest People* the reader learns there were two systems of morality within which the Ituri Pygmies lived. The first was their own; this was the world of the forest, of game-hunting, of nomadic bands that moved and set up camp quickly using materials to hand, a lifestyle that went back unchanged to the Late Pleistocene Era. The second was the world of the village, inhabited by tribes with different rituals and beliefs. The villagers were farmers, not hunters. They cleared land for agriculture. The hunter-gatherer Ituri spent most of their time in the forest, but regularly returned to the village to live among the tribe there.

While they were in the village, Turnbull observed, the Ituri Pygmies adopted the moral code of the villagers, a quite separate code from their own, which involved them becoming, apparently, slaves to the villagers. The relationship between villager and Pygmy was based on an exchange of foodstuffs. Turnbull, living among the Pygmy tribe and accepted as one of their own, describes the transition as the Ituri moved from their own world, the forest, into the world of the village –

> We got a warm reception as we emerged from the plantations among the neat rows of mud houses. The villagers eyed the baskets on the women's backs and tried to estimate how much meat they were bringing. They called out offers of free meals into the favour of people whom they theoretically regarded as slaves. (Turnbull, 159)

Meanwhile the Pygmy received from the villager 'generous portions of rice, beans, groundnuts and manioc leaves and a few of the tiny bitter tomatoes which blend so well with manioc leaves and groundnuts in the making of a sauce' (161).

It was a form of co-operation that was based on an exchange between different types of agriculture, between the hunter-gatherers and the farmers, but to allow it to happen the Pygmies had to pretend to be the villagers' slaves, while the villagers had to pretend to include 'their' Pygmies in rituals such as the '*nkumbi*', the circumcision ceremony that villagers believed cemented the relationship between the living and the dead. The Pygmies only pretended to believe this; for the sake of the two groups being able to join together and co-operate they would put their sons through the agony of circumcision, but, as Turnbull observed, the

Pygmies would cheat, insofar as they could, in order to lessen their sons' suffering.

Turnbull found himself observing a unique situation, in one particular year. Among the boys of a suitable age for *nkumbi* there were eight Pygmies, but no villagers, therefore 'the villagers were faced with the alternative of having no initiation at all, or having one for Pygmy boys alone … it meant that the villagers would have to go through all the work and expense purely for the Pygmies' (219), whom they regarded as a slave class. It was unthinkable not to have the *nkumbi*, because this would offend the villagers' ancestors.

This unusual circumstance led to an example of cheating in which the reader can take a moral delight. The *nkumbi* ritual takes place over a period of two weeks, with many strict rules. The boys can't eat with their hands, they are forbidden to eat with their relatives, they can't wash or even be outside while it is raining, they have to perform certain dances and songs. One by one the boys are cut, and their pain is horribly increased 'because after the operation the wound is wrapped in a leaf containing a native medicine that is full of salt' (222).

During the nights, the boys who are to be circumcised are kept separately, sleeping in 'the place of the *nkumbi*' (223) and only the fathers of the boys are allowed to be with them. During this particular year, because only Pygmy boys were initiates, the villagers found themselves bound by their own rules, and only Pygmy fathers were allowed to sleep in the same place as their sons. Turnbull himself was deemed to be a 'father' to all eight of the boys, and so witnessed what took place –

> [At] night, when all the villagers had left, I learned what the *nkumbi* really means to the people of the forest. The moment their instructors were gone, and only Pygmies were left, the boys leaped from the bed where they were supposed to be sleeping and joined their fathers around the fire, eating forbidden foods in forbidden company and in a forbidden manner, using their fingers … A shower of rain was an invitation to run outside and wash off all the dirt that had accumulated during the day. (223)

The reader rejoices at this story of cheating because our morality is aligned with Turnbull and the Pygmies. If the same story were to be told by a villager, with a wholehearted belief in the supernatural powers of long-dead ancestors, and if it were to be told to an audience of villagers with the same beliefs, their reaction would have been the opposite: instead of rejoicing in the cheating, they would have felt that blush of anger.

Turnbull summarises the moral situation –

> Far from illustrating the dependence of the Pygmies upon the villagers, the *nkumbi* illustrates better than anything else the complete opposition of the forest to the village. The Pygmies in the forest consciously and energetically reject all village values. When they are in the village they temporarily adopt its values and customs, not wanting to desecrate their sacred songs in the village … There is an unbridgeable gulf between the two worlds of the two peoples. (227)

The temporary bridge is built in the name of co-operation between the two tribes.

Similar examples of wholesale moral cheating can be found when one moral code subsumes or conquers another, for instance when the communist USSR forbade religion. Underneath the surface, religious belief persisted. When Gorbachev granted freedom of religion to the citizens of the USSR, church services sprang to life within days, reaching the Kremlin's own St Basil's Cathedral in just two weeks. Islam was given the same go ahead and money poured into Russia from Islamic countries such as Libya and Saudi Arabia in order to build mosques, schools and other religious institutions throughout the Asian republics controlled by Russia. The moral code that had been hidden, repressed, came to the surface and showed itself immediately.

Also in *The Forest People* is an example of a cheat who arouses the anger of the Pygmies (and the reader). It's the story of a Pygmy hunter called Cephu and the events, as witnessed by Turnbull, are retold by Christopher Boehm in *Moral Origins, the Evolution of Virtue, Altruism, and Shame* (2012). The Mbuti Pygmy is of interest to Boehm because the tribe counts as 'Late Pleistocene-era Appropriate' or LPA; their living conditions can be fairly judged not to have changed since this geochronological age, a hundred and twenty-five thousand years ago, during which modern man was established on all continents except Antarctica.

Boehm's account of Turnbull's witnessing of Cephu's crime adds to the telling, for our purposes. Both texts should be read in their entirety. Harry Shapiro, Chairman and Curator of Physical Anthropology at the American Museum of Natural History at the time of publication of *The Forest People*, opened his foreword to the work with the following advice, 'The book is exceptional.' He goes on, 'its author … knows the Pygmies intimately from years of living among them … As a result the reader can enter into some understanding of their lives and enjoy the exhilaration of participating in a culture other than his own'.

Christopher Boehm is a cultural anthropologist with forty years' experience of fieldwork with the Navaho, the Montenegrin Serbs and wild chimpanzees, and he is Director of The Jane Goodall Research Centre at The University of South California. As much as anyone he understands the way in which morality provoked our instinct for storytelling. The following story is therefore a piece of gossip from the 1950s, retold by Boehm, and retold again here. Perhaps it's on its way to becoming a myth.

Cephu was always on the edge of the tribe. He was a Mbuti Pygmy, but he kept his family group housed on the edge of whichever camp they happened to make, and there was an aloof quality to him and his relatives. From the outset he was regarded as egotistical in nature. He appeared superior, and arrogant, and what was going to happen next would prove how egoism might damage the interests of the group.

For the hunter-gatherer, large game is a prized food because of its high fat content and its savoury protein. But large game requires co-operation between hunters to bring it down, and the deal is that whoever actually makes the kill must share the spoils.

All over the world, mobile hunter-gatherers use social control guided by moral rules to see to it that when a successful hunter kills a large mammal, his ego is held in check. To this end, he is not only precluded from decisively favouring his family and kinsmen with larger portions of the meat, but usually he is forbidden by his fellow egalitarians even to preside over and distribute the meat – for fear that he might use his position to gain political or social advantages. Rather, the band sees to it that some neutral person will distribute the meat fairly and equitably, according to the rules. These rules are, of course, moral, and it is virtuous, as well as mandatory, to give over one's kill to the entire group. By the same token, it's danger-ously deviant to play the possessive meat bully – and downright shame-ful to sneakily cheat on the system. This last is precisely what Cephu did. (Boehm, 37)

On this occasion, a band of hunters set out to hunt game not with spears or bow-and-arrow, but with nets. This method involved the whole band: some of the men positioned the very long nets in a large semi-circle in the dense forest. The women and children started from some distance away and acted as beaters, thrashing the undergrowth to chase any prey, such as antelope, towards the nets. The antelope would run, become ensnared, and then be despatched by the men.

The mood was already running against Cephu. His reputation was poor. 'Cephu will spoil the hunt completely – you'll see' (Turnbull, 103). He had a reputation for watching the nets of other hunters more closely than his own.

The method of sharing out the spoils of the net hunt were well known and accepted by the tribe: each net was the same length, and positioned the same distance away from the beaters, so each net would catch more or less the same amount of game, when averaged out over time. Therefore, what they caught and killed in their net, they could keep.

Except – the egotistical Cephu moved his net.

[He] quietly decided he wasn't getting his due. As fleeing animals randomly rushed into other nets and were speared by their owners, Cephu decided to improve his luck. When he thought no one was looking, in the dense forest he repositioned his net so that it would be well ahead of all the others, and the driven animals would run into his net first. (Boehm, 38)

Cephu scored highly in this particular hunt, and took home a bounty that was above the average. He was pleased with his success. He was unaware that his cheating had been observed.

Colin Turnbull had taken part in the hunt, but hadn't seen Cephu move his net. However, as the band of hunters made their way home, Turnbull was aware of a cloud that hung over the tribe. Instead of the usual cheerfulness and anticipation after a successful hunt, there was a sour mood among the Mbuti. Back in the camp, he overheard men and women cursing Cephu. An adult male, Kenge, said to the group, 'Cephu is an impotent old fool. No, he isn't, he is an impotent old animal – we have treated him like a man for long enough, now we should treat him like an animal.' (Turnbull, 104)

There followed 'some serious gossiping' (Boehm, 39) as Cephu's moral reputation was put under intense scrutiny – 'the way he mistreated his relatives, his general deceitfulness, the dirtiness of his camp, and even his own personal habits' (39).

When Cephu returned from the hunt, he stopped at the entrance to his hut, and the same male, Kenge, shouted at Cephu, and repeated his accusation that Cephu was 'an animal'.

Cephu came over to the meeting place, the *kumamolimo*, where everyone was gathered.

> Trying not to walk too quickly, yet afraid to dawdle too deliberately, he made an awkward entrance. For as good an actor as Cephu, it was surprising. By the time he got to the *kumamolimo* everyone was doing something to occupy himself – staring into the fire or up at the tree tops, roasting plantains, smoking, or whittling away at arrow shafts. (Turnbull, 105)

Cephu the egoist was among the group of co-operative hunters, and they showed their displeasure in a particular way. It was customary for the young males to give up their seats to more senior males, but Cephu –

> went up to where a youth was sitting in a chair … (and) the youth continued to sit there in as nonchalant a manner as he could muster. Cephu went to another chair where Amabosu was sitting. He shook it violently when Amabosu ignored him, at which he was told, 'Animals lie on the ground'. (105)

They were shaming Cephu; and one can imagine his blush at this blatant exclusion, or punishment, from a young man much lower down than him in the pecking order.

Finally, the accusation came to light.

> Ekianga leaped to his feet and brandished his hairy fist across the fire. He said that he hoped Cephu would fall on his spear and kill himself like the

animal he was. Who but an animal would steal meat from others? There were cries of rage from everyone, and Cephu burst into tears. (106)

This sociable band of hunters, for whom co-operation was a matter of life and death, were determined to bring Cephu to account, to make him aware of his egoistical crime. Turnbull, deeply embedded in this tribe over a long period, is gripped by this unusual turn of events.

> I had never heard of this happening before, and it was obviously a serious offense. In a small and tightly knit hunting band, survival can be achieved only by the closest cooperation and by an elaborate system of reciprocal obligations which insures that everyone has some share in the day's catch. Some days one gets more than others, but nobody ever goes without. There is, as often as not, a great deal of squabbling over the division of the game, but that is expected, and nobody tries to take what is not his due. (107)

Cephu tried to wriggle out of the accusation. First of all he told a lie, saying that he'd got lost, and hadn't known where the others had been positioned with their nets, but he'd heard the beating begin and so had thought it best to set up his net anyway. When his lie didn't work, he changed tack and boasted that he was a better hunter than the others and so deserved a better position with his nets. He was a chief in his own right, he said, with his own family group within the band of hunters.[2]

Cephu's fellow hunters used sarcasm (humour always such a powerful method of shaming) to puncture Cephu's ridiculous boast –

> Manyalibo said there was obviously no use prolonging the discussion ... Cephu had his own band, of which he was chief, so let him go with it and hunt elsewhere and be a chief elsewhere. Manyalibo ended a very eloquent speech with 'Pisa me taba' (pass me the tobacco). Cephu knew he was defeated and humiliated. (107)

---

[2] Boehm compares this display to modern-day psychopaths: 'Cephu's next acts were to cover his deviance with a lie and then engage in some egoistic boasting, which, to me, seems almost worthy of the sometimes megalomaniac, fast-talking, recklessly-lying psychopaths described by Hare and Kiehl.' (Boehm, 40)

3 The Line in the Sand   137

They had called his bluff. Cephu knew it was over – because he and his family group were too small in number to hunt effectively. They would never survive on their own. 'He apologised profusely, reiterated that he really did not know that he had set up his net in front of the others, and said that in any case he would hand over all the meat.' (107)

This was Cephu's climbdown, an acknowledgement of his guilt. The group had won out over the individual. They went with him to his family's camp and ordered his wife to hand over all the meat. 'She had little chance to refuse, as hands were already reaching into her basket and under the leaves of the roof where she had hidden some liver in anticipation of just such a contingency. Even her cooking pot was emptied.' (Turnbull, 107)

They searched all of the family's huts and took all the meat and shared it out among themselves. Thus Cephu's whole family would go without. This pro-social punishment would encourage Cephu's family not to follow him in his cheating ways. The Mafia use a similar system: if an individual strays, the whole family is punished.

> Cephu tried hard to cry, but this time it was forced and everyone laughed at him. He clutched his stomach and said he would die; die because he was hungry and his brothers had taken away all his food; die because he was not respected. (Boehm, 42)

The cheater is shamed, punishment is meted out.

However, forgiveness was quick, in order to keep Cephu within the group.

> [W]hen the evening *molimo* singing was at its height I saw Cephu in our midst. Like most of us he was sitting on the ground, in the manner of an animal. But he was singing, and that meant he was just as much a BaMbuti as anyone else. (Turnbull, 108)

Boehm sums up how the shaming of Cephu was likely to have resonated with the group –

> Once ridicule has been used to shame someone, say for behaving arrogantly, others with a similar penchant are likely to stay in line almost automatically – just to avoid similar humiliation. More than fear is at work here, for the

potential deviants have internalised egalitarian group mores that condemn self-aggrandisement, have personally experienced shame feelings while growing up, and fear being further ridiculed or shamed as adults. They also have language, so the learning of moral lessons can be vicarious. Any Pygmy who later heard the story of Cephu would think twice before shifting his net ahead of the others. (Boehm, 43)

Cephu's story showed how gossip, day-by-day, minute-by-minute, seeks out cheats like Cephu (the most extravagant recent example was the cheating within the upper ranks of FIFA) and destroys their moral reputations, all in the service of fighting destructive egoism and offering lessons in egalitarian co-operation. The best gossip turns into stories, which then, in order to strengthen their impact, will be exaggerated to become myths and legends. The purpose of storytelling is to exercise our moral instinct, train our right-mindedness.

4   The thief

A young boy lies face down in the dust, unconscious, surrounded by nothing except a wasteland of sand, a hot desert. The logic-work begins immediately: we have been given the effect – a boy lies dead or injured, or perhaps asleep, and our instinct to complete the logic paradigm means we need to find out what caused this – what happened, and why.

A young boy (perhaps the same one as we've just seen, but perhaps not) waits in the dark, his hungry eyes fixed on a sheep that bleats occasionally in the back yard of someone's house. The boy is thin, young, and when we glimpse the owner of the sheep he is fat, middle-aged. The title of the film (only twenty-four minutes long) is *The Sheep Thief* (1997), written and directed by Asif Kapadia. Sure enough the boy steals the sheep; he picks it up bodily and runs through the deserted village (the film is set in Rajasthan). The line in the sand shifts: he is a thief, yes, but he is young and thin and needs feeding, whereas the owner is overfed and middle-aged. We instantly measure the pattern of right and wrong, and each new piece of information adds a new judgement that colours the pattern of our moral 'heart-reading'.

The sheep-thief is pursued by the owner, as well as others. One of their number catches up with him, and he drops the sheep and strikes out with his stick to the man's face. When the stick is dropped the audience can observe that a nail has been driven into the end of the stick, and the nail went into the man's eye. It's a vicious weapon, too vicious, and our judgement swerves against the sheep-thief; the nail drips with gore. The line in the sand shifts. That was excessive force; the sheep-thief was in the wrong.

The sheep-thief is now hiding under the footings of a building while the owner runs heavily past. A coin glints in the dust, and the sheep-thief, in his poverty, reaches out to pick it up.

The owner sees, and his smile is cruel. Our judgement starts to move back in favour of the sheep-thief. His poverty earns our forgiveness.

The owner heats a branding iron among the hot coals. He lifts the branding iron and holds it up, smiling grimly. The sheep-thief is held down by the owner's tribe and his head is gripped hard; he must be kept still. The owner presses the red-hot iron brand to the sheep-thief's forehead. That was excessively cruel; our mirror neurons ensure our observation of this scene mimics our taking part in it –

> [O]ur brains don't differentiate between a person in need in a flickering image and a person in need in front of us. This is why we can be moved by great movies, great music, and great art. Through oxytocin release, these products of the human imagination connect us to the entire human family. This is what we want most as social creatures. (Zak, 58)

Thus our sympathy rushes towards the sheep-thief. There was nothing pro-social about that punishment, no element of forgiveness or moral training. There was too much testosterone.

The boy is lying face down in the dust. We are pleased to perform the logic-work and lace together the cause and effect: the boy we saw earlier, we now know, is lying there because he is the sheep thief, and has been too-harshly punished.

A passer-by stops his camel to go and help. He turns over the unconscious body, and sees the fresh burn on the boy's forehead. We can surmise that the branding says, 'Thief'. The passer-by lets go, stands up, re-mounts his camel and rides off. He leaves the sheep-thief in the dust. He is not going to help, after all.

All four of our narrative instincts are entertained: the logic-work has allowed us to answer the mystery of a boy lying in a desert and attach his crime to his punishment; the boy's habitual, evident, vigorous desire to eat has earned our sympathy and involvement; our moral sensibility has been exercised, teased back and forth; and lastly we feel pity for him, and are ready to feel increased pity. This is dramatic writing, and it arrives neatly done, in just a couple of minutes, with no dialogue, but merely the poetry of events.

Rain falls on the upturned face of the sheep-thief and we appreciate its life-giving force, because he regains consciousness. He wanders alone through the arid landscape. He finds water to drink, and this interlude increases our pity for him and thus our involvement because he is so young, alone and, with that branding burnt into his forehead, helpless.

He steals again; from beside its dozing owner he takes a square of red fabric. He makes a bandana out of it, and ties it around his forehead. The strip of red cloth now obscures the branding that we already know would prevent anyone from helping him.

At a stroke, dramatic irony is invoked; two strands of logic open up. The sheep-thief and the audience work along one strand of logic because they know he is a thief; anyone else who meets him will occupy a different strand of logic and see only a boy on his own, hungry, wearing a red bandana. We have already witnessed how a passer-by refused to help him because of the verdict burned into his forehead; now we will see people do the opposite, help him, because they cannot see it. Our experience in narrative tells us this latter, unknowing group will find out, and both strands of logic merge together, sometime during the length of this film.

The audience's moral instinct is enlivened, now, because, with the stealing of the bandana and tying it around his forehead, the sheep-thief has an opportunity: he can avoid being ostracised. He can, perhaps, re-join his group. He has acted selfishly, against the interests of his fellows, in stealing sheep, but he has been punished severely. He might or might not have learned his lesson; we want to find out whether or not he steals again.

The feeling (the subject of Chapter 4, hereafter) we have for him is pity, because he is young and poor and alone, and because that punishment was too harsh.

Thus all four instincts are in play; the audience is involved.

He wanders for a while, and comes across a poor family, a mother and her two sons, aged around six or seven, collecting mangoes. They have a ramshackle trailer and one of its wheels has fallen off. He helps them; working together, for the good of the group, they can lift the trailer and re-attach the wheel. He sets off with them; he has become part of their group.

They arrive at their village. A gang of idle young men spot the newcomer, and give him hard stares.

At the hut belonging to the family, the sheep-thief is given a small amount of rice and gruel as a thank-you for his help. He doesn't go into the house; he is still an outsider. The two younger boys look at him with curiosity and interest, and the mother is judging him. We can ascertain her kindness, but also her caution.

He's received his reward of food, so now he will take his leave. But we have been given a glimpse of what is possible, given co-operation between individuals. Instead of stealing, he has given his help, and he's received the reward of a small meal, and inclusion in a small group, a family. Our hope for him is that he sees the story he is in, in effect, and learns his lesson.

On the outskirts of the village the young men drive him out with their stares. He's not a member of the group, not yet. He is back where he started: alone, out in the cold, with no shelter, no group or family.

The next day, good fortune visits him. He is asleep out in the open and the small boy, from the same family, sees him and dribbles some water in his mouth – again, it is water that revives our thief. The family are out here collecting mangoes again. The sheep-thief, wearing his red bandana, helps to gather the mangoes from the tree. He is sharing his labour, and we can presume he will be rewarded with another meal.

When he brings three mangoes to the cart, he slips one in his pocket. He steals it.

The audience feels dread. We rush to forgive him, but at the same time urge him to mend his ways, not to be a thief, because the mother looks kind, and the two boys could be his younger brothers. An aura of calm good humour surrounds this family and if the sheep-thief changes, if he doesn't steal, membership of this family group can be his reward. The causes that demand that he change, that he becomes not-the-sheep-thief, exert more pressure. But if he is not going to change, despite these changed circumstances, then the audience prepares itself for pity, for tragedy.

The mother and her two sons form a small, nepotistic group, the family, and their survival depends on their co-operative effort, the gathering of this fruit, and they are unwittingly inviting a sheep-thief to join them – but will he make a contribution to their co-operative effort, or will he steal from them? The unspoken agreement will be that he must control his own selfish agenda and join the co-operative one.

They shake the tree and the mangoes fall to the ground. The sheep-thief carries the fruits to the cart. Perhaps that theft of the mango was just the last small one that he will make. Perhaps it will slide past, and he will learn his lesson.

The dramatist, writer-director Kapadia, is dealing in the stuff of all stories. 'The problem of co-operation, then, is the problem of getting collective interest to triumph over individual interest, when possible. The problem of co-operation is the central problem of social existence.' (Greene 2012, 20) And the underhand nature of the stealing, the pretending to help, the obscuring of his branding, means that he is a cheat as well as a thief, so he now performs two of the story archetypes. Yet he is still the protagonist of this story, rather than the antagonist, because he earns our moral support, and moreover our narrative commitment. The story has previously shown us his precarious existence, how he almost had to steal to survive, and it also showed us his unfairly harsh punishment, so although we disapprove of his actions we see how small the theft is, and we wholeheartedly wish for his redemption, for him to be able to join this group, and thus our pro-social instinct for forgiveness allows us small, immediate measures of oxytocin, every now and again, which fuel our involvement in the story.

His theft of the mango remains undiscovered and the sheep-thief is able to return to the house for a second time, and the meal he is given is larger than before. After the meal the two younger boys begin to edge closer to him. The sheep-thief asks for their attention, and he holds up a small square of paper, into which he has made a tear that reaches half way through. He pretends to take a hair from the head of the younger boy, and with this imaginary hair it appears that he pulls back and forth one half of the torn section of paper. It moves by itself. It's a piece of magic that enchants the boys.

There will be another piece of magic, later on, when the family group is selling the mangoes at the market. Trade is steady, but quiet, and the younger boys hanker for more magic. They wear bandanas, now, in imitation of the bandana worn by the sheep-thief. This is a deliciously ironic agitation of the dramatic irony in the film, because the bandanas worn by the boys are white, the colour of innocence, whereas the sheep-thief's is red, the colour of danger. The boys' innocent admiration of the bandana as a fashion item comments on its use as a mask by the sheep thief, but the latter's thieving is a way of life that seems to be fading into the past, given the generous sharing of this family group.

The boys want more magic, and the sheep-thief claims to be able to make it rain, and he points upwards into the sky. The younger boy's gaze points upwards, and he feels drops of rain, miraculously, although we know the drops of water come from the water-bottle, flicked in the air from the sheep-thief's fingers. We attach this rain to two previous scenes: when the sheep-thief lay unconscious in the dust, face up, and rain from the sky fell onto his lips, and brought him back to life, and when the younger boy poured water into his mouth to wake him. Here, in this scene, the magic of the water cements the relationship between the sheep-thief and the boys who are becoming, in effect, his younger brothers. Later, rain will again perform its work as a metaphor for life itself.

The 'moral machinery' (Greene, 28) of the film is then tested in the darkness of the Rajasthan night, when the lighting conditions are similar to the scene at the beginning of the film. Once again the sheep-thief's face is seen close-up, with just a slice of light thrown across it at an angle. As before, he is carefully watching, listening, except this time he is lying down in what might become his home. As before, the soundtrack offers that bleating, but of a goat this time. The narrative is testing the sheep-thief. His circumstances have changed to this extent, but will his character change? Will he steal the goat? The sheep-thief's face is watchful, alert; he's thinking about it.

But then he turns onto his other side. He doesn't steal. He is no longer a thief. This might be his own home.

The oxytocin injects itself into our bloodstream as we experience this sympathy for, and approval of, the sheep-thief. He is now a member of a family; he has two younger brothers and a mother; and, as a member of this family, he is also a member of the village. The village elder has heard his story, and his moral virtue is spoken for by the mother; she will take responsibility for him.

Has he changed, then?

The family is selling its mangoes at the market, but no one is buying. There is a sense of urgency. The mangoes are offered more vigorously to passers-by in the market, but still no one is buying. The younger brothers need some magic from their elder brother, in order to answer this problem.

He rises to his feet. We sense he is going to help, and that he is now working not just for himself but for his family. This will be nepotism, a first step towards reciprocal altruism, which in turn might lead to altruism, the help that we might give not to our family, nor to our group, but to those outside our group, at some cost to ourselves and with no possible benefit. None the less, despite his progress in turning away from being a thief during the night, we are concerned that he will steal, given the mangoes aren't selling, and bring the tragedy of being a thief down on his family, who have agreed to take responsibility for him.

He moves quickly away. The younger brothers watch him go, wondering how the magic will manifest itself.

The sheep-thief leaves the village and walks quickly through the rocky, desert landscape. He arrives at the temple or mosque, set on its own; there is no one to see what he will do here.

He goes into the temple. A gold-coloured jug rests on a stone shelf. Is it gold? We know it's valuable, a relic of some kind, and we know it trades in the belief-system of this village, which we might guess to be Muslim, with its attached moral code. We don't need to know much to realise this will be a bigger theft than any that's gone before – if he steals it.

Yet it is also a naïve theft. How will he sell such a thing? He is almost bound to be caught.

Next, he is running, with the jug in his grasp. We have to leap over the gap in time, the missing event, the act of stealing, and so that event becomes our own because we have been required to find it for ourselves, and fix that small gap in the logic. He has stolen it; he is still a thief despite all the changing circumstances that demand his character must change; he must stop being a thief.

We felt dread when he stole the mango but we forgave him because he had been, not so long before, a starving, abandoned child. We felt a rush of approval and love for him when he turned away in the night from stealing the goat. The audience now feels a redoubled dread because he has stolen the relic from the temple, but he is stealing in the interests of his family, not just himself, and because this well-meaning theft is naïve, doomed to failure.

None the less he is trapped in the logic of his character. He is the sheep-thief, and he cannot change even though his changed circumstances suggest he must, and should change. It arouses our pity.

There is further logic-work arranged for us in this sequence by the writer-director, or perhaps the editor. The sheep-thief is spotted running away from the temple by the young men of the village who previously gave him such hard stares. They rise quickly, and we see a bare foot hurriedly thrust into a sandal. They are going after him.

We have already been trained to expect jumps back and forth in time, none the less we are expecting to see, next of all, a fight between the sheep-thief and the village youths, and then his arrest and punishment. Instead we skip over this event, and see a strange old man, someone we've not met before, sitting respectfully before the woman we have come to know as the village elder, who settles all matters and is the crowning moral authority in the world of this film. The old man is telling her what's happened, and we are surprised; we furiously have to adjust the logic attached to this situation, because it isn't what we were expecting to hear. This young man, says the storyteller, indicating the sheep-thief, is to be applauded. He stopped the young men from stealing the relic from the temple. If it hadn't been for him, they would have got away with it.

We assemble the new reasoning even as the film travels backwards to show us what happened: there had been a fight, and it was witnessed by this man who had gone to break it up, but the sheep-thief had lied to him; the sheep-thief had said it was the young men who were stealing, and he had been trying to stop them, and luckily he had succeeded, because the relic is here, intact, and can be returned to the temple.

His lie had worked. The red bandana obscured the true character of the sheep-thief from the elderly villager, and the tragedy of the sheep-thief had been averted, or, we suspect, merely delayed.

The whole village has no doubt heard about this young man who saved the relic from being stolen from the temple, and so it is like magic, after all, because suddenly, at the market, everyone buys mangoes from this family. The mother, the two brothers and the sheep-thief, the family unit, can't take the money fast enough.

The moment comes, next, which our narrative experience told us had to come. The sheep-thief is protected by his red bandana, but he looks up from his market stall to catch the eye of the only person who knows what is underneath the bandana: the man who performed the branding. The cruel, overfed owner of the stolen sheep looks at him, frowns, and recognises him. The man's smile – more of a leer – is slow to come. The sheep-thief has been unmasked.

The village elder is again consulted, and the sheep-thief, without his red bandana, is revealed as a thief, and is banished from the village. The two younger brothers and the mother have lost the new member of their family who appeared to have brought them luck, but whose true nature is now revealed.

The two young boys escort their magical older brother to the outskirts of the village. They lie down, all three, their backs to the earth. When it starts to rain, it's impossible to distinguish between the first drops of rain, symbolic of life itself, and the first tears, emblematic of sorrow, that issue from the downhill corner of the younger boy's eye.

When the rain turns into a downpour, the two younger boys rise to their feet and run to take shelter.

The sheep-thief lies there and soaks it up; he has nowhere to go.

There is a brief postscript to the story that makes the tragedy more poignant. The younger boy sits in his classroom, among his fellows, but he is distracted. He has a square of paper with a tear in it, and he pulls a hair from his own head, but he cannot make the flag of paper move back and forth, as could the sheep-thief. The magic has gone and can't be recreated.

It is a perfectly realised short-form dramatic narrative filmed for twenty-five thousand pounds by a student of the RCA in London as his graduation film. Kapadia took his crew to Rajasthan and worked in collaboration with the Indian Film School in Pune, using local actors. It won the Grand Jury Prize at Cannes in 1998, among many other awards on the international film circuit. Abdul Rehman played Tashan, the sheep-thief, and Kokila Mahendra played Safia, the mother. The two boys, Ya Ya and Zed, were played by Soaib Karimbhai and Jigar Bikhabhai.

5   Conclusion

With the ability of modern neuroscience to measure our biological activity at a sub-molecular level it has become clear that 'our moral behavior is embedded in cells throughout the body, and ... morality is not some civilising afterthought, or a frill that runs counter to nature, but, in fact, something deeply connected with basic survival' (Zak, 29). Therefore morality takes its place as a human instinct, along with willpower, desire, the subject of Chapter 1, and logic, the subject of Chapter 2, but perhaps uniquely among the four instincts described in this book morality is the reason that stories exist, and why we are so compelled to keep telling, reading and watching them. Stories are an extensive and continual training programme that is demanded by morality if co-operation is going to overcome, or at least work alongside, our tendency towards egoism, selfishness, aggression. Powerful stories are thus made up of four moral ingredients: the benefits of co-operation; the perils of egoism, the effect of sanctions or punishments; the role of forgiveness in maintaining the group.

4

Moods and Mental States

In *Moving Viewers* (2009) Carl Plantinga asks that film scholars should never again 'use the tired literary metaphor of a "reading" to describe the viewer's encounter with a film ... [because] it implies that film viewing is a cool, intellectual experience' (2) and he asks for intellectual prejudice against emotion to be stripped away –

> [F]or the vast majority of film spectators, movie going is first and foremost a pleasurable experience, suffused with affect. Audiences are willing to pay for this experience with money, time and effort, and in return they expect to be fascinated, shocked, titillated, made suspenseful and curious, invited to laugh and cry, and in the end given pleasure. On this foundation of pleasurable affect rests the multibillion dollar international media industries. (2)

Plantinga's 'pleasurable affect' is made of emotions, and emotions are a family of powerful instinctive behaviours that contribute to our survival and thriving. They are explosive accelerants to the instincts that have made up the previous three chapters of this book.

Chapter 1 looked at the instinct of willpower or desire, volition, which is intensified by a collection of negative and positive emotions – ambition and greed, love and lust, admiration and envy or jealousy – and desire also forms the end-game of any other emotion, given that an emotion is

149

inevitably a motivation for action of some kind – as in Hume's 'hybrid theory', explained by Prinz: Hume 'thinks that emotions have motivational force. They contain desires, which are a special class of feelings that compel us to act' (Prinz 2004, 11).

Chapter 2 examined logic, and the feeling of narrative tension, the most powerfully sustained and commercially valuable emotion in drama, is created by the patterns of logic described therein. Hanich includes interest (a synonym for narrative tension) in his reckoning of emotions – 'And if we stress the role of cognitions, *interest* turns out to be an emotion.' (Hanich 2010, 18)

Chapter 3's subject matter, morality, right and wrong, is accelerated by feelings of anger at injustice, and the feeling of *elevation* ('which modern psychology has only begun to take seriously' (Boyd, 114)) when justice falls into place, whether a natural variety or a justice organised by a society's institutions. Prinz, in the Preface to his *The Emotional Construction of Morals* (2007), takes as his starting point David Hume's *Treatise on Human Nature*, which argues that 'our moral concepts have an emotional foundation'. Given that Zak has traced his 'moral machinery' back to a time before we crawled out of the ocean, it might be put the other way around, that our emotions have a moral foundation.

Neuroscience is building an increasingly detailed understanding of how emotions work. Jesse Prinz's description, in *Gut Reactions* (2004), of Schachter and Singer's famous 1962 experiment will be envied by film marketers who would love to be able to inject adrenalin into their audiences –

> In a famous experiment … subjects were injected with a substance that they were told was a special vitamin that was being tested for its ability to improve eyesight. They were then asked to sit in a waiting room for twenty minutes before an eye exam, so the injection could begin working. In reality, the substance was adrenalin. (Prinz 2004, 13)

The adrenalin caused an increased heartbeat and breathing patterns in all the subjects, but some of them were told that this eyesight drug would have these side-effects, while others weren't. Each subject was then sent into one of two different waiting rooms, which subjected them to very different experiences.

In one waiting room, they were made to feel angry. They were presented with a questionnaire and asked to fill it in. The questions started off as banal, inoffensive, but slowly became unreasonable. The final question asked, "'With how many men (other than your father) has your mother had extramarital relationships?" The multiple choice options for answering the question are "(a) 4 and under; (b) 5–9; (c) 10 and over'" (13).

Also in the room was a stooge employed to impersonate one of their number, filling in the questionnaire. The stooge becomes increasingly and volubly angry at the questions, and 'finally tears it up and storms out' (13).

Meanwhile, in the other waiting room, the subjects of the experiment, with the same dose of adrenalin in their system, are encouraged to feel joy, euphoria – 'They receive no questionnaire and are accompanied by a stooge who makes paper airplanes, stands on a table, and plays with hula-hoops' (13). The results were fascinating. Those who had been told about the side-effects to the drug demonstrated little change in their emotional state. They felt the difference in their bodies but made the appraisal, the judgement, that it was the drug that had caused it, and so they didn't join in with the anger or the euphoria. The others, who had not been warned to expect any 'side-effects', felt the emotion that they were exposed to – those in the 'angry' room joined in with the stooge's anger and felt the same outrage at the intrusive questions, those in the 'euphoria' room celebrated the euphoria.

> Schachter and Singer use these results to argue that emotion depends on interpretation of bodily states. They say that the bodily states produced by the injection are the same for all subjects, but they are interpreted as signs of anger by some, as signs of euphoria by others, and as mere drug side effects by others. Context and background knowledge are used to label bodily states, and the labelling process is presumed to be cognitive. (Prinz 2004, 13)

The experiment proves that we identify emotions only after our appraisal of the circumstances in which they occur and thus begins to disentangle what is termed 'The Problem of Parts', which asks what *is* an emotion? The experiment tells us that an emotion is not just the bodily change that we register as 'a feeling' – although the 'Feeling theory' (Prinz 2004, 4) puts the sensation on its own and the 'somatic feeling theory' (5) announces that 'emotions are feelings of bodily state changes' (5). Julian Hanich traces how the experiment was worked through in the 1990s by cognitivists such as Noel Carroll – 'Their key assumption is: emotions involve cognitions. Apart from a bodily feeling (a) and an *object* to which the person in intentionally directed (b), there must be a thought, belief, evaluation, or judgement involved that connects (a) and (b)' (Hanich 2010, 12).

Is the emotion, then, the *judgement* that causes that bodily feeling? The neuroscientist Damasio, quoted in Prinz and widely elsewhere, describes emotions as an 'internal milieu' which strikes me as an affectionate term, like a charming town that one might visit.

Advances in neuroscience have led to a growth in the manner and type of such experiments that help to describe how emotions work mechanically but for the purposes of writing drama it is most useful to wrap up all the 'parts' into one system and describe emotions according to what Prinz calls 'cognitive cause theories' (2004, 13) –

Perception – appraisal – emotional state – impulse for action

Thus you see a snake (perception), you judge it to be dangerous (appraisal), your heart races and you identify that as fear (emotional state) and you turn and run (impulse for action). Or, you see a particular man (perception), you judge him to be absolutely what you want (appraisal), your heart races and you identify that as love (emotional state) and you freeze, can't say a word (impulse to action, but fear of such action).

The next task will be to make a list of emotions, and there are as many lists as there are psychologists to make them. Plutchik organised a wheel of 'basic emotions' (2001, 348); Ekman made a list of emotions based on facial expressions, 'anger, disgust, fear, happiness, sadness and surprise' (Prinz 2004, 150). Prinz divided up emotions into negative and positive types, 'On the negative side we have frustration, panic, anxiety, physical disgust, separation distress, and aversive self-consciousness. On the positive side, we have satisfaction, stimulation and attachment' (2004, 157).[1] But for the writer of drama the drawing up of such a list of emotions should be pertinent to the task in hand, this writing of a screenplay or play, and therefore the writer should enquire first into the relationship between emotion and film genre.

Academics have a way of handling genre as a classification system, as do audiences; I propose that screenwriters have a different relationship with genre, controlled by the idea that viewers, in buying any particular genre of screen drama, sign up for a particular emotional 'ride' in the same way that they would choose a ride in a fairground. Therefore emotion, feeling, is closely allied to genre.

For the academic, chiaroscuro lighting is an ingredient that makes up the genre of a 'noir' film. A general audience might not use such a finely tuned terminology, but they will see that quality within their generic understanding of what constitutes 'noir'. The screenwriter will absorb this classification system because the screenwriter is a committed member of the audience and also enjoys a similar enslavement to their subject as the academic, but the screenwriter, in setting her- or himself the task of writing a 'noir' film, will know that she will be expected to write either a mystery (in which she must arouse the feeling of intense curiosity) or a thriller (excitement). For the writer of drama, therefore, 'noir' is not a genre, it's a style, within which are customarily deployed one of those two different genres.

Similarly, the academic might define 'Dogma' as a genre, whereas the screenwriter will see it as a production ethic; an audience member might define a 'Western' as a genre but the screenwriter will see it as a setting, and if the writer is to write *Blazing Saddles* then she or he is writing a comedy, if it's *High Noon* then the feeling the writer is tasked

---

[1] It might seem that screenwriters and audiences would mostly trade in positive emotions but it's immediately evident this can't be true: films trade overwhelmingly in fear, sadness, pain, loss – but as will be seen there are important stipulations attached to our taking pleasure in these emotions in a work of fiction.

with arousing is along the moral axiom – feelings of anger or sorrow at injustice, as well as pride and love, *elevation*, when justice triumphs. An audience will describe 'fantasy' as a genre, the screenwriter will absorb this qualification, also, but as a setting, and then ask – what genre will it be? The writer will then define the genre according to the predominant feeling or mood that the film proposes to arouse. *The Lord of the Rings* (Jackson 2001–2003) is a three-part action-adventure. Similarly, science-fiction would thus be regarded as a setting; *Galaxy Quest* (Parisot 1999) is a comedy, a parody of the setting of science-fiction.

Screenwriters, faced with the creation of a drama rather than analysis of it, are best served if they classify genre according to the dominant emotion they intend to evoke. Any one emotion has a psychological architecture, specific to its use in drama, which will make demands on the structure of the work.

Many films serve more than one emotion, and perhaps this is nowhere more evident than in Bollywood films. If an emotion is like a ride in a fairground, then it has a particular quality and the audience pays for the ticket because they want that kind of ride, whether a roller coaster or the ghost train. Bollywood films, born out of the Sanskrit tradition of storytelling, offer a single ticket that insists you take every ride in the fairground, one after another. In *The Pleasure of The Spectator* (2003) Anne Ubersfeld has described the effect of this on the audience – 'This combination produces a global experience different from individual feelings ... It can be compared to a delicious drink which is a mixture of various ingredients but whose flavour is unlike that of any single ingredient' and she quotes K.M. Varma, '"the spectator's total experience of this combination ... is pure, unique and completely peaceful. Such an experience is called *rasa* and it is nothing short of beatitude"' (Ubersfeld 2003, 246).

A Western audience is not so willing to take this more objective, distanced, position (Ubersfeld comments, 'Even Brecht might subscribe to it' (247)). For a Western audience subjective engagement rather than an objective, beatific *rasa* is the tradition. With films like *Lunchbox* (Batra 2013), a love story, the indie class of films in India offers dramas that are more closely aligned to the tastes of Western audiences for single linear narratives featuring one dominant emotion.

A list of emotions that will be most useful to the screenwriter therefore holds hands, at all times, with genre –

* Love/attachment is aroused in the love story, the movie about friendships or that concerns itself with love between family members.
* Fear is aroused in the horror story, with its subdivision of types – psychological horror, supernatural horror, the revulsion in slasher films or gore movies.
* Excitement is the dominant feeling offered in the different categories of thrillers and action/adventure films.
* Curiosity is the feeling evoked in mystery stories.
* Anger is aroused at injustice; and the feeling of elevation is provoked by the settling of justice on the world of the story – it's a genre that might be called the legal drama, for want of a term that might encompass natural justice also.
* Cathartic pity or sorrow is aroused in tragedy; laughter is provoked by comedy. They are the matched pair, the grandparents of all genre.

This is not a comprehensive list of emotions, but they are the ones that a dramatist will want to evoke in an audience. Others such as jealousy, shame, remorse or avarice, are those that might be felt by the characters *in* the drama, in whichever genre, but a writer won't want an audience to feel jealousy themselves. Many other feelings, such as patriotism, can be regarded as subdivisions of the ones listed above (patriotism is a form of 'elevation'). Others, like surprise, can be regarded as a technique rather than an emotion that builds the overall mood of the film.

It would seem to be part of our daily lives to control our emotions, to look for the positive and to avoid the negative ones, but all emotions, even positive ones, have penalties attached; the suffering they might bring threatens us; experience might teach us to lock our emotions away.

Drama allows us the opportunity to take out our emotions and, without penalty, exercise them. Anne Ubersfeld describes 'this pleasure specific to the narrative form: to see, in safety, presented through simple words or flat images, what could produce anxiety or dangerous desire' (237–238) and she goes on to say, 'It is agreeable to experience through another person, feelings, passions, pain which, as chance would have it, we have been spared in our day-to-day existence.' (243) Plantinga quotes from Roger Manvell – 'The Cinema makes it possible to experience without danger all the excitement, passion and desirousness which must be repressed in a humanitarian ordering of life.' (Plantinga, 1)

1   Fear

Most of us are frightened of the dark. I'd include as 'dark' that sense of void or emptiness, death, and what might be on the other side of death: the zombie, vampire or ghost. 'The pleasure of theatre is having the spectator touch (but from a safe distance) anything he fears, or feared as a child – the fear of death, for example' (Ubersfeld, 245).

We are frightened of what will physically hurt us – snakes, spiders, a maniacal killer, a dentist who doesn't use anaesthetic, a jealous lover, poverty and homelessness, an enormous truck with darkened windows that seems intent on following us. We are also frightened of what will hurt us mentally: the love or abandonment of a loved one, the onset of madness (films like Polanski's *Repulsion* (1965) and *The Tenant* (1976) draw us into madness) or dementia (there is real dread on behalf of Alice (Julianne Moore) in *Still Alice* (Glatzer and Westmoreland (2014)).

Plantinga remembers, aged seven, cowering behind the dashboard of the family car at a drive-in and doesn't underestimate the importance of horror films. 'The images and sounds of *The Birds* and *Alien* have been seared into the memories of generations of moviegoers, becoming cultural icons.' (1)

Julian Hanich reminds us of Gumbrecht's division of aesthetic experiences such as watching films – 'aesthetic experiences oscillate between a *presence*-dimension and a *meaning*-dimension, between experiential and semantic levels ... Compare music and reading: while the former tends towards the presence-dimension, the latter is dominated by the meaning-dimension' (16). It would seem that fear, as an emotional currency, like music, also pertains more to the presence-dimension.

The presence of fear in real life, because it means immediate danger, is perhaps the emotion most strongly to be avoided. The human animal, for the most part, builds a life that is protected from fear; perhaps it's why the genre of horror is so popular.

And the 'presence-dimension' sounds as if it is easier to write than the 'meaning-dimension'.

It would seem that the shape of a drama that seeks to arouse fear will entail merely writing the presence of the fearful. This is too easy: a door silently opening at night, a translucent figure at the window, spiders breeding in the basement.

The challenge for the writer of fearsome material is twofold – to over-write the genre, and to write a good drama that occupies the domain of the fearful.

To overwrite any genre demands a deep love and knowledge of what has been written before. The audience has been copiously exercising its fear in cinemas and in front of televisions for many years. Given that we are all afraid of the same things, the writer of fear is essentially playing the same music as has been played many times before and a way must be found to embrace the cliché but then, by virtue of the writer's invention, reinvigorate the genre, refresh the audience's pleasurable exercise of fear. This demands novelty, the upending of convention.

The conventions of the vampire film suggest that a vampire will be a senior male and will prey on young girls and thereby recruit them also to be vampires. *Let The Right One In* throws these ingredients in the air and looks for the opposite. The vampire appears as a twelve-year-old girl and an elderly male, old enough to be her grandfather, is her assistant.

The generic vampire film also offers, as its story, the overcoming of the vampire: the stake through its heart. *Let The Right One In* recruits us to the opposite quest: for the vampire to continue undetected, to succeed, and because she is immortal, this young girl, she must replace her now-elderly male assistant with a new, younger model.

The presence of fear is easy to write: the blood drained from the neck, the knife, the strange rules of the game that sees the vampire bleed from her eyes if she steps over a threshold uninvited. To refresh the cliché is difficult and involves (as so often in dramatic writing that celebrates the logic patterns created by irony), the search for opposites, in this case the opposite of convention. The difficult part is to write a drama that answers the demands of the other three instincts previously described in this book. *Let The Right One In* addresses all four of the instincts we examine –

> *Desire*: with our emerging empathy for the vampire, the film intensifies our involvement in her habitual, evident, vigorous desire to keep going, undetected, and Oskar's desire to escape from school bullies.
>
> *Logic*: the writer arranges for us a slow but sure dawning of comprehension, allowing us to be able to bolt together the mystery, to find more causes to add to the effects that are first given to us, until we have a complete understanding.
>
> *Morality*: our recruitment into the foreign morality of this strange creature, who has to murder often enough to stay alive, who must therefore stay hidden, unrecognised, who has lived for a countless number of years, and who finally earns our wholesale moral approval when she saves her new young friend from violent school bullies.
>
> *Emotion*: the same old fear, but freshly minted so as to have its effect renewed.

Dread, fear for the certain fate of a character, would be generated by suspense but within the narrower definition offered previously (on page 77) suspense isn't evident in this film. Within the broader definition of suspense described by McKee and Carroll, which I have called narrative tension and which is modelled on uncertainty rather than certainty, on mystery rather than dramatic irony, it is prevalent throughout.

How difficult it is to generate originality in this well-worn genre can be measured by how seldom a horror film occupies the major prize lists. *The Others* (2001), a Spanish-American horror film written and directed by Alejandro Amenábar, won a Bafta for Best Original Screenplay among other awards. It, too, seeks for opposites in order to refresh the genre, but in a very different way, and it recruits our involvement in the protagonist's evident, habitual, vigorous desire to save the lives of her own children. It draws a wonderful pattern of logic that changes in front of one's eyes like a pattern in a kaleidoscope, and, as does *Let The Right One In*, it trades on our empathy for children.

2 Pity and laughter – tragedy and comedy

If the horror film operates, as described above, in the presence-dimension, then tragedy and comedy occupy the meaning-dimension. They are the most cerebral of genres, and in Chapter 2 I described the architecture of these emotions in *There Will Be Blood* for tragedy, and in *Borat* for comedy (pages 65 and 69 respectively).

None the less I'd like to make some further observations.

The first is to repeat how closely related are tragedy and comedy. 'Laughter is the counterpart of crying' (Prinz 2004, 167). Laughter sounds like crying; tears fall with the feeling of both. It is as if the whole of human suffering, of *wrongness*, is in an enormous pit, on the edge of which stands the screenwriter, and across that pit is strung a tightrope. If the writer edges along the tightrope facing in one direction, he or she is writing comedy; if the writer faces in the opposite direction then he or she is writing tragedy. In either case the writer is always looking closely at what is wrong with people, and what is wrong with the world. What is funny about a character is what is wrong with them (and a pattern of irony increases this effect if what is wrong with them is also what is dead right, or good, about them); what is sad about a character is what is wrong with them; and what is funny or sad about a situation is what is wrong about that situation. The extra magic that comedy has above tragedy is that comedy uses various logic-tricks to allow us to escape from the devastating effect of what is wrong, and instead gives us relief, in understanding most beautifully what is wrong but with intense pleasure, which effect is accompanied by admiration for the writer – 'Playful humour outruns others' expectations not to defeat but to delight them' (Boyd, 331).

Most admirable to me are those writers who can write a piece of drama that looks in both directions at once, and delivers a sorrow that is sweetened by laughter, and comedy that is made poignant by sorrow. A recent example is the TV series *Fleabag* (2016) written and performed by Phoebe Waller-Bridge, and it joins that rich vein of comedy that is performed by its writers.

As for tragedy, it's notable that an audience pays money in order to feel the suffering of others created in a fictional scenario. If we observe suffering in real life, particularly unmerited suffering, we join up with the story in an entirely different way, and pity is easy to arouse. Catharsis is the mechanism by which sorrow becomes pleasurable in a work of fiction, as described with regard to *There Will Be Blood* (cf. on page 69). Without catharsis, an audience has the sense that a writer has stood a character up in a story only in order to throw rocks at the character, and will turn away in disapproval.

3   Excitement

The genres which offer excitement are the various categories of thriller and action adventure and they set out to squeeze adrenalin into audiences as directly and obviously as did Schachter and Singer in their famous experiment.[2] Above and beyond the narrative excitement offered by suspense, mystery, dramatic irony and twists (already described in Chapter 2) thrillers and action adventures excite adrenalin when they successfully include in their architecture the race or the chase, or both. The difference between them is that the chase is one person or entity after one thing, the race is when there is a competition between more than one person for the same thing.

Successful examples of the chase scenario are the Coen brothers' *No Country for Old Men* (2007), in which Llewelyn Moss (Josh Brolin) is chased by Anton Chigurh (Javier Bardem), who is in turn chased by a police officer Ed Tom Bell (Tommy Lee Jones), or *Terminator 2: Judgment Day* (Cameron 1991) in which a new, advanced Terminator chases an outdated model as well as the family protected by the latter. The architecture of the chase is particularly satisfying if the two entities are chasing each other (because of the circular irony, the pattern of logic), as in the *Bourne* (Greengrass 2002–2016) series (except for the unfortunate fourth film), and in *The Fugitive* (Davis 1993) written by David Twohy and Jeb Stuart. This effectively turns two chases into a race – who is going to get to the other, first? A race or chase is only exciting if it is a close-run thing and if what's at stake becomes increasingly important; it's the invention

---

[2]See page 151.

of the *closeness* of the chase, its timing, the variety of the pacing, as well as the value of the result, that is the challenge for the screenwriter.

A successful example of a race, when two or more people are after the same thing, is in *Fargo*. Jerry Lundegaard (who is being chased by police officer Marge Gunderson), is in a race between himself and his father-in-law Wade, as well as the pair of kidnappers, either to get the money or to keep hold of it.

In addition to this, the Coen brothers have in effect orchestrated a race between Jerry's various different financial scams. It's a four-horse race, with four different sums of money.

Three minutes into the film, the first horse is set running, a big, bad horse, the kidnap scenario, and it's worth forty thousand dollars.

Seven minutes into the film, another horse is set running: Jerry has identified a plot of land, and if his father-in-law can be persuaded to put up the money for him to buy it, that'll be a big win. The land could be a turned into a parking lot.

These two big horses are out of the starting gate and running alongside each other.

Nine minutes into the film and a third horse is set going, and this one's a tiny, comical horse, galloping for all it's worth — only a few hundred dollars — in order to try and keep up. Jerry works in a car dealership and sells cars including a 'Truecoat' option that the customer never ordered, which allows Jerry to rake off the amount for himself. The customer is outraged and complains — 'These guys, it's always the same, it's always more!' — but has to pay up before he can get the keys to his car.

Twelve minutes into the film, horse number two, the land deal, overtakes the kidnap horse. It's a bigger, faster horse, worth seven hundred and fifty thousand dollars, and Jerry's father-in-law agrees, his voice crackles over the phone, the deal is 'pretty sweet' so this horse takes the lead. It's a good horse — legitimate, whereas all the others are illegal. Immediately Jerry tries to rein in the kidnap horse, but it's too late, his wife has gone, that horse is out of control.

Fifteen minutes into the film, the fourth horse joins the race, but it's exhausted, knackered, worth *minus* three hundred and twenty thousand dollars, and it's about to stumble and fall. Jerry has been applying to finance companies on behalf of non-existent customers to buy cars that don't exist, and taking the money for himself. The money is all gone and the hole where it was meant to be has been spotted. We realise that all the other horses have been set running because this one's about to fall and if Jerry can't put the money back into the account the race is over.

The Truecoat horse skips along winningly, twice crossing the line, but it's too small, it will never be enough.

The kidnap horse is running wild but heading in the right direction; however, apparently, it won't be enough even if it does win.

Twenty minutes into the film, the land deal horse is ahead. Jerry is called to the office of his father-in-law. His car pulls up, the only one to occupy the snow-covered parking lot outside the building. He goes in, and his smile turns to a full-on beam when he learns it's all going ahead. The figures stack up; his father-in-law is in. 'All that's left,' says Wade, 'is for us to know your fee.'

Jerry is confused. This was his deal; he found it. He's willing to pay for the loan, 'Heck, say, one over prime?'

It's the turn for the father-in-law, Wade, to be confused. 'We're not a bank, Jerry.' They will only give him a finder's fee.

The smile falls from Jerry's face. His seven-hundred-and-fifty-thousand-dollar horse is pulling up, just as it was approaching the winning line.

Wade and his sidekick, Stan Grossman (Larry Brandenburg), are the ones who are smiling, now. 'Well, if you're not going to move on it, you won't mind if we do?'

They steal the horse out from under him.

Jerry leaves the building. He goes outside, to his car, the only one that stands in this waste ground of cold, white snow. He has to scrape off the windscreen, and the back and forth of the scraper in his hands speeds up as his frustration shows itself, and he ends up beating the hell out of his own car windscreen with a plastic scraper, just for a while, before he burns out, and just has to carry on.

We've lost one horse, but we're forty minutes into the film and the kidnap horse is still running hard, but uncontrolled and dangerous – Jerry is struggling to control it. His father-in-law, who is the one paying the ransom for his daughter, Jerry's wife, wants to deliver the money to the kidnappers himself and this will spoil Jerry's plan. Jerry tries to stay in the saddle. He says, 'This is my deal here, Wade … ' They are the same words he used when he was riding the other horse, the land deal horse, which was just stolen from under him twenty minutes ago – although no one notices. Jerry nearly gave himself away as the architect of the kidnap rather than the victim.

Wade insists; he is going to deliver the million dollars himself.

The size of the horse increases hugely – it's worth a million dollars, now. Jerry told the kidnappers it was only forty thousand dollars. But we already sense Jerry is a loser, so he's going to be found out and doubtless, again, he will lose.

Fifty minutes into the film, we can appreciate the valour of the little Truecoat horse, who's still going, and Jerry is still trying to get the GMAC finance horse off its knees. The winning post for all the horses is set for tomorrow afternoon.

The film is labelled as a thriller but a comic tone underlies every beat; and this race between scams feels like an episode of *Wacky Races* (Hanna and Barbera 1968–1969) with Dick Dastardly and Muttley in the Mean Machine, The Gruesome Twosome in the Creepy Coupe and The Slag Brothers in The Boulder Mobile.

The skill required for the writer of an exciting race or chase is to engineer, just like in *Wacky Races*, the reverses in fortunes, the roller coaster ride, plus the narrowness of any change in the competition, as well as to affect the moral landscape in a way that secures and increases our involvement.

More important than speed or pace is to make the race or chase a close thing – 'we wish for a closely fought match that contains many satisfying reversals, but which can be seen, retroactively, to have always tended toward a satisfying and inevitable conclusion' (Mamet, 8). That *closeness* of the race or chase will tax the invention of the screenwriter.

Morality, as always, must have its effect if it's going to be a race or chase that we care about. In simplistic terms a mainstream thriller or action adventure 'points to two logically opposed outcomes, one of which is evil or immoral but probable or likely, and the other of which is moral, but improbable or unlikely or only as probable as the evil outcome' (Vorderer et al. 1996, 77).

It goes without saying that suspense is a sharpener of excitement, just as it is a sharpener of any emotive scenario.

4 Curiosity

Some lists of emotions don't include curiosity. It doesn't appear in Plutchik's wheel of 'basic emotions' (348) for instance, and doesn't appear in Solomon's *True to Our Feelings*, but it is among the most important, and in *Gut Reactions* Prinz confirms, 'curiosity or interest … are frequently included on lists of emotions' (2004, 164). The genre that gives rise to the feeling of curiosity is mystery, but it is a technique as well as a genre; as described earlier, in Chapter 2, it functions as the interruption of the logic paradigm, the leaving out of one part or another, either cause, change, or effect, in order to trigger our compulsive interest and our ambition to complete the logic paradigm and cement our understanding of the whole truth. Therefore mystery writing, as a technique, is found in any genre, and in Chapter 2 I described how the technique of mystery, among others, was used in Michael Haneke's *Amour*, a love story. It is equally prevalent in storytelling as its sister technique, dramatic irony, which is the multiplying of strands of logic, and if one combines instances of mystery as a technique across all genres, and as a genre in its own right when it stands as the dominant emotion evoked in the drama, it might be the most popular form of dramatic writing.

Mother (Bong Joon-ho 2009), written by Bong Joon-ho and Park Eun-kyo, is a South Korean film that executes its mystery on a strong line of desire from the eponymous Mother (Hye-ja Kim), whose nerves are strung tight from the outset by her love for her son, Do-joon (Won Bin), who is an amnesiac. He is arrested on suspicion of the murder of a schoolgirl and the evidence is overwhelming: a golf ball that he has signed with his name was found at the scene, but he 'can't remember' what happened. The audience knows that he followed her that night, that she disappeared into a pitch-dark alley, and then she threw a rock at him as he passed by, but he turned away and continued on his way. The next we see of him is when he arrives home and, untroubled, calmly goes to bed – and he shares his bed with his mother. The police tell him he must have done it, and they have prepared a confession. The pad of ink waits on his knee – he will press his thumb in the ink and imprint it on the confession, agreeing that he is the murderer – because they tell him that's the truth of the matter. He suffers from amnesia, and he believes them. They lock him in jail to await trial, and the case is closed.

In a frenzy of care for him, the mother sets out to uncover the truth. What happened in those moments after the girl threw the rock, after her son turned away, that led to the girl being murdered and draped over the parapet on the roof of the building for the whole town to see? This short gap in the time sequence is the focus of an intense mystery. The mother must find out what events filled this gap in the middle of the night in a small town in South Korea. She must find out how and why the girl went from alive to dead, and who did it. She must do so before her son goes to trial, and she pursues the mystery with a relentless, gritty, selfless, manic determination. The film intensifies her desire by making the police useless, and the lawyer she spends her savings on worse than useless. On the other side of the scratched Perspex that divides them she rails at her son, 'Why did you sign that confession?' He answers dumbly, 'If I killed her, I should have signed it.' He can't remember, as he so often can't remember – inside his head exists probably vital clues as to who killed the girl, Moon Ah-jung, and why. He must rub his temples (he and his mother have a word for this trick; they call it 'The Temples of Doom') until it comes back to him.

Meanwhile she fixes on Jin-tae (Ku Jin), the friend of her son, as a likely killer because he was in the army and is known to be violent. She betrays him to the police but she got it all wrong; it wasn't blood on Jin-tae's golf club, it was lipstick. She tearfully apologises to Jin-tae and after she has paid him 'settlement' he agrees to help her. Why was the body positioned up on the roof? It is as if it were displayed as a warning, for everyone to see…

In the prison yard, Do-joon rubs his temples, trying to remember. He rubs and rubs. Other inmates tease him: one advises another to 'call him a retard and see what happens'. Do-joon attacks wildly, just like he did before, at the beginning of the film, when someone called him a retard. They beat him up, badly. His eyes open … he can remember something, now.

The Mother's questioning of the mystery surges forward when she finds out that the victim, Moon Ah-jung, slept with many different men and secretly recorded her encounters on a 'pervert phone' so she could blackmail them. Wherever that phone is now, one of the pictures on it is undoubtedly that of her killer. The Mother unleashes Jin-tae on some glue-sniffing thugs who know something about the phone; and the Mother steps in front of the bloodied thug for the final bit of interrogation, which gives her the clue as to where to go and find the phone.

Do-joon, meanwhile, yes, remembered something when he was beaten up in the prison yard. Something important. He urgently calls for his mother to visit. She leans forward and begs him to tell her. He talks from behind his Perspex screen. This is it. 'When I was five, you tried to kill me. You gave me a Bacchus bottle with insecticide in it.'

The Mother is mortified, but it seems that it's true, she did try to kill him. She had been going to kill herself, too, and when she couldn't do it, she had rescued him, and forever afterwards she'd given him nothing but the best food, and cared for him with all the willpower at her disposal. This portrait of their desperate but loving relationship gives an ironic poignancy, now, to her vigorous desire to save his life, to get him out of jail.

She goes to where she thinks the pervert phone is, and she won't stop until it's found; she has it in her hand, opens it up. It switches on and the screen comes to life. There are the pictures – and she recognises one of the faces among the victim's lovers. It's the middle-aged man who gathers scrap from around the place; he lives out on the edge of the town. Fearlessly, without delay, alone, she hurries there.

The scrap-man is underneath a vehicle, fixing something. Cautiously she edges towards broaching the subject of Moon Ah-jung's murder. She is ready to defend herself, aware that she might be talking to the killer, or someone who knows the killer. He seems happy to talk about it. In fact, he feels really bad. Because he saw something that night, and he ought to tell the police.

He calmly relates how he saw the man who killed Moon Ah-jung – it was the man they have in jail, Do-joon, the Mother's son.

Her face tells us – she can't believe it.

Carried by the scrap-man's narration, a flashback fills in the gap in the logic: Do-joon followed the girl; she hid in a darkened alley. He passed by, and she threw the rock at him; that much is known already. He turned to continue on his way, because he was always a placid, peaceful man. But then, from her darkened alley, Moon Ah-jung had called out one single, accusing word, 'Retard!'

We seize on the word and lace together the points of logic arranged for us by the writers. Do-joon attacked because, when he's called a retard, he always does. We see what happened: Do-joon picked up the rock that she had thrown, and struck her. Afterwards, he'd tried to wake her up, and had carried her up to the roof, trying to make it all right for her.

It's a perfect twist:[3] the audience is riding along one strand of logic, and suddenly jumps to another, different strand of logic that suddenly becomes visible, although it was there all along, throughout the length of the previous events. Both strands of logic were always available, but we can *see*, now, how the other one is the true one.

The scrap-man is telling the Mother this, but without knowing who she is. Now he really should do his duty and call it in, make his statement, especially if, as seems to be the case, they are listening to new evidence and they are about to release Do-joon from custody. The police should know they have the right man. He must do his duty as a witness and call it in.

The Mother's singular, vigorous, evident desire – to save her son's life – won't be stopped now. It was her opinion that to uncover the truth would save her son, but now, to save her son, she must bury the truth, immediately. The pattern of irony is intensely satisfying. She finds a heavy wrench and strikes the scrap-man's skull even as he is dialling the police station. She herself becomes a murderer in order to save her son.

It is easy to put in front of an audience an inexplicable event and therefore to ask a big, initial question – who murdered Moon Ah-jung, and why? The writers' skill is evident in the way in which they create, in *Mother*, a pattern of mystery, by writing underneath the big question, which can't yet be answered, smaller questions that can be immediately answered, that lead towards the answer to the bigger question, complete with satisfying ironies and cognitions working across the events of the story.

---

[3]Cf. Chapter 2, page 87, 'Creating Strands of Logic – The Twist'

5   Anger and elevation – the legal drama

In *True to Our Feelings* (2007) Robert Solomon finds an unusual description of the way in which anger is sponsored by injustice or perceived injustice. It comes from Lewis Carroll's *Alice in Wonderland* – 'In a section called "The Mouse's Tail" he quips, "I'll be judge, I'll be jury, Said cunning old fury." This is, it turns out, a brilliant analysis of anger.' (Solomon, 23)

If we consult our own episodes of anger, it will be to find always an incidence of a wrong, or perceived wrong, committed against our person, or against another person for whom we feel sympathy.

> It is easy enough for us to appreciate the important role anger plays in life when other people do not always play by the rules, where one's territory and one's dignity are often trespassed against, in which our needs and desires are often frustrated. (Solomon, 14)

A further instance might be when we feel anger having observed *wrong-headed* anger in another person, if their anger is founded on a reading of justice with which we can't agree. Such wrong-headed anger is what gives this emotion a bad name. 'It is one of the seven deadly sins. It is demonised by the ancient Stoics, rejected by the Buddhists as among the worst "agitations," and has an awkward place at best in the Christian tradition.' (Solomon, 13) Our own anger is always deemed by us to be correct, of course, and given our vanity we are likely to overdo it, which further exacerbates the problem – leading to 'acts of retaliation and schemes of revenge' (16).

The flip side of anger is elevation – the sense of lift, ascension, when justice, *rightness*, is restored.

> Psychology has recently begun to study the emotion of elevation, a feeling that we all know but that science has hitherto spurned: the admiration for moral beauty, and the desire to emulate it, that we experience when we witness a singular act of kindness, gratitude, fortitude or the like – and that we feel no less intensely when we encounter it in fiction. (Boyd, 196)

It was Haidt (quoted in Prinz) who 'proposed the existence of an emotion that he calls elevation, which he describes as a positive response to moral beauty' (Prinz 2007, 81).

Chapter 3 described how the genesis of story was gossip, and the role of story in our evolution has been to groom the moral sensibility that will cement co-operative, egalitarian behaviour – fairness – and therefore reward a more successful group or society. The production of oxytocin on receiving or granting co-operation is the same hormone as rewards us for love, and this term 'elevation' is identical to the feeling of love – it is our appraisal of the circumstances that divides the same feeling and calls it on the one hand love, and on the other hand justice, or elevation.

Given that stories exist in order for us to comb through, to rehearse, scenarios of right-and-wrong, it goes without saying that almost all stories of whatever genre involve the invigoration of this principle and its attached feelings in an audience (let's call it the anger-elevation axis), but to identify any work as being specifically in this genre, what might be termed a legal drama (as long as we can include in that term the idea of natural justice), means that within this drama the anger-elevation axis takes its place as the predominant set of feelings that the writer works to arouse.

It is the screenwriter's task to observe the architecture of these feelings, how they can be built. There is a top-down and a bottom-up approach.

In bands of hunter-gatherers, egalitarian behaviour within the band was easily achieved because each day started afresh with the simple requirement to catch prey, and the people they saw on any given day would probably be the same people they saw every day for the rest of their lives. Thus 'natural justice' worked; it was enough to gossip and therefore maintain or alter reputations, to repeat or invent stories, and punish offenders by shaming, by ridicule, or, as a last resort, by exclusion. 'Natural justice' works from the bottom up.

With the advent of farming, and land ownership, wealth could be stored, either in the form of land or of crops, and that same wealth could be raided, stolen, overrun, and a growing population meant an increased likelihood of meeting strangers, who might be cheats, thieves or bullies. With ownership of lands and crops, armies and defence became inevitable, as well as forms of hierarchy, and of central concern in the new model of fairness would be the coaching of an individual's acceptance of their place in that hierarchy. The bottom-up method of ensuring egalitarian behaviour (gossip and shaming and stories – 'natural justice') had to be reinforced by top-down structures: the law, with its army of enforcers, the police and prison systems; and also religion, with its powerful, mythical, exaggerated stories and its elevating rituals and buildings, as well as its punishment structures. Such a top-down determination of moral structures might be termed 'societal justice'. However, societal justice is often a mask worn by bullies to enforce co-operative behaviour in a resource-gathering project of some description, and it is still, as it ever was, the work of storytelling to coach our appreciation of natural justice and thereby instil in our society or group the benefits of co-operation, both from the top down and the bottom up. In this sense storytelling is always a political act.

The legal drama, as a genre, can therefore be defined as one that takes for its principal mood or feeling the dramatic expression of justice, either natural justice, from the ground up, or societal justice, from the top down, or, most commonly, both ends are played against the middle, against each other, in our continual attempts to argue true right from wrong, to groom ourselves and our societies to operate with perfect, elevating egalitarianism, and therefore achieve trust, and success.

A film that plays out a story of natural justice right next to one of societal justice is *To Kill a Mockingbird* (Mulligan 1962), adapted by Horton Foote from Harper Lee's novel.

The film opens with the two forms of justice, natural and societal, meeting, as it were, in an allegorical handshake. A farmer, Mr Cunningham (Crahan Denton), impoverished by the 1929 financial crash, arrives with a sack of hickory nuts to pay the town's lawyer, Atticus Finch (Gregory Peck), for legal services that Atticus performed for free. From the ground up, the farmer is sharing his produce. From the top down, Atticus has shared his expertise in societal justice with a farmer, who is below him in the hierarchy of wealth and position.

'He's paying me the only way he can,' Atticus explains to his daughter, Scout (Mary Badham). 'The crash hit them the hardest.'

Scout blithely accepts the farmer's nuts on behalf of her father. She is more concerned, this summer, with spying on a neighbour, Arthur 'Boo'

Radley (Robert Duvall), who is never seen, whose very name – Boo! – gives the idea of a fright.

Children occupy more visibly the territory of natural justice – they are more obviously the bully, the cheat, the thief and the free-rider because they have not yet learned how to hide these traits or quell them. And they are more obviously the genuinely kind, the generous-hearted. Immediately we can judge Scout to be an optimistic, adventurous, fair-minded child, quick to give and quick to fight. Her occasional piques of selfishness are just the seasoning that allows us to enjoy more the sweetness of her nature.

Scout and her brother Jem (Phillip Alford) are frightened of Boo Radley. They have listened, awestruck, to the gossip that has gone around the town for years, which has cemented Boo's reputation as a monster. In terms of dramatic archetype, a monster is a bully with supernatural powers.

Jem describes Boo's father. 'There goes the meanest man that ever took a breath of life.'

How come, asks Dill (John Megna), the boy who is spending the summer next door with his aunt.

'For one thing,' answers Jem, 'he has a boy named Boo, that he keeps chained to the bed in a house over yonder … Boo only ever comes out at night, when you're asleep and it's pitch dark.'

'Wonder what he looks like?' asks Dill.

'Well, judging by his tracks, he's about six-and-a-half feet tall. He eats raw squirrels and all the cats he can cage. There's a long scar that runs all the way across his face. His teeth are yellow and rotten, his eyes are popped, and he drools most of the time.'

It's a wonderfully inventive description that we can judge is exaggerated gossip. Dill doesn't believe it, but his aunt comes over and warns him off the house. 'There's a maniac lives there and he's dangerous.'

This is natural justice – gossip circulating and accreting until it leads to moral disapproval, anger and the exclusion of the offending individual from society.

The audience, however, reads the exaggerated nature of the gossip, and at the same time as enjoying the inventive description we read it as probably wrong, and thus we are ready to judge this society, the town itself, as acting unfairly.

It's confirmed that the town of Maycomb has a vicious element when Scout kindly says to an elderly neighbour sitting on her porch, 'Hi, Miss de Bose,' and Miss de Bose screeches back, 'Don't you say "Hi" to me, you ugly girl.'

Atticus doesn't become angry with Miss de Bose, and therefore demonstrates his forgiving nature. Instead he stands admiring Miss de Bose's flowers, and his generosity to Miss de Bose stops the old lady in her tracks. We can see how generosity, acts that are beyond fair, positively inclusive, might mend the situation – this kind of pro-social forgiveness will be subtly repeated in this film.

When Atticus tucks Scout into bed that night his instruction echoes our moral reading of the situation. 'Leave those poor people alone,' he advises her, talking of the Radleys. 'Stop tormenting them.' His disapproval is the mildest form of pro-social punishment, but it counts, and furthermore it is followed by an episode of sharing, of generosity, in one of the most touchingly acted scenes in the film. Scout, lying back against the pillows, fiddles with her father's pocket watch, and hears again how it will be left to her brother, Jem, when her father dies, while she, on the other hand, will receive a necklace that belonged to her mother, who died not long after Scout was born.

At around eighteen minutes into the film, while Atticus is on his own, taking the night air on the porch, Judge Taylor (Paul Fix) arrives and appoints Atticus to the 'Tom Robinson case'. Nothing is said about the case itself, and Atticus merely replies, 'I'll take the case.' This 'notwriting' evokes our curiosity, especially since the register and tone of the dialogue allows us to judge the subtext – the Tom Robinson case is a dangerous one.

The legal battle between Tom Robinson and Bob Ewell will be the topdown dramatisation of societal justice, and it will be a story of prejudice and persecution that ends with anger, injustice. Meanwhile the story of the children, Scout, Jem and Dill, versus the 'monster' Boo Radley, will dramatise natural justice, from the bottom up, and it will be the story of prejudice and persecution that ends with elevation, justice.

The two stories will run alongside each other, intertwine, and they will comment on each other – natural justice the province of the children's story and societal justice the province of the adult's story.

The children are running their usual persecution of Boo Radley – Scout rolls herself up in a tyre and accidentally bumps up against Boo's porch step, whereupon Jem cries, 'Get out of there,' and he runs up and bangs on Boo's door, just for the sake of it. Dill, their friend (who in real life is based on Lee's childhood friend, Truman Capote), makes a suggestion, 'Let's go down to the courthouse and see the room they left Boo locked up in. They say he nearly died from the mildew.' The idea of Boo and the children's fear of him, prejudice against him, is carried right into the courthouse, where the children, hoisting Dill on their shoulders, can get a sense of what's going on in the adult courtroom.

Dill, looking through the window, reports down to them, 'The judge looks like he's asleep', which is an early indicator that societal justice is dangerously undermined in this town, especially given the following observations granted to us by Dill –

'I see your daddy and a coloured man. The coloured man looks to me like he's crying … There's a whole lot of men standing on one side, and one man is pointing at the coloured man and yelling. They're taking the coloured man away.'

Atticus is seen standing with the coloured man, which must be Tom Robinson. The writers are generously not-writing to allow us small cognitions.

Atticus sees the children spying on the courtroom and demands to know what they're doing. Scout says, 'We came to see where Boo Radley was locked up. We wanted to see the bats.' The innocence and humour contribute to the irony of these two stories, juvenile and adult, running alongside each other.

As the children disperse, the camera lingers to introduce Bob Ewell (James Anderson) – the father of the girl, a white girl, whom Tom Robinson (Brock Peters), a black man, is accused of raping. Ewell is there to make sure Atticus is going to join in with the same kind of racial prejudice that infects every word and every expression of this drink-fuelled farmer. 'Kill him myself!' Ewell says of Tom Robinson, which would save the state some time and money. Ewell wants to be able to reassure his friends that 'Mr Finch ain't taking his story again ourn… '

When Atticus firmly positions himself as a fair upholder of the law, Ewell is angry, slighted; an injustice has been done to him, is his perception. 'What kind of man are you, you got chillun of your own,' rages Ewell.

The audience's anger is aroused at the wrong-headedness of Ewell's anger.

Meanwhile the children, in their innocent way, persecute Boo Radley. Late at night they determine to creep up to his windows, 'To get a look at Boo Radley.'

Jem steals up to the house … and Boo is a huge shadow pouring over him as he cowers against the side of the house. It's terrifying and the audience can remember the words of the narrator, an adult Scout looking back, that opened the film – the town of Maycomb had 'Nothing to fear but fear itself.'

The children run in terror, leaving Jem's trousers behind, stuck in the fence.

Time rolls forward, and it's Scout's first day at school; and she has to wear a dress.

At school, the first thing Scout does is attack a boy. It's a mystery as to why, but we snatch the name 'Cunningham' from the scuffed-up dialogue and remember the farmer who delivered the hickory nuts to the Finch household at the beginning of the film. Is this his son?

Jem pulls Scout off. 'He made me get off on the wrong foot,' Scout points at the Cunningham boy. 'I was trying to explain to the teacher why he didn't have any money for his lunch. And she got sore at me.'

Jem finds out that the boy is Walter Cunningham, the farmer's son. Jem is wearing a tie, and school uniform, and we observe his father's generosity filter down to his behaviour, just as we can understand Boo Radley might be a monster because his father has treated him so meanly. Like his father, Jem mends the situation by giving, being generous – 'Well, come home and have dinner with us, Walter. We'll be glad to have you.' Silence from Walter. 'Our daddy's a friend of your daddy's.' We are moved, elevated, by this evidence of what is beyond fair – a generous, reciprocal altruism.

In the very next scene a plate of food is put in front of Walter, and he pipes up, 'I don't know when I've had roast. We've been having squirrels and rabbits lately.' The sense of elevation continues, as Walter asks for syrup.

Around the dinner table, Atticus tells the children the story of his first gun. Apparently his father 'rather I shot tin cans in the yard.' But after a while the older man could see that the temptation would be for thirteen-year-old Atticus to go after birds. Atticus remembers how his father laid down the ground rules. 'I could shoot all the bluejays I wanted, if I could get 'em. But to remember, it was a sin to kill a mockingbird.'

'Why?' asks Jem.

'Because mockingbirds don't do anything but make music for us to enjoy … they don't do one thing but just sing their hearts out for us.' It's a story that delivers its narrative pleasure on two counts: we enjoy the piece of logic work that always comes with the appraisal of metaphor or allegory, and we have heard the title of the film repeated to us and we understand that this town, Maycomb, is a town of bluejays, screeching and acquisitive, territorial, aggressive, attacking and killing other birds and destroying their nests, while Atticus and his family are among the mockingbirds, who never harm anyone. The music in the film is now tied to the use of music in the allegory, as the song of the mocking-bird (which often imitates the songs of other birds in an expression of what might be empathy) causes that identical sense of elevation as in the narrative.[4]

Calpurnia or 'Cal', the maid (Estelle Evans), brings the syrup, now, and we might deduce that the sack of hickory nuts brought to the house in the film's opening scene has been used to make hickory syrup and therefore Walter's father's sharing his produce with Atticus is now precisely repaid in an act of reciprocal altruism visited on Walter, the son, when the latter nearly empties the whole jug onto his plate. 'He's gone and drownded his dinner in syrup,' says Scout and gets a sound ticking off from Cal in the kitchen. She runs from the house.

Atticus goes to soothe Scout and we now hear the story of the fight in the school yard. A teacher had seen that Walter didn't have money for a

---

[4]Boyd describes how any art causes elevation, as it 'promises pleasure, commands attention, stirs the senses and emotions, and arouses pride and awe at the effects produced and the mastery exhibited' (118). Also see Boyd pages 114–125 for a description of how religion sequesters art in order to harness its effect and create for itself that same elevation, *rightness*, ascension.

school lunch and had tried to give him a quarter, 'But everyone knows the Cunninghams won't take nothing from nobody' – and Scout had interfered and got off on the wrong foot.

The Cunninghams are the noble poor, with a sound reading of the ethics of reciprocal altruism – they won't agree to receive because they can't give back.

It is around forty-one minutes into the film, and Atticus gives the story's defining message, 'You never really understand a person until you consider things from his point of view', which is a definition of empathy. Empathy is the emotion that fuels co-operation, trust, justice. Empathy is the currency of storytelling; we pick up stories and use them to coach ourselves in empathy; it is the feeling that underpins natural justice and it is written into the fabric of all drama.[5]

Atticus explains how compromise works – an argument results in a bargain being struck; it's a reaching for synthesis and agreement – co-operation. A successful society. Maycomb isn't a successful society; its only hope is to follow the example of Atticus (and the town's black community, as will be seen later).

Suddenly a rabid dog is staggering in the street. The dog is sick with a mad kind of aggression, just as Maycomb is. Atticus doesn't own a gun and has always refused to give one to his son, Jem, but now a rifle is put in Atticus's hands. He aims carefully and shoots the dog. It turns out that Atticus is a crack shot – 'Best shot in this town' – which earns him a new, grave respect from his son. America has always upheld the gun as an instrument of justice, but Atticus never uses a gun.

Positioned right next to the scene of the mad dog staggering in the street is a scene that shows a mad white man staggering in the street – mad with drink and prejudice, just as dangerous as the rabid dog.

Atticus is visiting the household of his client, Tom Robinson, and while Atticus is in the house his son, Jem, waits in the car. A boy his age, a black boy, approaches the car, which is a status symbol far out of the

---

[5]Widely cited research shows empathy is the one quality missing from the criminal mind and there-fore story initiatives in prisons (e.g. Storybook Dads, Stories Connect and the programme run by the Royal Literary Fund) suddenly appear to be of critical importance.

reach of this family. The black boy and the white boy, looking at each other from either side of privilege, share a simple wave, an expression of greeting and respect, that evokes a strong feeling of elevation in the audience, given that Atticus (a lone example in this town of societal justice also being an instrument of natural justice) is defending Tom Robinson, who is black. It is a moment of grace, ascension.

The father of the rape victim, Bob Ewell, the mad dog, staggers into view and approaches the car. He is drunk.

Atticus is called from the house. Ewell accuses Atticus angrily, 'You nigger lover!'

Atticus drives the car away, and Ewell is left staggering in the street, precisely the image of the dog that we saw in the scene before. Atticus's aim in the courthouse, in the upcoming trial, is going to be just as precise, but the mad dog will not die; Tom Robinson does.

Solomon finds in Aristotle's *Rhetoric* that 'anger is a distressed desire for conspicuous vengeance in return for a conspicuous and unjustifiable slight of one's person or friends' (Solomon, 20), and furthermore, in distinguishing anger from irritation or annoyance, anger 'necessarily involves a moral judgement' (20). In this case the audience is angry with Ewell's racism, his prejudice; and it is prejudice that means that the society of Maycomb is divided, unco-operative, failing. If, however, a member of the audience subscribes to the same racial prejudice, the affect of the film's story on such a member of the audience would be different. 'In anger, the subject casts him or herself in the superior role of judge and jury. Thus the phenomenology of anger involves a sort of courtroom scenario.' (Solomon, 20)

Just beyond fifty minutes into the film, Jem is left guarding the house at night, and is led a short distance from the house to find, in a hole in a tree, a gift or offering of some kind. It looks like a medal. We are generously allowed by the writer our cognition that this gift has been left there by Boo Radley. There are more of them: this time, two small figures portraying Jem and Scout, carved out of soap stone.

The mean-looking, wordless father, Mr Radley, blocks up the hole in the tree with cement.

It's revealed that gifts have been left in the tree over a period of years and Jem has been secretly keeping them. We recognise the items from the film's title sequence. Among the treasures that have been left in the tree, and that Jem has been keeping in a special box, is a medal awarded for spelling in school, and a broken pocket watch. We have already learned that a pocket watch is a symbol of family love, passed from father to son, and Boo Radley, the young man who is never seen although he lives next door, has given his watch, a broken one, to Jem. Our delight in playing the logic-game of metaphor or allegory leads us to attach the watch to what must be, then, Boo Radley's paternal love for Jem and Scout. This is confirmed when we hear from Jem that when he went back to get his trousers that were caught in the fence, he found they were no longer tangled in the wire, but 'they were folded across the fence, sort of like they were expecting me.' It's a feeling of familial love that is precisely the same, biologically the same, as elevation, or justice. Thus props, or properties – the gifts in the tree, the trousers tangled in the fence – to the extent that they are suffused with meaning by the writer, evoke in drama a precisely engineered emotion.

On the bottom-up, 'natural justice' side of the film, the children's (and the audience's) perception of Boo Radley is changing, and thus, the audience instinctively feels, is moving towards truth, fairness and co-operation. The top-down 'societal justice' side of the story, the trial of Tom Robinson, is moving the opposite way, towards truth and *in*justice, unfairness, lack of co-operation.

'His trial is tomorrow,' Atticus tells his children. Tom Robinson, accused of the rape of Ewell's daughter, has, for his own safety, been kept in a jail in a neighbouring town. This evening, the day before his trial, he has been moved back to the dysfunctional town of Maycomb. Even in the town's jail Tom Robinson will be in danger from the men 'out at Old Sarum.'

Atticus decides to spend the night on the steps outside the jail in order to guard Tom Robinson and protect societal justice from the wrong-headed natural justice that is felt in the anger of Ewell and his like out at Old Sarum, a name that is close to 'scarum'.

In the middle of the night the men from Old Sarum descend on Maycomb in convoy. The sound of their car engines is exaggerated; it's like a squadron of aircraft are descending on the steps leading to the town's jail where Atticus shines in the darkness in his white suit.

Unknown to Atticus, Scout and Jem are watching from the bushes over the road as the men form a mob and approach the steps of the jail.

Atticus is one man; they are many. Atticus is unarmed (although we know he's the town's best shot); they are armed.

These are the town bullies. Their anger in this scene is a negative emotion, almost a 'severe personality disorder' (Solomon, 20) because it promotes bullying and exclusion, the opposite of co-operation, whereas *our* anger at *their* anger is a positive emotion, because our anger promotes inclusion and co-operation, and therefore makes it *rightful*.

'Get aside from that door, Mr Finch.'

It's Walter Cunningham, who brought the hickory nuts, whose hungry son 'drownded' his meal in the syrup made from those nuts. The children's and the adults' stories touch together and we gain intense satisfaction from lacing together the moral irony.

The children rush across the road, worm their way through the crowd and stand next to Atticus to defend him. Movingly, he instructs them to go home, and just as powerfully, they refuse to do as they're told.

Scout sees in the crowd someone she knows. 'Hey, Mr Cunningham,' she says and the script is now filled with multiple strands of irony – the hickory nuts, the syrup, Scout trying to defend Walter but then attacking him, their taking Walter home and feeding him. We piece together the pattern of sharing, co-operation, and its opposite, the bullying behaviour, mean prejudice and violence. Dramatic irony also is in play, because we understand more than Scout about life, about prejudice. And thus we are so deeply moved by Scout's innocent, goodhearted greeting.

'How's your entailment getting along? Don't you remember me, Mr Cunningham? I'm Scout Louise Finch. You brought us some hickory nuts one morning, remember? We had a talk. I went and got my daddy to come out and thank you. I go to school with your boy. I go to school with Walter. He's a nice boy. Tell him hey for me, won't you? You know what, entailments are bad ... '

The shame of Walter Cunningham fills us with a stirring elevation. Scout asks him, 'What's the matter? I sure meant no harm Mr Cunningham.'

The bullies have been floored by Scout's innocence and friendship. Their shame reads in their faces. 'I'll tell Walter you said hey,' says

Mr Cunningham. The bullies disperse. We are elated at the righteous type of natural justice protecting, just for a while, Atticus's right-minded execution of societal justice.

A little over an hour into the film, the trial scene forms a drama in its own right. In a packed courtroom Atticus's children can only find enough space to stand with the 'coloured folk' up on the balcony, and the children are welcomed there particularly by a man with a silver cross showing against his waistcoat. This is racial tolerance, inclusion, the opposite of the prejudice, exclusion and violence that will be so evident in the courtroom below.

The trial scene is remarkable for the gracefulness with which it allows the audience to piece together the truth of the story and the righteousness of Tom Robinson, represented by Atticus.

Bob Ewell swears on the Bible to tell the truth. He was collecting wood and came back to hear of something going on in his house. He ran up to the window. 'I seen him with my Mayella,' he cries. He witnessed Tom Robinson beating up and raping his daughter. He ran around and chased after him in the dark. 'But I seen who it was all right.'

Atticus focuses the court's attention on the injuries to Mayella: she had bruises all the way around her neck, and, Ewell agrees, yes, 'her right eye, I remember she was beat up on that side of her face.'

Atticus asks if Ewell can read and write. Yes, says Ewell, and is pleased to demonstrate, laboriously writing his name. He writes with his left hand. We lace together the logic: the bruising was on the right side of Mayella's face. It was Ewell who beat up his own daughter.

'Call Mayella Violet Ewell.'

Mayella (Collin Wilcox), the victim, takes the stand, but the fact that she doesn't put her hand actually on the Bible, but instead lets it hover an inch above, allows the audience to infer that she is going to lie. 'I fought him hard … but he hit me … again and again.'

Atticus asks, 'Is your father good to you?'

'Tolerable … Except when he's drinking.'

'Has he ever hit you?'

Mayella is distressed, almost incoherent. 'My Pa's never touched a hair of my head in my life.' She is lying. 'I got something to say and then I ain't go to say no more. He took advantage of me.' She loses it, curses everyone in a virulent, long outburst, and then runs from the courtroom.

When Tom Robinson takes the stand, he is invited by Atticus to catch a glass. Atticus throws it. Tom's right hand lifts instinctively to catch the glass. He's right handed. Moreover, Tom admits, 'Can't use my left hand at all.' It was caught in a cotton gin and 'All my muscles were tore loose.' The audience can now confirm their earlier guess: Tom Robinson could not have inflicted those injuries on Mayella.

Tom gives his version of events: Mayella, alone and friendless, habitually greeted him. 'I'd tip my hat when I passed by,' he says. She'd invite him to come into the house and he'd perform chores for her, 'chopping kindling, or drawing water.' He'd do these chores for free. On this occasion, she invited him in the house, telling him that a door needed fixing – but the door was all right. It was unusual because the house was so quiet; there was not a child on the place. 'Where the childrun?' he'd asked her. She'd answered that it had taken her a year to save the nickles to send them to town to buy ice-creams.

She invited him to fetch a box down from on top of the chifforobe, then she'd grabbed him round the legs. He was scared and hopped down. 'And I turned around and she sort of jumped on me, hugged me around the waist, kissed me on the face. She'd never kissed a grown man before … '

Bob Ewell had seen them. He'd 'cussed her from the window and said he's gonna kill her.'

'Did you rape Mayella Ewell?' asks Atticus.

'I did not.'

Atticus has exposed the lies of the prosecution case but still is graceful in his pity for the victim, Mayella. 'I have nothing but pity in my heart for the chief witness for the state … But my pity does not extend so far as to put in danger a man's life.' He points out that Mayella's only crime was to have broken a moral code – 'She is white and tempted a black man … she kissed a black man.' To have broken this code was such a severe transgression that 'She must destroy the evidence of her offence' and lie, in concert with her father. 'The defendant is not guilty,' asserts Atticus, 'but someone in this courtroom is … ' He means the cheat and bully, Bob Ewell. Robinson must be released, and Atticus makes sure of it with his instruction to the jury. 'In the name of God, do your duty. In the name of God, believe Tom Robinson.' Surges of elevation, of lift, are granted to the audience at this expression of the justice system at work – natural justice and societal justice working together.

Two hours later the jury are called back in after their deliberations. 'Have you reached a verdict?' asks Judge Taylor.

'We have, your honour.'

'What is your verdict?'

'We find the defendant guilty as charged.'

Justice does not prevail. The story relentlessly persecutes Tom Robinson. The truth of the matter – racial prejudice corrupting the justice system – wins out, and through our dismay, our appraisal of bare-faced injustice, we applaud the writers for revealing the truth.

The courtroom empties. Upstairs, in the gallery, the black spectators are all still there. They stand for Atticus, a lone figure below. Their lack of anger (the feeling that has been so destructive when deployed negatively by the whites), and their silent appreciation of Atticus's efforts, arouses intense feelings of elevation, catharsis, in the audience. The world is all wrong, but the writer knows exactly how it is wrong, and has showed us the truth.

The suffering continues. Atticus has to carry even worse news to the family: Tom Robinson is dead. 'They were taking him to Abbotsville for safekeeping' and a guard 'shot at him to wound him, but missed his aim. Killed him.'

Ewell appears again, outside the house. He spits in Atticus's face. Atticus holds onto his anger, doesn't let it go. He takes out his handkerchief and wipes his face.

The top-down story of societal justice has been completed, with societal justice apparently performed but wrongly, brokenly, with true, natural justice denied in the case of Tom Robinson. It remains to finish the story of Boo, the bottom-up story of natural justice.

The narrator – Scout as an adult – rolls us forward to September. 'I still looked for Boo.' Scout is dressed as a ham in order to attend a pageant celebrating agricultural produce. Her costume only has a slot for her eyes; otherwise she is completely covered.

Scout is walking with her brother Jem through the woods in the dark. 'Hush a minute, Scout. I thought I heard something.'

Scout hears it as well.

A figure attacks – a figure dressed in black. Jem is knocked out. Scout, in the ham, is caught up in a wrestling match between a figure in black and a figure wearing white. Scout's reduction to just a pair of eyes emphasises that it is what we see, and how we see, that makes all the difference. There is emphatic use of the image of the hand, in this scene – because it is what we do, with our hands, that also makes all the difference.

The figure with the white trousers wins the fight. This figure can be seen carrying the unconscious Jem back to the house. Scout runs after them, to find Jem in bed, still unconscious.

Golden-haired Boo Radley is behind the door. He was their saviour.

'Hey Boo,' says Scout.

'Mr Arthur Radley.' Atticus accords Boo his full name and title.

The gentle kindness of Boo Radley is confirmed. He has saved the lives of the children by defending them from this murderous attack by Bob Ewell, who lies dead, a knife in his ribs.

Societal justice failed, but natural justice found a way to exert its power and kill Bob Ewell. And natural justice still prevails – it would be 'a sin' to drag Boo Radley through the courts. 'Sort of like shooting a mockingbird, wouldn't it?' says Scout. They will keep quiet, and allow natural justice to take effect.

Atticus shakes Boo Radley's hand. 'Thank you for my children,' he says.

The narrator, Scout as an adult, sums it up. 'He gave us two soap dolls, a watch, a knife, and our lives.'

6   Love

The fact that oxytocin is the biological reward granted both for feelings of love and for feelings of elevation (following any other type of sharing or co-operation) accounts for the similarity in effect of *Agape*, the love of rightness, usually described as love between God and humankind, and *Eros*, sexual love (and what is *eros* if not the most intimate sharing). This euphoric chemical should thus be doubly available as a reward for the love story that also (as all stories should) grooms our moral understanding.

Love Is Strange (2014), directed by Ira Sachs and written by Sachs and Mauricio Zacharias, squares up to the problem faced by most writers in order to evoke any kind of feeling of love in an audience: to create a rush of feeling it's first necessary to create its opposite, a vacuum empty of the prescribed emotion, in order that its effect will be felt when the vacuum is filled. This structural problem creates the architectural question of all love stories – what keeps the lovers apart? Clichés abound, on all sides, in this most valuable of genres.

Sachs and Zacharias refresh the cliché by looking for opposites: if the cliché of a love story is to have a young man and young woman as protagonists, they will have two old men; if the cliché asks for boy-meets-girl, they'll have their two old men having already, at the outset of the film, spent thirty-nine years living together. However, the question is the same: what keeps the lovers apart, how is the *absence* of love created, the vacuum? The moral play of events is usually invoked here – in *Romeo and Juliet* and in *West Side Story* and in Blackman's *Noughts & Crosses*, one title forming the inspiration for the next, it is the prejudice of different groups, their refusal to co-operate between groups, to mix their blood, that creates the separation of the lovers across the divide between different tribes. In *Love Is Strange* the writers find the architectural design of the story is available in an area where society's moral code, the law, has recently changed. Two elderly men are now legally allowed to marry, and are happy to do so in the film's opening scene. However, George (Alfred Molina) is a music teacher in a Catholic school and his sudden visibility as a homosexual means he loses his job. This act of intolerance, the bullying of a top-down religious moral structure, means the two old men lose their income and can no longer afford their comfortable apartment and, given how crowded the city is, when their friends and family get together to work out where the two men can go, the result is that George must stay in one apartment with two gay cops, Roberto and Ted, while Ben will stay with his nephew Elliot, Elliot's wife Kate and their son Joey. The lovers are thus separated, and their desire to be together is expressed in their placid, evident and singular desire to find an apartment they can afford. The recruitment of the audience and the intensification of the audience's desire for the two men to be together again is created by the moral scenarios played out in each of these two apartments.

George must sleep on the sofa at Roberto and Ted's apartment, and given that Roberto and Ted are sociable, party-loving young men, the film portrays an increasingly glum George as the parties become louder, and more crowded, and he must wait even longer for his bed, the sofa, to be available for him to sleep on. It's heartbreaking.

Meanwhile, on Ben's side, the pattern of sharing and co-operation also becomes increasingly difficult as Ben, every night, has to sleep in the bottom bunk of the bedroom occupied by his grand-nephew, Joey, who at thirteen is just the wrong age to be asked to share his bedroom with an old man. Joey has a Russian friend called Vlad, and Ben's offering to paint Vlad on the roof of the apartment causes Joey to become increasingly rude and in the end unforgivably aggressive towards the older man, his great-uncle. Joey's bullying behaviour is only lifted once, when Ben, from the bottom bunk, asks him if he's ever been in love. Joey answers that perhaps he was, but didn't dare say a word to the girl concerned. Ben gives the softest, most obvious piece of advice – talk to her.

During the day, when Ben can occupy the living room, he instead trespasses on the concentration that Kate must give to the writing of her novel at a desk in the same room. Each gentle, affectionate phrase that Ben politely utters, as he sits there, prevents her from working, and with a final, excruciating irony Ben says that he himself can't work, as a painter, if there is someone else in the room. Blind irony, that wonderfully two-handed display of logic, lifts the moral picture, the impossibility of sharing, into a more powerfully dramatic mode of expression.

The audience is mortified at the undignified position in which the film puts these two elderly lovers, Ben and George, and increasingly longs for them to be allowed back together, the more that the sharing environments in both their temporary apartments deteriorate.

This vacuum, this absence of love, finally looks like it's going to be filled, given a lucky break with a rent-controlled apartment belonging to a new acquaintance suddenly offered to them, but a further irony pitifully disallows our satisfaction when the film skips forward in time, deliberately misses out events, and shows only one of the old men, the younger, George, finally occupying the longed-for new apartment. The break in logic generously allows us to work, to scrabble for the missing event, and earn our place in the story by working out that Ben, the older man, is dead, his funeral already behind us.

However, a rush of oxytocin, of love, is allowed to us after all – but from an unexpected source. George receives a visit from thirteen-year-old Joey, who brings the picture that Ben painted of the Russian friend, Vlad, on the roof. Joey simply leaves the picture with George, but then, in the stairwell on the way down from the new apartment, carrying his skateboard, Joey stops, dead still, utterly alone, and is taken over by a sudden, intense episode of tears. The audience rushes to understand this, and we know for certain we are watching the boy's remorse at his bullying of his late great-uncle. Our love for the remorse that shows itself so privately in Joey provides the sense of elevation, of rightness, of love, that we were expecting to gain from the two old men finally living together again. This wrong-footing of the audience's expectations, combined with the evoking of the feeling of elevation (identical to love), is further celebrated when Joey leaves the building and, out on the street, skateboards carelessly, easily, in the company of a girl of his own age. We lace together the sight of this girl with the one good conversation that occurred between Joey and his great-uncle, and we realise – Joey must have, yes, talked to her. It is as if the older man's wisdom about love has been handed down to create the new love that would seem to have sprung up between the two teenagers moving so freely down the city streets.

The architecture of the love story depends more than in most genres on the wholesale obstruction of the emotion for the extent of the film before the graceful removing of the obstruction to create in the audience a consequent rush of that emotion, so the screenwriter's chief work will be to invent the obstruction, and keep it in place in such a way as to deploy the moral fibre of the story.

The hunger in the audience for such a pleasurable emotion as love has created a large population of clichés – the genre is thick with them. Love 'is, in a word, *hypercognised*' (Solomon, 51). Moreover, a modern audience's attitude to love is complicated by a realism, or cynicism, that rubs away at the Western, historically Christian, fairytale model for romantic love that C.S. Lewis advised us was born in medieval France. There has always been a professional cynicism about love among psychologists.

Prinz paraphrases the evolutionary psychologist Robert Frank's (1988) analysis –

> Love is a way of signalling that you are devoted and that you would incur a great cost (misery) if the relationship should come to an end. If two individuals 'fall in love' they make the cost of a break-up prohibitively high, which makes the risk of investing in the relationship seem worthwhile. Love forges commitments by saddling infidelity with mutually assured despair. (Prinz 2004, 109)

This is the cynicism of the reductionists, but there is also the cynicism of the constructionists, who believe emotions are skills that one can improve at, like sport, with love being particularly good fun, not to mention competitive. Both analyses might be termed cynical – 'It is hard to know which is more cynical, reductionism or constructionism. On the former, love is an evolutionary insurance policy, and on the latter, it is a French fad that happened to stick.' (Prinz 2004, 113)

However, realism (or cynicism) has bled into the public domain not because audiences have been reading evolutionary psychology textbooks but because romantic love has failed often enough, badly enough, that a species awareness of the reality has seeped into our appraisal of love.

On top of that, further difficulties arise for screenwriters setting love stories in the West because more liberal, tolerant social mores have created fewer opportunities to invent obstacles that will keep lovers apart. Some writers (like Sachs and Zacharias, above) have found their material in these changing social mores (another example is *Brokeback Mountain*) but on the whole love stories are more rare (although they can be found as a more or less slight component within almost all films), and often the love story is combined with another genre, for instance comedy, to make up for the difficulty in writing a story that evokes purely love.

7   Conclusion

It is clear that the four instincts described above are not separate but instead are intertwined. A desire is an emotion; the 'appraisal' part of an emotion often involves a moral judgement; the moral judgement is in itself the operation of logic's pulleys and levers, and 'high level cognitive processing can reach down in to the emotional systems' (Rolls 2007, 451).

The writer's and the audience's instinct for plot, for story, meet in the middle, in the drama, and both are experts, but it is the writer's work to labour for long hours to create the belief system that is a story, only for the quick and greedy consumption by an audience in an hour or two.

It is difficult to have written this book without coming to the conclusion that to watch films and to write them is not only an entertainment but a grave responsibility. Morality in the human creature was born out of a biological imperative to co-operate, first within families and then within groups, and the fight against selfishness depends on a continual assessment of oneself and others in the group. But the challenge of our age is defined by the next step in the evolution of story: if co-operation grew *within* families and then *within* bands or groups, then the opposite impulse has sprung up *between* groups: competition, enmity and aggression. Co-operation was and still is the key to survival, and to thriving, as the reality TV show *The Island with Bear Grylls* attests. But can the human creature foster co-operation between groups as well as within them? To achieve this end is it possible to create a group-of-groups? Or can groups dissolve their differences? It's a much harder task but it might be evolving now – or not. At the time of writing Britain has just voted to leave the European Union. The argument was always a moral one: co-operation within which group, competition between which groups?

Evolution was the 'blind watchmaker' that orchestrated the use of story as the mechanical tool for tightening co-operation, but evolution can lead to unexpected after-effects. It is an unlooked-for result that clever and manipulative bully/cheat figures can turn the process on its head, and use stories to create a group, recruit a population and harness the group's supernaturally willing, energetic co-operation in a project, an apparently religious or a racial/political project, but usually, in fact, a sequestering of resources, of wealth, which might be punishing to the individual, at worst fatally destructive to the individual, let alone to other groups with which it comes into contact. It seems only logical that the most fantastic levels of co-operation can only be created by the most fantastic and incredible stories.

Zak and other moral philosophers note that morality has grown from the bottom up; however, it is easy to see that our internal biological workings, the instinct for morality and therefore for story, inevitably created religious stories that provide a set of symbols and a methodology, a system of morality, that is then prescribed from the top down. Religious stories, fictional myths, did not create our moral instinct but merely trade on its effects. Religious movements therefore can be seen as the product of evolution, but a destructive one as well as a constructive one. They are one way in which that particular archetype of selfishness, the bully, smuggles his (and it nearly always is a 'he' due to the female's disposition towards oxytocin, and the male's disposition towards testosterone) self-aggrandising agenda into a hyper-co-operative scenario. Similarly a suite of laws or political ideals can also be a method by which a bully smuggles into a population a selfish project.

It can easily be seen, therefore, how many stories concern themselves with a battle between on the one hand 'natural' justice, what might be termed our biological instinct for co-operation, bottom-up morality, and on the other hand 'societal' justice, imposed from above either by a religious entity or a law-making political structure. These stories, like all stories, continue our training in the benefits, rewards both sensual and practical, of co-operation, empathy, forgiveness, and love.

The recruiting power of religious and political storytelling has led to the achievement of some of the greatest co-operative projects, not least in construction (pyramids, temples, cathedrals, churches, mosques, palaces and parliaments). These buildings put one in mind of the structures routinely built by other creatures that co-operate with one another even more efficiently than we do: ants, bees and wasps.

> They, too, may outdo us in contributing 'selflessly' to their societies, but if we look for homologies, we are sorely disappointed: basically, they are doing this in the absence of anything like an internalising conscience, gossip, group social pressure, shameful blushing, or moralistic capital punishment by angry, morally outraged bands. (Boehm, 329)

As Boehm says, evolution has found more than one way to arrive at the benefits of co-operation. The co-operation of wasps, bees and ants 'provide a striking analogy, which shows that natural selection can stumble into the making of a collectively oriented species in more ways than one' (Boehm, 329).

The co-operation of ants and bees is built on the use of pheromones, a chemical system rather than a moral one, and is therefore automatic and incorruptible; the unlooked-for tragedy in the co-operative machinery that evolved in humans is that, given language, storytelling has become the most powerful tool in our moral training, a resource for the emphatic deployment of morality, and it can therefore be corrupted as a method by which bullies can recruit and coerce a population into contributing to a project on any enormous scale that can be imagined. Storytelling becomes a method for enforcing top-down coercion, rather than an expression of bottom-up 'natural' morality. It is one of the challenges of our age, perhaps, for stories themselves to address this subject.

It's a question that's urgently being considered at the time of writing here in Europe with the UK having voted to leave the European Union and with migrant populations fleeing from violently untrustworthy, bullying political systems towards the more trustworthy societies. How do we evolve our co-operative efforts from here onwards? If it's true to say that 'Morality is a set of psychological adaptations that allow otherwise selfish individuals to reap the benefits of cooperation' (Greene, 20), then it's also clear, as stated above, that –

> this conclusion comes with an important caveat. Biologically speaking, humans were designed for cooperation, but *only with some people.* Our moral brains evolved for cooperation *within groups,* and perhaps only within the context of personal relationships. Our moral brains did not evolve for cooperation *between groups.* (Greene, 26)

Greene calls it 'the modern tragedy' (26), and points out how human co-operation is designed to further the survival of the fittest group as opposed to the neighbouring group, and so the 'very same moral thinking that enables cooperation within groups undermines cooperation between groups' (26).

The referendum in the UK in 2016 sponsored hours of discussion on television and reams of print journalism, and the 'Remain' camp mostly focused on the economic benefits, but the central argument in the hearts and minds of the population was a concern about the threat to the group, the British group, and so the issue of economic benefits was secondary. The powerfully entrenched group that called itself British could see itself being diluted by a quarter of a million people every year from dramatically different 'other' groups and this was in their eyes a matter of survival. The 'Remain' campaign fought in vain if it could not answer this problem, and the only way to have achieved it was to redefine our group as European rather than British, and they failed even to try and do this, despite a European football championship playing out across the continent, and a centenary of the First World War remembered in rituals throughout Britain. The 'Remain' camp spoke only about money.

The modern digital age allows inhabitants of unsuccessful, untrustworthy societies to know about and observe first-hand, via screens, the more trustworthy, co-operative societies, and if they can't engineer political change, or trust, in their own countries they will move with all speed, with more or less urgency, before it's too late, towards those societies where trust and co-operation can be more easily found. The only answer might seem therefore to be to export trust and co-operation.

With overpopulation and with our climate now being altered for the first time as a result of human activities, there is a reason for human groups to coalesce, to form one group. That will only be achievable if we can grow a new kind of morality. 'What we in the modern world need, then, is something like morality but one level up.' (Greene, 26) Greene proposes as an answer what he calls a 'deep pragmatism' but he doesn't underestimate the enormity of the task – no less than the complete remoulding of our moral sensibility. Zak is optimistic – 'as a species, we are far less self-interested – and, on balance, generally far kinder and more cooperative – than the prevailing wisdom has ever acknowledged' (xvi).

Sometimes, with powerful stories, we feel as if we are clinging by our fingernails onto life itself.

References

Alfredson, Tomas (Director). 2008. *Let The Right One In.*

Amenábar, Alejandro (Director). 2001. *The Others.*

American Film Institute. 1970. *Alfred Hitchcock on Mastering Cinematic Tension.* www.youtube.com/watch?v=DPFsuc_M_3E. Accessed 20 November 2014.

Anderson, Paul Thomas (Director). 2007. *There Will Be Blood.*

Batra, Ritesh (Director). 2013. *Lunchbox.*

Boehm, Christopher. 2012. *Moral Origins, the Evolution of Virtue, Altruism, and Shame.* New York: Basic Books.

Bordwell, David and Thompson, Kristin. 2001. *Film Art – An Introduction.* New York: McGraw-Hill.

Bordwell, David and Thompson, Kristin. 2011. *Minding Movies – Observations on the art, craft, and business of filmmaking.* London: University of Chicago Press.

Boyd, Brian. 2010. *On the Origin of Stories: Evolution, Cognition, and Fiction.* Cambridge: Harvard University Press.

Cameron, James (Director). 1991. *Terminator 2: Judgment Day.*

Carroll, Noel. 2001. *Beyond Aesthetics.* Cambridge University Press.

Cauvin, Jean-Pierre. 1982. 'Introduction'. In *Poems of Andre Breton: A Bilingual Anthology*, by Andre Breton. Austin: University of Texas Press.

Charles, Larry (Director). 2006. *Borat.*

Crichton-Browne, James. 1871. 'Letter no. 7658'. In *Darwin Correspondence Project.* 3 April. http://www.darwinproject.ac.uk/DCP-LETT-7658. Accessed 29 April 2016.

Coen, Joel (Director). 1996. *Fargo.*

Coen, Joel and Coen, Ethan (Directors). 2007. *No Country for Old Men.*

Cukor, George (Director). 1964. *My Fair Lady.*

Darabont, Frank (Director). 1994. *The Shawshank Redemption.*

Darwin, Charles. 1871. 'Letter no. 6160'. *Darwin Correspondence Project.* 7 April. http://www.darwinproject.ac.uk/DCP-LETT-6160. Accessed 28 April 2016.

Davies, Stephen. 2012. 'The Artful Species: Aesthetics, Art and Evolution'. http://0-www.oxfordscholarship.com.lib.exeter.ac.uk/view/10.1093/acprof:oso/9780199658541.001.0001/acprof-9780199658541-chapter-4. Accessed May 2014.

Davis, Andrew (Director). 1993. *The Fugitive*.

Dayton, Johnathan and Faris, Valerie (Directors). 2006. *Little Miss Sunshine*.

Delaney, Frank. 1993/2001. *Telling The Pictures*. London: Harpercollins.

De Palma, Brian (Director). 1976. *Carrie*.

Doxiadis, Apostolos and Mazur, Barry. eds. 2012. *Circles Disturbed*. Princeton: Princeton University Press.

Egri, Lajos. 1942/2004. *The Art of Dramatic Writing*. New York: Touchstone.

Field, Syd. 2013. *www.sydfield.com*. 1 January. http://sydfield.com/writers-tools/the-paradigm-worksheet/. Accessed 15 August 2014.

Foley, James (Director). 1992. *Glengarry Glen Ross*.

Mulligan, Robert (Director). 1962. *To Kill a Mockingbird*.

Forster, Edward M. 1962. *Aspects of the Novel*. London: Pelican Books.

Gilligan, Vince (Director). 2008-2013. *Breaking Bad*.

Girard, Rene. 1961/1976. *Deceit, Desire and the Novel*. London: The John Hopkins Press.

Glatzer, Richard and Westmoreland, Wash (Directors). 2014. *Still Alice*.

Gledhill, Christine. 2003. *Reframing British Cinema, 1918–1928: Between Restraint and Passion*. London: BFI Publishing.

Gold, Joseph. 2002. *Story Species*. Markham, Ontario: Fitzhenry and Whiteside.

Gottschall, Jonathan. 2013. *The Storytelling Animal*. New York: Mariner Books.

Greene, Joshua. 2012. *Moral Tribes: Emotions, Reason and the Gap Between Us and Them*.

Greengrass, Paul (Director). 2002–2016. *Bourne*.

Haneke, Michael (Director). 2009. *The White Ribbon*.

Haneke, Michael (Director). 2012. *Amour*.

Hanich, Julian. 2010. *Cinematic Emotion in Horror Films and Thrillers*. New York: Routledge.

Hanna, William and Barbera, Joseph (Directors). 1968–1969. *Wacky Races*.

Hazanavicius, Michel (Director). 2011. *The Artist*.

Hegel, Georg. 1969. *Hegel's Science of Logic*. London: George Allen and Unwin.

Hitchcock, Alfred (Director). 1940. *Rebecca*.

Hitchcock, Alfred (Director). 1963. *The Birds*.

Hooper, Tom (Director). 2010. *The King's Speech*.

Jackson, Peter (Director and Performer). 2001. *The Lord of the Rings: The Fellowship of the Ring*.

Jackson, Peter (Director). 2001–2003. *The Lord of the Rings: The Motion Picture Trilogy*.

Jackson, Peter (Director). 2005. *King Kong*.

Joon-ho, Bong (Director). 2009. *Mother*.

Joyce, James. 1948. *The Essential James Joyce*. Edited and with a preface by Harry Levin. London: Jonathan Cape.

Kant, Emmanuel. 1963. *Introduction to Logic*. London: Vision Press Ltd.

Kapadia, Asif (Director). 1997. *The Sheep Thief*.

Leigh, Mike (Director). 1996. *Secrets and Lies*.

Levinson, Barry (Director). 1988. *Rain Man*.

Macdonald, Ian W. 2013. *Screenwriting Poetics and the Screen Idea*. New York: Palgrave Macmillan.

Makhmalbaf, Samira (Director). 1997. *The Apple*.

Mamet, David. 2002. *Three Uses of the Knife*. London: Methuen.

Marinis, Marco de. 2003. 'Dramaturgy of the Spectator'. In *Performance – Critical Concepts in Literary and Cultural Studies, volume 4*, ed. by Philip Auslander, 219–235. London: Routledge.

McGinn, Colin. 2000. *Logical Properties: Identity, Existence, Predication, Necessity, Truth*. Oxford: Oxford University Press. http://0-www.oxfordscholarship.com.lib.exeter.ac.uk/view/10.1093/0199241813.001.0001/acprof-9780199241811. Accessed 14 August 2014.

McKee, Robert. 1999. *Story*. London: Methuen.

Pakula, Alan J. (Director). 1982. *Sophie's Choice*.

Parisot, Dean (Director). 1999. *Galaxy Quest*.

Parker, Philip. 2006. *The Art and Science of Screenwriting*. Bristol: Intellect Publishing.

Paterson, Don. 2000. 'Aphorisms'. In *Strong Words*, by W.N. Herbert and Matthew Hollis, 282–286. Northumberland: Bloodaxe Books.

Plantinga, Carl. 2009. *Moving Viewers: American Film and the Spectator's Experience*. Berkeley/Los Angeles: University of California Press.

Plutchik, Robert. 2001. 'The Nature of Emotions'. *American Scientist* 344–350.

Polanski, Roman (Director). 1965. *Repulsion*.

Polanski, Roman (Director). 1976. *The Tenant*.

Pollack, Sydney (Director). 1982. *Tootsie*.

Potter, Cherry. 2001. *Screen Language*. London: Methuen.

Price, Steven. 2013. *A History of the Screenplay*. New York: Palgrave Macmillan.

Prinz, Jesse J. 2004. *Gut Reactions – A Perceptual Theory of Emotion*. New York: Oxford University Press.

Prinz, Jesse. 2007. *The Emotional Construction of Morals*. New York: Oxford University Press.

Rinder, Robert (Performer). 2014–2016. *Judge Rinder*. Directed by Various.

Rolls, Edmund T. 2007. *Emotion Explained*. Oxford: Oxford University Press.

Romano, Andrew. 2011. 'Breaking Bad: the Finest Hour on Television'. *Newsweek*, 6 June: Culture.

Rouyer, Philippe, interview by TFI. 2012. *Introduction to Amour*.

Rowe, Kenneth Thorpe. 1939. *Write That Play*. New York: Funk and Wagnallis.

Russell, David O (Director). 2012. *Silver Linings*.

Sachs, Ira (Director). 2014. *Love is Strange*.

Schopenhauer, Arthur. 1818/2010. *The World as Will and Representation, volume 1*. Cambridge: Cambridge University Press.

Scott, John. 1868. 'Letter no. 6160'. *Darwin Correspondence Project*. 4 May. http://www.darwinproject.ac.uk/DCP-LETT-6160. Accessed 29 April 2016.

Shklovsky, Viktor. 1925/1993. *Theory of Prose*. London: Dalkey Archive Press.

Sibley, Adrian (Director). 2014. *Joanna Lumley meets Will.i.am*. Performed by Adrian Sibley.

Sippy, Ramesh (Director). 1975. *Sholay*.

Solomon, Robert C. 2007. *True to Our Feelings*. New York: Oxford University Press.

StackExchange. n.d. 'What Significance does Mike Yanagita Have in Fargo?' http://movies.stackexchange.com/questions/290/what-significance-does-mike-yanagita-have-in-fargo. Accessed 13 October 2014.

Stern, Tiffany. 2009. *Documents of Performance in Early Modern England*. Cambridge: Cambridge University Press.

Terruso, David. 2007. 'Tension Holds Your Screenplay Together'. *Absolute Write*. 1 January. http://www.absolutewrite.com/screenwriting/tension.htm. Accessed 12 May 2014.

Truby, John. 2008. *The Anatomy of Story*. New York: Farrar, Straus and Giroud.

Turnbull, Colin M. 1962. *The Forest People*. New York: Simon and Schuster.

Ubersfeld, Anne. 2003. 'The Pleasure of the Spectator'. In *Performance – Critical Concepts in Literary and Cultural Studies*, ed. by Philip Auslander, 236–248. London: Routledge.

Vorderer, Peter, Wulff, Hans J. and Friedrichsen, Mike. 1996. *Suspense: Conceptualizations, Theoretical Analyses and Empirical Explorations*. New York: Routledge.

Waller-Bridge, Phoebe. 2016. *Fleabag*.

Weimann, Robert. 1967/1978. *Shakespeare and the Popular Tradition in the Theater*. Baltimore, MD: The John Hopkins University Press.

Weir, Peter (Director). 1998. *The Truman Show*.

Weir, Peter (Director). 1991. *Thelma and Louise*.

Welty, Eudora. 1948. *One Writer's Beginnings*. London: Faber and Faber.

Wenders, Wim (Director). 1987. *Wings of Desire*.

Wittgenstein, Ludwig. 1914–1916/1961. *Notebooks 1914–1916*. Oxford: Basil Blackwell.

Wittgenstein, Ludwig. 1953/1976. *Philosophical Investigations*. Oxford: Basil Blackwood.

Wittgenstein, Ludwig. 1958. *The Blue and Brown Books*. Oxford: Basil Blackwood.

Yorke, John. 2013. *Into the Woods*. London: Penguin Books.

Zak, Paul J. 2012. *The Moral Molecule. The Source of Love and Prosperity*. New York: Dutton.

Index

16230951R00123

Printed in Great Britain
by Amazon